A Brief History
of Ancient Israel

A BRIEF HISTORY
OF ANCIENT ISRAEL

Victor H. Matthews

WESTMINSTER
JOHN KNOX PRESS
LOUISVILLE • KENTUCKY

Cover design by Mark Abrams
Interior design by Sharon Adams
Cover photograph by Richard Nowitz

First edition
Published by Westminster John Knox Press
Louisville, Kentucky

This book is printed on acid-free paper that meets the American National Standards Institute Z39.48 standard. ♾

PRINTED IN THE UNITED STATES OF AMERICA

04 05 06 07 08 09 10 — 10 9 8 7 6 5 4 3 2

Library of Congress Cataloging-in-Publication Data is on file at the Library of Congress, Washington, D.C.

0-664-22436-9

To
Dwight W. Young
James C. Moyer
Don C. Benjamin Jr.

Whose friendship and encouragement
have contributed so much to my career

Contents

List of Illustrations   ix

Introduction   xi

Abbreviations   xv

1: The Ancestral Narratives: A Sea of Names and Places   1

    Tales of Origins and Heroes   2

    The Ancestral Narratives   3

    Precedents and Constitutional Experiences in the
       Ancestral Narratives   5

      Covenant Making   5

      Abram/Abraham Builds an Altar   6

      Abraham Purchases His Family Burial Plot   6

      Jacob Obtains the Covenantal Blessing   7

      Jacob Makes a Treaty with Laban   8

      The Israelites Move to the Delta Region of
      Lower Egypt (Goshen)   9

    Dealing with the Wealth of Names   9

    Conclusions   13

2: Exodus and Settlement Period   15

    Putting the Story Together   17

      Superpower Politics and Diplomacy   17

      Aids to Chronology and Historical Reconstruction   23

    Archaeological Data   30

    Precedents Important for Later History   33

3: Early Monarchy Period (ca. 1030–900 B.C.E.)   35

    Judges Period as a Political Transition   35

    Saul and the Establishment of a Chiefdom   39

    David and the Kingdom of Israel   41

    Solomon and the Organization of a Monarchy   45

Reconstruction of the Tenth-Century Monarchy   47
Precedents Formed in the Early Monarchic Narrative   49
4: Period of the Divided Kingdom (ca. 925–586 B.C.E.)   53
Extrabiblical Sources and Historicity   55
Division of the Kingdom   55
Jeroboam's Sin and the Pattern of Leadership in Israel   60
Dynastic Changes in the Northern Kingdom   63
    The Household of Omri   65
    The Eighth Century and the Mounting Assyrian Threat   70
5: Judah Stands Alone (ca. 720–586 B.C.E.)   77
Hezekiah's Reform   80
The Last Days of Judah   85
Josiah, Reform, and Disaster   88
The Last Kings of Judah   94
6: From Exile to Alexander (ca. 597–322 B.C.E.)   101
Aftermath of 587   104
    Those Who Remained Behind   104
    Those Taken into Exile   105
Restoration Period   112
    Those Who Returned   113
    The Role of Ezra and Nehemiah   119
Alexander of Macedon and the Beginning
    of the Hellenistic Age   125

Major Events During the Monarchy Period   129
Glossary   131
Bibliography   137
Index of Ancient Sources   157
Author Index   163
Subject Index   167

Illustrations

Figures

1.	Treaty elements (Genesis 31)	8
2.	Heirs of the covenant promise	10
3.	Biblical cities	11
4.	Chronology of Mesopotamian history	19
5.	Chronology of Egyptian history	19
6.	Ancient Near Eastern texts and the Exodus account	23
7.	Archaeological periods	30
8.	Recurring themes	33
9.	Formative events prior to the monarchy	36
10.	Steps toward monarchy	50
11.	What you need to know about the divided monarchy period	54
12.	Extrabiblical parallels during the monarchic period	56
13.	"Jeroboam's Sin" (1 Kgs. 12:26-32)	61
14.	Major differences between Judah and Israel	61
15.	Shalmaneser III's monolith inscription	65

16. Events in the fall of Samaria (723-720 B.C.E.)   73
17. Kings of the divided kingdom   75
18. Political leaders in the late eighth and seventh centuries B.C.E.   78
19. Elements of Hezekiah's reform in 2 Chronicles   81
20. Josiah's reform   89
21. Discovery-report motif   91
22. Judas's last days   93
23. Archaeological surveys   98
24. What you need to know about the exilic and postexilic periods   103
25. Neo-Babylonian rulers   106
26. Elements of the Jewish identity movement   108
27. Isaiah and Cyrus   114
28. Persian rulers   115
29. Persian imperial policies that shaped provincial activities in Yehud 117
30. Nehemiah's mission and activities   122

Maps

1. Israel and its neighbors   12
2. Ancient Near East   18
3. Egypt   25
4. Monarchic period Israel   42
5. Mesopotamia   74

Introduction

In a conversation with one of my colleagues who teaches at another university, he expressed the wish that his students could be supplied with a short volume that would provide them with an up-to-date historical supplement to courses on the Hebrew Bible/Old Testament and the history of ancient Israel. He and I shared the same frustration that many of our students were basically unaware of the sequence of events found in the biblical narrative, and that the world of the ancient Near East was, for the most part, a complete mystery. We both agreed that what students could use is a straightforward summary that would help them understand such basic things as:

What are the most important events in Israelite history?

Which characters and places are the most important to learn about?

What is the basic chronology used by historians and archaeologists?

What extrabiblical documents exist to help write a history of Israel?

What can archaeology contribute to the recreation of the history of ancient Israel?

This volume is an effort to answer, in a concise format, these questions and many others about the history of Israel during the period from ca. 1800 to 332 B.C.E. While there are many other histories of Israel available, this one is particularly student oriented. I have studied and taught these materials for over twenty-five years, and I must admit that I have sometimes frustrated students with the shear amount of data in my courses. It is very easy to step into the role of "sage" and to overawe a class without really teaching them very much. As a result, I have tried here to keep scholarly arguments to a minimum and concentrate on what can be said about the reconstruction of ancient Israel within its historical and cultural context. I have also not attempted to provide as broad or detailed a coverage of Israelite history as J. M. Miller and J. Hayes in *A History of Ancient Israel and Judah* (Philadelphia: Westminster, 1986) or as the multiauthored *Ancient Israel,* revised edition, edited by Hershel Shanks (Washington, D.C.: Biblical Archaeology Society, 1999).

Rather than serving as a stand-alone text, this volume is a supplement to the Bible and will complement other introductory textbooks. Its value will be found in its various teaching aids (inset boxes, keyword cues, extensive parenthetical documentation and bibliography) and a sense for what will be most helpful in a classroom situation. In particular, students are directed to note the terms highlighted in **bold print.** They will be defined in the glossary and are keys to understanding that portion of the text. The insets also provide a guide to the accompanying material and serve as basic outlines to the chapter sections.

WRITING A "HISTORY" OF ANCIENT ISRAEL

In recent years the terms "history" and "historical" have become somewhat problematic when used to describe the ancient Near East and especially ancient Israel. Historians generally define their work as scientific investigation and therefore verifiable (Roth 1988). For instance, some claim to seek "a succession of events whose historicity is beyond doubt" (Soggin 1978, 51), and others make "demands for scientific stringency" (Lemche 1991, 103) and set a high standard of objectivity (Lemche 1988, 52). Drawing on this perspective, some claim to seek "historicity as the measure of the truth and reality of falsifiable historical statements" (Thompson 1996, 39–40). More simply put, at least one scholar has stated that history consists of "what is really there" (Davies 1992, 29).

Those biblical scholars who are now dubbed "minimalists" maintain that it is not possible to discuss an event in the biblical account as "history" unless its historicity is proven through scientific methods. On the other hand, those termed "maximalists" hold the position that the biblical account is basically historical in character and should be considered as such unless disproved by verifiable means

(Grabbe 1997b, 192; Malamat 2001, 411). Both sides of this debate have their origins in nineteenth-century German scholarship and specifically the work of Leopold von Ranke (Maier 1999,195; Sasson 1981, 8–11). They are dependent on conceptions of "historicity" and "verifiable proof" and the relationship between history and nation (Younger 1990, 25–28; Dever 1997b, 178). For them, such terms as "probability" or "plausibility" have no place within the discussion of the ancient cultures of the Near East (Smelik 1992, 3–4; Davies 1997, 119–20). However, subjective judgments such as these and the critical analysis of "narrative history" (Younger 1990, 25) have become a part of the more recent conversations on what "history" is within the broader field of the discipline (R. D. Miller 2001).

As is often noted by scholars, one key to the reconstruction of the past is the ability to immerse oneself in the available, relevant data, and then make a well-reasoned argument for "meaningful interconnections" (Edelman 1991, 14–15; Elton 1967, 98). Defining what is relevant may be as simple as identifying what is at hand. While recognizing that ancient writers had a different perspective on history writing and engaged in what we would term exaggerated, propagandistic, or theological reasoning, it seems illogical to disregard their stories completely and thus deprive ourselves of a potential source of information (De Moor 1996, 214). By employing the full range of materials available to us, we can reconstruct "possible pasts" (Halpern 1997, 331; Trigger 1998, 29; Grabbe 1997a, 21; Barstad 1998, 126). Taking this a step further, it then becomes possible to establish "working hypotheses that approximate accurate knowledge" (Hallo 1990, 188), which can be tested and examined (Kincheloe and McLaren 1994, 151, 153–55; Grabbe 1997a, 31). These in turn, when compared with other scenarios set forth by scholars using a similar critical process, can be used to produce a plausible reconstruction of events (Trigger 1998, 23). Throughout this endeavor, it is important to clearly describe what data is being used and what is being excluded. With this in mind, one may more reasonably establish "what it is possible to know" (Grabbe 1997a, 36). This simple statement is crucial to the understanding of how Israelite history is to be approached as a discipline and will be the basis upon which this volume will attempt to reconstruct the world of ancient Israel.

Abbreviations

Key Resources Cited

ABD   D. N. Freedman, ed. *Anchor Bible Dictionary,* 6 vols. New York: Doubleday, 1992.

ANET   J. Pritchard, ed. *Ancient Near Eastern Texts Relating to the Old Testament,* 3rd ed. Princeton, N.J.: Princeton University Press, 1969.

Ant.   Josephus, *Antiquities of the Jews*

COS-2   W. W. Hallo and K. L. Younger, eds. *The Context of Scripture: Monumental Inscriptions from the Biblical World,* Vol. 2. Leiden: Brill, 2000.

Cowley   A. Cowley. *Aramaic Papyri of the Fifth Century B.C.* Osnabrück: Otto Zeller, 1967 [1923 reprint].

EA   El-Amarna letters

ISBE   G. W. Bromiley, ed. *International Standard Bible Encyclopedia,* 4 vols. Grand Rapids: Wm. B. Eerdmans, 1979–1988.

OTP   V. H. Matthews and D. C. Benjamin. *Old Testament Parallels: Laws and Stories from the Ancient Near East,* 2nd ed. Mahwah, N.J.: Paulist Press, 1997.

Chapter 1

The Ancestral Narratives: A Sea of Names and Places

In approaching material that holds significance for a specific community, it is very easy to simply adopt that community's view and treat its story uncritically as historical. In fact, what is contained in the book of Genesis is a set of narratives, genealogies, and cultural signposts that tell the official Israelite version of the origin of the universe, the foundations of human civilization and diversity, and the beginnings of a people that will come to be known as the Israelites. Much of this material was composed and edited in the monarchic period (post-900 B.C.E.) and functions as an explanation for and justification of the political and social institutions that existed at the time. This is not to say that the stories of the ancestors are completely ahistorical. It is evident that the descriptions of ancient pastoral nomadic groups, social and economic conditions, and legal practices are quite authentic within their ancient Near Eastern context and recognizable as part of a traditional village or rural-based society (see Matthews and Benjamin 1993, 52–63). It will be the task of this chapter to describe how this material illumines our understanding of the premonarchic Israelites. Since there are no direct extrabiblical links available in ancient Near Eastern texts, much of our discussion will be focused on what is available to us: the literary, archaeological, and

1

sociological data that can be used to help interpret the biblical text (Grabbe 1997a, 35).

TALES OF ORIGINS AND HEROES

The first issue that arises in our examination of the ancient Israelites in Genesis centers on what purpose the primordial history and the ancestral narratives serve within the traditions of the people that will eventually come to be known as Israel. With regard to the epic stories of creation, flood, and the table of nations (Gen. 1–11), it is more likely that these narratives function to explain the origin of the world and society (**etiology**) rather than provide scientific or objective historical accounts. Elements of these stories would have circulated in oral tradition for many years, but they would not have been written down prior to the establishment of the monarchy (ca. 1000 B.C.E.). The creation and flood epics in the Bible also drew upon the literature of Egypt and Mesopotamia, using familiar archetypal images such as creator, hero, and trickster. However, they submerged, for theological purposes, direct references to cosmic battle and the dragon archetype so commonly used as the enemy of order in the older, polytheistic epics (Batto 1992, 44, 76–78, 131). Because creation stories are often tied to the political fortunes of major cities or nations in Mesopotamian literature, it is also quite likely that when the biblical stories in Genesis 1–11 were edited into a standardized form, they also received a political flavor—at least to the extent of introducing Yahweh as the creator deity and providing the genealogical link to the establishment of covenant with Abram/Abraham and eventually to the creation of the nation of Israel.

POLITICAL ELEMENTS IN CREATION EPICS

"Geb, the earth, commanded the Ennead to assemble. At first, Geb proposed to end the war between Horus and Seth by dividing Egypt equally between them. Horus would rule over Lower Egypt in the north and Seth would rule over Upper Egypt in the south. Then Geb proposed that the land of Horus should rule over the land of Seth, and that Horus, son of Osiris, should unite Upper and Lower Egypt into one land." (*OTP* 3–4, "Hymn to Ptah," the creator god and patron of Memphis)

"If I agree to serve as your deliverer, if I am successful defeating Tiamat, if I save your lives, you must proclaim me the ruler of the divine assembly. My word, not yours, must determine all things. What I create must not change, what I command must not be revoked or altered." (*OTP* 13, "Enuma Elish," proclaiming Marduk, the patron god of Babylon, as lord of the gods and creator)

If this is the intent of the primordial history, then it does fulfill its role as a provider of "origins" stories. It clearly establishes which God is responsible for creation, how human culture began to develop, why there are many nations, and, ultimately, how Yahweh chose to act in "history" to form an identifiable group to worship and obey the deity's commands. With this in mind and in order to create a basic, generational chronology from the materials in Genesis, one may easily read them as received annals, drawing a time sequence from what the biblical editors have done. This is not to say that we are dealing with history writing as defined by modern scholars (see Barstad 1997, 39–45). However, giving the ancient storytellers their due, we can both outline events and take note of cultural developments, as ancient audiences did, and thereby see how these narratives were shaped to provide a foundation for later Israelite traditions.

THE ANCESTRAL NARRATIVES

During the first half of the twentieth century, W. F. Albright (1957; 1968) and G. E. Wright (1962; 1968) attempted to create a scholarly consensus that would place the ancestors of the Israelites in a historical setting. These scholars and many of their students argued for the basic historicity of the narratives involving Abraham, Isaac, Jacob, and Joseph (Gen. 12–50). According to the Albright/ Wright "consensus," the most likely time period to assign to the ancestors was the first half of the second millennium B.C.E. (i.e. 2000–1500 B.C.E.). This was based on alleged parallels with the eighteenth century B.C.E. royal documents from Mari (a major site on the upper Euphrates that dominated much of that area), and the fifteenth century B.C.E. family/legal documents from Nuzi (a Mitannian site east of the Tigris) that mention pastoral nomadic tribal groups, kinship relations, and legal documents such as adoption contracts and inheritance decrees.

While this view has never been universally accepted, its first serious challenge came in the mid-1970s with the publication of works by Thomas L. Thompson (1974) and John Van Seters (1975). These two books created a climate of doubt that required a fresh look at what had been the general view. Subsequently, these scholars (Thompson 1999; Van Seters 1992), as well as others (Davies 1992; Lemche 1998) expanded on their argument that the evidence, which biblical archaeologists used to search for the history of the ancestors, was flawed. Their "minimalist" position has been successful in convincing a segment of the academic community that archaeology today is not, and may never be, an effective tool in the search for the history of the ancestors. Despite this fact, they have been unsuccessful in establishing a consensus that the biblical traditions are not historical. The debate goes on, but the most recent book rebutting their position, *What Did the Biblical Writers Know and When Did They Know It?* (Dever 2001b), has once again argued against relying too heavily on skepticism as a starting point for the examination of ancient materials. Since he did not choose to deal with data outside the books of the Deuteronomistic History (Dever 2001b, 97–101), future treatments are likely to expand their reconstructions to take into account the value of the data presented in the Pentateuch, Chronicles, and the prophetic materials (Vaughn 2001).

There are also a number of scholars who are of the opinion that the biblical materials should be given the same value as ancient Near Eastern literary texts (Barstad 1998, 127). Like the cuneiform and hieroglyphic texts, the biblical materials serve as cultural data that can be drawn upon to reconstruct the past (see Kitchen 1995; Millard and Wiseman 1980). This information sheds some light on the ancestral stories in Genesis, but it is still best to treat it as an indication of similar legal, economic, and social responses to common problems and situations. These cuneiform texts written on clay tablets cannot be used to authenticate or prove that the biblical stories are historically accurate. In fact, to date no extrabiblical, direct mention of any of the ancestors has come to light. Some initial attempts were made to tie personal and place names in the Ebla texts (major mid-third millennium B.C.E. Syrian site) to the Genesis accounts (see Freedman 1978), but this has now been discounted and as such adds nothing to the discussion at this time (see Krecher 1993 and Millard 1992).

It is best, therefore, to maintain a balanced view, tempering enthusiasm for a comparative approach with the realization that the process of writing down the biblical narratives dates no earlier than the period of the monarchy (ca. 900–600 B.C.E.) and must be used with caution. In addition, there is a question whether actual social precedents from the Middle and Late Bronze Age (2000–1200 B.C.E.) are laid down in these stories. The characters may simply be constructs or composites whose actions represent biases, customs, and attitudes of a later period.

Given these uncertainties, it is not possible to say with confidence that Abraham, Isaac, Jacob, and Joseph, as well as their wives and children, were real persons. They are shadowy figures as far as historians are concerned and may be composites of several persons or tribal leaders. However, for the purposes of this volume, these characters will be treated as heroes, or founding ancestors of the ancient Israelites. While there may be more of legend than fact in their stories, the ancestral narratives represent for this period of Israelite history virtually all the data we have at present. To be sure, they are referenced in later periods and thus serve as signals of an earlier time. For ancient Israel, the places where Abraham, Isaac, Jacob, and Joseph are said to dwell, to do business, to make their devotions to Yahweh, and to be buried are all part of the larger matrix of Israelite traditions and in many cases appear to set precedents for later happenings in the biblical narrative (see figure 3, p. 11). It is possible, of course, that these are contrived precedents embedded into the ancestral narratives by later writers who wished to add authority to places and customs in their own time. However, that cannot be proven and thus, until more information becomes available, it is just as useful to consider that the majority of the events, cities, and social customs described in the text do in fact reflect either authentic data or very good cultural memories edited into a coherent set of stories.

PRECEDENTS AND CONSTITUTIONAL
EXPERIENCES IN THE ANCESTRAL NARRATIVES

The following is an annotated outline of significant events in the ancestral narratives. It will highlight actions as well as places associated with the ancestors and will briefly note how these precedents function in Israelite tradition. This section is not designed to retell the biblical story, only to highlight those events that will be most significant to later periods. It should be noted that the biblical writers seem less concerned with a sequence of events than they do with providing a set of cultural precedents that will serve as the basis for actions in later stories.

Covenant Making

The point made in Genesis 12:1–3 is to place the first ancestors within a particular geographic region and then to provide the basis for their migration to Canaan. Ethnographic studies of Arab and bedouin groups have provided similar examples of immigration due to clan conflicts, economic difficulties or opportunities, and political instability (Zevit 2001, 624). The events described in these narratives indicate that the earliest cultural memories of the people who will eventually be known as the Israelites have their origins in Mesopotamia and northern Syria. Harran, the starting off point for Abram's journey to Canaan, is located on the upper reaches of the Euphrates River in what is today northern Syria. It was part of the territory administered by the kings of Mari during the period between 2000 and 1780 B.C.E. and is very different culturally than the urban-based civilization of southern Mesopotamia. The Mari kingdom included both an urban population in cities ranging from two thousand to ten thousand inhabitants and a variety of pastoral nomadic tribal groups who engaged in mixed farming and herding to maintain themselves. If Abram's family had migrated to Harran from a southern Ur of the Chaldees, then that would have involved a journey north approximately four hundred miles (Millard 2001, 52–53). It should be noted that the use of the term Chaldees is an **anachronism** referring to the Neo-Babylonian period (post-1000 B.C.E.) and was most likely placed into the narrative by the biblical editors as a clue for the benefit of later readers of this story. On the other hand, if the Ur mentioned in Genesis 12:1 was actually a northern Mesopotamian city, then ties to the more culturally developed south can be discounted. Abram and his family would not have had to undergo as much of a social transformation when they set out as migrating pastoralists for Canaan if they had their original home in a rural, pastorally based region.

The principal genre represented in the stories in Genesis 15 and 17 is one of covenant making. Ancient Hittite treaty documents contain a strict protocol that includes the setting of terms for all parties concerned, obligations for treaty partners, and a certification by the god(s) of the participants. While there are some similarities between this procedure and that described in Genesis, as well as elsewhere in the biblical text, at least in the case of Abram the terms seem to be more like an adoption formula in which Abram and his descendants inherit claim to property and assume membership in a designated group (McCarthy 1972, 11–12). In Genesis 15 and 17, the formulation of the covenant statement confirms the promise of land and children to Abram/Abraham. He and his descendants were to treat Yahweh as their patron deity and be obedient to divine command. Mesopotamian culture was polytheistic, but it did contain the concept of patron gods, so such a commitment to Yahweh would not have been unusual (Jacobsen 1976, 159). Because Abram/Abraham was a "founding figure," however, it would have been useful to Israelite storytellers to portray him as obedient to God's command and as a faithful worshiper of Yahweh (see Davidson 1989).

Abram/Abraham Builds an Altar

In the Genesis narratives, the cultic acts such as building an altar and making a sacrifice are not tied to a religious calendar (Nakhai 2001, 47). They are more attuned to either spontaneous actions (Abram in Gen. 12:8 at Bethel) or to commemorate the fulfillment of a promise (Noah in Gen. 8:20–21 following the flood) and Abram at Shechem (Gen. 12:6–7) and at Hebron (Gen. 13:18). These episodes in the ancestral narratives function as etiological stories that provide precedents for the worship of Yahweh within Canaan. They also add substance to the tradition of the cultic significance of ancient cities such as Bethel, Hebron, and Shechem (Lemche 1988, 65–66; DeVries 1997, 232). Physical and sacred space can be transformed by ritual acts and by defining these places as belonging to or associated with a god (Eliade 1959, 41). Thus, it is quite significant that the first named stopping point in Canaan is associated with worship. Thus, Abram/Abraham's first act upon reaching Shechem was to build an altar and make a sacrifice to Yahweh, thereby officially establishing God's presence in this place (Gen. 12:5–7). His act of thanksgiving could be compared to that in the flood epic (Gen. 8:20–21), in which Noah built an altar and made a sacrifice after surviving the catastrophe. On a political scale, Abram/Abraham, in essence, marks off the land when he also constructs and uses an altar at Bethel (Gen. 12:8) and plants a tamarisk tree at Beersheba (Gen. 21:33). All three of these places will be associated with important events in later Israelite history (see figure 3), and Abram's actions add authority to these subsequent events. Along these same lines, it is interesting to note that the change of Abram's name to Abraham (Gen. 17:5–6) is a similar transformation, with a person, rather than a place, being marked as associated with this particular God.

Abraham Purchases His Family Burial Plot

Land becomes identified with a particular people through their living there and as the resting place for their cherished dead (Deut. 5:33; see Knibb 1989, 400).

The story of Sarah's death and the efforts that Abraham makes to find a family burial plot (Gen. 23) provide the basis for a tradition of ownership and association with the area of Hebron, a city later tied to the political origins of the Davidic dynasty (2 Sam. 2:3–4). A similar association is made with Jerusalem and specifically the precinct known as the "city of David," where many of the kings of Judah were buried (Schmidt 1996, 252–53).

What makes the Machpelah incident remarkable, therefore, is that in the ancient world it was uncommon for land to be sold to nonfamily members. One way in which this custom was circumvented, however, is found in the legal transactions described in the Nuzi texts, dating to the fifteenth century B.C.E. These documents allow a landowner to adopt the purchaser of his property. This type of economic covenant making maintains the custom of keeping land within the control of the family while not preventing a family from benefiting itself economically (Maidman 1976). There is no evidence of an adoption ritual in the Genesis narrative. Instead, Abraham's success appears to be based on (1) his apparent wealth ("a prince among us") and (2) the assistance of the elders of Hebron, who agree to support this noncitizen's attempt to complete a land deal. The dialogue between Abraham and Ephron indicates a pattern of speech in which the purchase is proposed and a series of magnanimous statements are made (Tucker 1966, 78). First, Ephron offers it "for free," which obligates Abraham to be equally generous, inviting the owner to "set his price." Ultimately, when the sale is completed, a formal contract is drawn up and witnessed by the elders. By completing this transaction, Abraham creates a legal claim to a portion of the "promised land" and thereby authenticates the covenant promise by Yahweh of "land and children" (Gen. 12:1–3). The story also functions as a parallel to Jeremiah's redemption of a field during the siege of Jerusalem in 588 (Jer. 32:1–15). Thus, both when the people first enter the land and on the eve of their exile from the land, a contract is written down and witnessed to ensure that no one can deny their claim to that land.

Jacob Obtains the Covenantal Blessing

There is a long history of "younger sons" who rise to importance in Israelite tradition (see Joseph in Gen. 37:2–11; David in 1 Sam. 16:1–13; Solomon in 1 Kgs. 1:5–53; the "prodigal son" in Luke 15:11–32). This initial example sets a chronological precedent and perhaps provides a literary formula for later stories. It may also serve, in the case of the Davidic monarchy, as justification for the actions of these kings to supplant their older brothers as well as the Saulide dynasty (Halpern 2001, 17–18). In the case of Jacob, it should also be noted that the mother (Rebekah) engineers the events. She is the one who recognizes Jacob's merit over his older twin brother Esau. She convinces Jacob to perpetuate the deception and provides him with both a disguise as well as the meal that Isaac has requested (Gen. 27:5–17). There is a real practicality to this story that may be a reflection of the labor needs and collective concerns for the survival of the household. It is also an indication of a more influential role for women in ancient Israel (C. Meyers 1999, 40; 1997, 24–25). Thus, it is possible to portray Rebekah moving independently and decisively to engineer what she believes is in the best interests of her household. This couples with the dimension of pragmatism found in other stories in which Israelite women make decisions without consulting their husbands or fathers (Matthews 1994; see Tamar in Gen. 38:13–26; Jael in Judg. 4:17–22; Abigail in 1 Sam. 25:14–35; Bathsheba in 1 Kgs. 1:15–21). It also contributes to political strategizing when David comes to the throne. During his administration, both he and his military adviser Joab employ deception as a tool to ensure the success of their plans (see 2 Sam. 3:6–30; 15:32–37; 20:4–10).

Jacob Makes a Treaty with Laban

On its face, the treaty between Jacob and Laban is little more than an establishment of boundaries (Gen. 31:44–55). However, it also contains a nonaggression pact similar to the much fuller example of ancient Near Eastern treaty formulae contained in the thirteenth-century treaty between the Hittite king Hattusilis III and the Egyptian pharaoh Ramesses II (Hillers 1969, 29–42). It will also have legal echoes in Joshua 24, where the assembled tribes of Israel renew the covenant after completing the conquest of Canaan, and in the divine instructions found in Deuteronomy 9–10 and 29, where the Israelites are reminded that their conquest of the land is based on the covenantal promise and the aid of the divine warrior Yahweh. In each of these passages, covenants are formally renewed and the stipulations of the compact are spelled out for the community (Davidson 1989, 333–34).

Figure 1: Treaty Elements (Genesis 31)

1. Proposition (v. 44): "Come let us make a covenant."
2. Pillar and boundary marker (vv. 45–46): Pillar (divine image) and heap of stones create a recognizable border between territories.
3. Covenant meal (v. 46): "They ate there by the heap."
4. Naming (vv. 47–48): Laban and Jacob each name the heap as witness of treaty.
5. Divine invocation as witness (vv. 49–50): "The Lord watch between you and me."
6. Stipulations (vv. 51–52): "I will not pass beyond this heap to you."
7. Oath (v. 53): "May the God of Abraham . . . judge between us."
8. Sacrifice (v. 54): Sacrificial meal solemnizes occasion.

Throughout Israel's history, the covenant, both its promises and its obligations, will provide the basis for the Israelites' relationship with God. The Israelites considered themselves to be covenant partners. As a result, they were repeatedly reminded to obey the covenant, and their failure to do so formed the basis for God's judgment against them and their punishment (**theodicy**).

The Israelites Move to the
Delta Region of Lower Egypt (Goshen)

While there is no mention of the movement of the Israelite tribes into Egypt in extant Egyptian records, a report from a border official during the late thirteenth century (Papyrus Anastasi VI) describes a similar case. In this instance, it is reported that Shasu tribal people from Edom have been allowed to enter the borders of Egypt at the eastern end of the Wadi Tumilat "to keep them alive and to keep their cattle alive" (*ANET* 259). Ecological disasters (famine and drought) may have made this necessary, or it may be connected with either a military action or marauding bands.

The Joseph narrative is the most carefully crafted of all of the ancestral narratives. It is held together by a "garment motif" in which Joseph is successively given a new set of clothing and then loses it—each time marking a change in his social status (Matthews 1995). It also contains an additional example of a contest between gods (Gen. 41), first found in the wife-sister story in Genesis 12:10–20, which allows Joseph to rise to a high position of authority and to demonstrate the power of Yahweh in comparison to the helpless, manipulated Pharaoh. His ability to interpret dreams also serves as the precedent for the stories of Daniel in Nebuchadnezzar's court (Dan. 2, 4).

Embedded in this transition story is the emergence of the two major tribes that will dominate politically the later history of the nation. Judah, highlighted in the story in Genesis 38 and blessed in Genesis 49:8–12, and Ephraim, Joseph's younger son (Gen. 48:17–22), are designated by Israel as the leaders of the future. Quite likely this is a political tradition inserted into the text to justify later political realities, but that is the case with many of the precedents set in these early narratives.

DEALING WITH THE WEALTH OF NAMES

One major challenge for the student in dealing with the biblical narrative is attempting to keep all of the personal and place-names straight. The episodes in Genesis weave together a complex kinship web that successfully outlines how the successive generations achieve through marriage and economic associations with the land the fulfillment of the covenant promise made to Abraham as the "father of many nations" (Steinberg 1993; Steinmetz 1991). Ethnic origin stories such as these legitimize the people's place among the nations and provide cultural precedents and legal claims to lands that will later be the seat of government for the nation of Israel. In the process, however, it can also become confusing.

The one thing that ties all of the ancestral narratives together is the pledge made to Abraham and his family. The narratives provide the genealogical data to demonstrate the fulfillment of this promise through a sometimes torturous "search for the heir" motif. These tension-filled episodes are designed to draw the audience into the search for the true heir of the covenant. It also provides them with the origins of their national identity as well as the basis for their claim to the land.

> Sarah and subsequent female ancestors are barren, and they and their husbands must wait for God to provide the child who will ensure the continuation of the covenant promise and the fortunes of the tribe. Any attempt on their part to circumvent this divine plan is set aside by God, who designates the children of slave women and concubines as secondary characters who are not heirs of the covenant (see Hagar and Ishmael in Gen. 21:8–21).

> The life of the heir is endangered (e.g., Isaac is almost sacrificed by his father in Gen. 22:1–20; Jacob is forced into exile for twenty years because of Esau's anger in Gen. 27:41–45; Joseph is sold into slavery in Egypt in Gen. 37:12–36).

Embedded into these same stories are the ancillary characters that serve as the ancestors of ancient Israel's neighbors. Abraham's nephew Lot and his daughters produce two sons, Ammon and Moab, through their incestuous relations (Gen. 19:20–38). Abraham, in his latter years and after the death of Sarah, fathers many children with Keturah and thereby peoples the desert area of Midian (Gen. 25:1–6). The expulsion of Ishmael (Gen. 21:8–21) provides a founder for several tribal peoples mentioned in the Assyrian and Neo-Babylonian annals, who inhabited the desert east of Canaan (Knauf 1992, 514). Esau's demotion as Isaac's heir in turn provides the origin story for Edom (Gen. 33:12–17; 36:1–14).

Figure 2: Heirs of the Covenant Promise

In each generation there is a couple that ultimately produces the heir of the covenant. In the process, other wives and children assume secondary roles. These characters remain part of the Abrahamic genealogy but are not considered direct links to the formation of the people of the covenant.

First Generation: Abram (Abraham) and Sarai (Sarah) = Isaac as heir
Second Generation: Isaac and Rebekah = Jacob as heir
Third Generation: Jacob and Rachel = Joseph as heir (northern kingdom tribes = Ephraim)

Spouses and Children

Lot and daughters = Ammon and Moab (Gen. 19:31–38)
Abraham and Hagar = Ishmael (Gen. 16:15–16) = Arab tribes (Gen. 25:12–16)
Isaac and Rebekah = Esau = Edom (Gen. 36:1–5)
Abraham and Keturah = various tribal groups inhabiting Midian and Arabia (Gen. 25:1–6)
Jacob and Leah, Zilpah, Bilhah = ten sons (Gen. 30:1–21), Judah = heir of southern kingdom

Figure 3: Biblical Cities			
Place Name	Initial Event	Subsequent Event #1	Subsequent Event #2	Subsequent Event #3
Shechem	Abram first arrives in Canaan, builds an altar to God (Gen. 12:6–7)	Rape of Dinah, massacre of men of Shechem by Jacob's sons (Gen. 34:2–26)	Joshua stages covenant renewal ceremony after the conquest (Josh. 24:1–32)	Rehoboam meets with tribal elders; kingdom divides (1 Kgs. 12:1–17)
Bethel	Abram builds altar to God (Gen. 12:8)	Jacob has a theophany and names the place Bethel (Gen. 28:11–22)	Jeroboam builds northern kingdom shrines at Bethel and Dan (1 Kgs. 12:29)	Amos prophecies against Israel at Bethel (Amos 7:10–13)
Hebron	Hebron Abraham buys burial cave of Machpelah (Gen. 23:2–19)	Hebron given to Aaron's sons (Josh. 21:13) or to Caleb (Judg. 1:20)	David becomes king in Hebron (2 Sam. 2:11; 1 Kgs. 2:11)	Absalom begins his revolt from Hebron (2 Sam. 15:7–10)
Gilgal	Joshua begins conquest, crossing the dry bed of the Jordan River (Josh. 4:14–24)	Saul made king at Gilgal after victory at Jabesh-Gilead (1 Sam. 11:5–14)	Samuel condemns Saul's dynasty (1 Sam. 15:12–23)	Amos (4:4) and Hosea (9:15) tie Gilgal to the evils of the monarchy
Shiloh	Joshua assembles the tribes, sets up the tent of meeting, and casts lots to apportion tribal territory (Josh. 18:1–10)	Shiloh cited as the location of the house of God (Judg. 18:31)	Eli and sons serve the shrine and ark until its capture by Philistines (1 Sam. 1:3; 3:21; 4:17)	Jeremiah warns Jerusalem, citing Shiloh as an example of a destroyed shrine (Jer. 7:12–14; Ps. 78:60)

In addition to the many personal names that can distract a reader, there are innumerable geographical names that sprinkle the text with even more items to keep straight. One way to deal with this is to take note of those place-names that are repeated in the narrative. This is done partly because Canaan is a relatively small land, and it would be natural for certain places to keep being used in the narratives. However, this also provides a link for the Israelites to their past. Later characters seem to delight in staging events in the same city or at the same site where major events occurred in the past. In this way they are able to connect with their ancestral stories and also draw upon the authority and power associated with these moments when God is invoked or directs their actions.

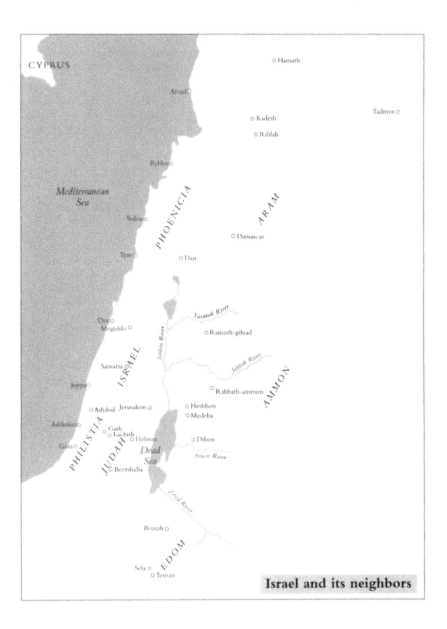

Israel and its neighbors

CONCLUSIONS

Because of the current lack of extrabiblical data corroborating the Genesis narrative, it is not possible at this time to date this period of Israelite history. It is clear, however, that the origin stories in Genesis 1–11 and the accounts of the ancestors in Genesis 12–50 are designed by the editors to provide the underpinning for a great deal of subsequent Israelite history and tradition. Of particular importance is the assertion that Yahweh is the all-powerful creator, who chooses Abram/Abraham and his descendants as his particular people. The covenant between them is the basis for the remainder of the legal traditions in the biblical text, the saving events of the exodus, the pronouncements of the Hebrew prophets during the monarchy period (ca. 1000–587 B.C.E.), and the destructive events of the eighth and sixth centuries that strip the Israelites of their political and religious institutions. In many ways, the ancestors that begin the relationship with Yahweh and the returned exiles in Jerusalem in the fifth century B.C.E. are much alike. Both are coming to know the full measure of Yahweh's power and both will start to build a culture with little more than a promise of divine assistance.

Chapter 2

Exodus and Settlement Period

At its heart, the narrative of the exodus event is a national origins story. While the cultural beginning of the Hebrew people is found in the covenantal narrative in Genesis 12–50, the story of the creation of a people referred to as Israel is the result of the exodus experience. No other single event is cited more often than the exodus, and this is a clear indication of how important the biblical writers felt it to be. The exodus was never just an event in time. It was a recurring experience in which the nation was renewed and recreated, regardless of who the oppressor nation might be. In fact, the exodus is always portrayed in later narratives and poetry as an epic happening and as an example of how Yahweh upholds the covenantal promises made to Israel.

For I am the LORD who brought you up from the land of Egypt, to be your God. (Lev. 11:45)

Then do not exalt yourself, forgetting the LORD your God, who brought you out of the land of Egypt, out of the house of slavery. (Deut. 8:14)

They did not keep in mind his power, or the day when he redeemed them from the foe; when he displayed his signs in Egypt, and his miracles in the fields of Zoan. (Ps. 78:42–43)

When Israel was a child, I loved him, and out of Egypt I called my son. (Hos. 11:1)

This narrative centers on the saving acts of Yahweh and is held together by a series of episodes in which Moses serves as the mediator between the Israelites and their God. The departure from Egypt draws the people into a loose confederation of tribes, gives them a common liberation story, and places them on the road to reclaim the promised land that is part of their covenantal legacy.

Put into theological perspective, the exodus and the wilderness story that follows may be viewed as either the origin of the people's obligation to Yahweh (see Exod. 19:4–6) or as a retrospective narrative that is a mirror image of the exilic experience of the sixth century. Current disputes centering on the context in which each story should be read and which one actually takes precedence cannot be resolved here. Suffice it to say that Israel viewed itself as a nation born out of enslavement and divine intervention, and in need of purification because of its inability to remain faithful to the covenant. This viewpoint works equally well for the exodus story as well as Isaiah's understanding of the purpose of the exile and the prospects of the return in his four "Servant Songs" (Isa. 42–53).

The question must therefore be asked: What can be drawn from the stories that would provide any relation to historical events? An attempt must also be made to determine, if possible, when these events occurred. There is also the mystery of why the Egyptians make no mention of the exodus and why there are no existing extrabiblical records of the movements of the Israelites in the wilderness or during their conquest of Canaan. A variety of answers could be given. For instance, the Egyptians may have removed all mention of the Israelites because this was an embarrassing episode, in much the same way that they removed the name of the heretic pharaoh Akhenaton from many of his monuments. Of course, it is also possible that no exodus event actually occurred and that we are dealing in the biblical account with an etiological legend rather than a historical occurrence. Taking a middle ground on this issue, one additional answer to all of these questions could be that we simply have not yet discovered what is still lying out there hidden away and waiting for the archaeologist's trowel. More realistically, it can be said that the survival of ancient manuscripts is extremely unlikely unless they were written, as in Mesopotamia, on clay tablets or, as in Egypt, carved into the walls of monuments or tombs. The Dead Sea Scrolls are the one major exception, but one cannot just reserve all judgment based on the hope that evidence will eventually turn up.

What we have in the biblical text is the eventual recording and editing of stories that most likely circulated for centuries as oral traditions. Naturally, their final form depends on these surviving cultural memories as well as the political and religious agendas of the editors. Therefore, when we attempt to create a chronology of the exodus story or trace the progress of Joshua's army as it conquers the cities of Canaan, we need to realize that we are not dealing with first-hand accounts. Nuggets of historical information may well be embedded in the biblical text, but sifting it out is very difficult and, quite frankly, disappointing for all serious students of the Bible. What appears below will of necessity be incomplete and in many cases inconclusive. It represents a synthesis of current understanding of the data and recognizes how little scholars currently know about this material.

PUTTING THE STORY TOGETHER

Superpower Politics and Diplomacy

The history of the ancient Near East has been determined by the realities of geography. Mesopotamia is an arid flood plain watered only by the Tigris and Euphrates Rivers. It has no natural barriers to invasion and has therefore been subject throughout its history to successive waves of invaders who have disrupted trade and the political order. Thus, the earliest civilization developed around **city-states** (Ur, Uruk, Lagash, Kish, Nippur) in the southern portion of Mesopotamia, an area known as Sumer, around 2900 B.C.E. Because this foundational culture was never able to successfully unite, it in turn was conquered and replaced by a **Semitic** group from the steppes of western Asia referred to as the Akkadians (Knapp 1988, 66–87). This destructive cycle was broken or at least slowed when empires developed in that large region. The unification of Mesopotamia from Mari south to Ur by Hammurabi (c. 1760 B.C.E.) made it less of a target for invasion by disorganized groups from less civilized regions, but eventually fostered sufficient political rivalry to spark major power struggles with comparable states in Anatolia, Egypt, and Persia.

Hammurabi's Babylonian realm in the eighteenth century B.C.E., the Assyrian Empire that spanned the tenth through the seventh centuries, the short-lived Neo-Babylonian Empire of Nebuchadnezzar (sixth century), and the huge Persian Empire (late sixth to mid-fourth century) all learned that to survive they needed to control as much territory as possible and exercise political hegemony over what they did not conquer. It was this concern to protect their borders and to maintain free access to the Mediterranean Sea that brought the Mesopotamian states into conflict with Egypt. In the process, Canaan, squarely placed between these two superpowers, became a battleground for their disputes and ambitions (Cline 2000, 6–28).

Egypt benefited from encircling natural fortifications. On the west was the Sahara Desert. The cataracts of the Nile River that prevented easy transport up that water highway guarded the south. To the east was the Red Sea, and in the north were the marshy reaches of the delta. Only a narrow bridge of land connected Egypt to the Sinai. Here the Egyptians concentrated a string of fortresses.

Canals were constructed as water barriers and aids to transportation, but they tended to silt up too quickly to serve as longterm defenses. As a result of these geographical gifts, Egypt for much of its early history chose not to expand beyond its borders except in the area of trade.

Certainly, as texts such as the nineteenth-century "Tale of Sinuhe" indicate, the Egyptians were familiar with "Asiatic" peoples, who inhabited the desert just beyond Egypt's border. However, it was only after Egypt was conquered by the Hyksos invaders about 1674 B.C.E. that the naturally isolated Egyptians resolved

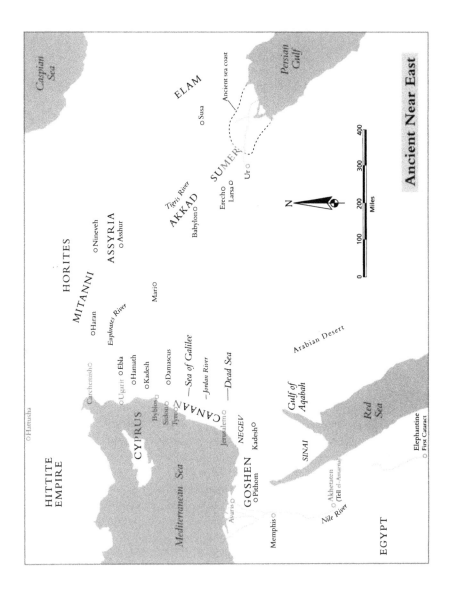

Ancient Near East

to take control of more than their own land (Redford 1992, 118–29). After the Hyksos were expelled in 1550, a new age of diplomacy emerged that dominated the remainder of the second and all of the first millennium.

At the heart of the emerging political struggle was the desire on the part of all of the superpower states (Egypt, the Hittites, and the various Mesopotamian empires) to control the land bridge that included Syria, Phoenicia, and Canaan. In addition to Lebanon's strategic value as a highway for trade and the movement of armies, the mountains of Lebanon contained the only major stand of cedars in the Near East. These forests are mentioned in the earliest texts from

Figure 4: Chronology of Mesopotamian History	
2900–2400	**Sumerian Period:** Independent city-states formed in southern Mesopotamia, cuneiform developed, monumental architecture employed for temples (ziggurats) and palaces as a sign of power.
2400–1200	**Akkadian Period:** First attempts at political hegemony by Sargon of Akkad and Naram-Sin; Ebla and Ugarit serve as major commercial links to Mediterranean trade.
2200–2113	**Ur III Period:** Sumerian cultural revival, codification of law by Ur-Nammu.
2006–1750	**Amorite Period:** First empire established by Hammurabi of Babylon, submerging Ur III and Assyrian dynasts and combining all of Mesopotamia under a single ruler.
1595–1168	**Kassite/Mitannian Interregnum:** Babylon's influence wanes while new, non-Semitic peoples establish smaller kingdoms in central Mesopotamia and compete with growing power of Hittite kingdom of Anatolia.
883–612	**Neo-Assyrian Period:** Eventually all of the Near East, including Egypt, is conquered and held under Assyrian hegemony by military force. Continual campaigning of kings such as Tiglath-Pileser III, Shalmaneser III, Sargon II, Sennacherib, and Ashurbanipal.
612–539	**Neo-Babylonian (Chaldean) Period:** Nebuchadnezzar conquers Assyria, competes with Egypt's weak rulers, but his successors cannot maintain his empire.
539–332	**Persian Period:** Cyrus, Darius, and Xerxes establish complete hegemony over the Near East, introduce new economic and communication methods, create *pax persica*.
332–63	**Hellenistic Period:** Alexander of Macedon conquers Persian Empire. His successors Ptolemy and Seleucus establish kingdoms in Egypt and Mesopotamia, creating a mixture of Greek and Near Eastern culture and ending with the emergence of Rome as an international power throughout the Mediterranean.

Figure 5: Chronology of Egyptian History	
2700–2200	**Old Kingdom:** Pyramid age, unification of **Nomes** under Pharaoh
2200–2050	**First Intermediate Period:** Decline and political restructuring
2050–1800	**Middle Kingdom:** Theban dynasties, expansion south to Nubia
1730–1570	**Second Intermediate Period:** Hyksos invasion, rule from Avaris
1570–1165	**New Kingdom:** Empire period, Amarna age
1150–663	**Post-Empire Period:** General decline, conflict with Assyria and Neo-Babylonians/Chaldeans

Mesopotamia. Each strong ruler began his royal annals and his career by staging campaigns to establish ownership over the cedar needed to help construct his palaces and temples. Egypt too depended on these gigantic trees, as attested in the tenth-century "Tale of Wenamon" (see below).

Gudea (ca. twenty-second century): "the en–priest of Ningursu, made a path in(to) the Cedar Mountain which nobody had entered (before); he cut its cedars with great axes." (*ANET* 268)

Thutmosis III (1490–1436): "Every year there is hewed [for me in Dja]hi genuine cedar of Lebanon, which is brought to the Court. . . . Timber comes to Egypt for me. . . ." (*ANET* 240)

Tiglath-Pileser I (1114–1076): "Upon the command of Anu and Adad, the great gods, my lords, I went to the Lebanon mountains, I cut cedar beams for the temple of Anu and Adad." (*ANET* 275)

Wenamon (ca. 1085): "I am here to buy timber for the great and noble ship of Amon-Ra. . . . The Mediterranean and the Lebanon mountains do not belong to Syria, but to Amon. He planted forests on the Lebanon mountains as a source of timber to build the most sacred ship on the face of the earth." (*OTP* 327–28)

Thus, the nation or empire that succeeded in controlling Syro-Palestine would also control the lucrative movement of trade goods and a wealth of natural resources, as well as the strategic routes that armies depend upon to respond to enemy attacks. However, such a prize required periodic military campaigns by the current dominant state/empire to "show the flag" and thus impress on vassal states and their rulers that no rebellion would be countenanced. In addition, a small army was also necessary to operate behind the scenes. Each of the superpowers constantly attempted to undermine the authority and loyalties of the other side(s) and thus strengthen its own hand in the region.

The movement of royal messengers, ambassadors, visiting dignitaries, merchants, and the exchange of royal or noble daughters as brides helped to facilitate diplomacy, but such persons also carried on a shadow war. It was understood that constant surveillance was a part of the job of these visitors. As a result, no unqualified friendships were possible at these levels of society. The exchange of information, like gifts, was kept at a parity level, with neither side willingly giving up more than it had to, and both parties always working to learn the other's political and military secrets (a situation that characterizes Israel and its neighbors during the first millennium). The growing cultural and economic exchanges experienced by both Egypt's cities and those of Mesopotamia in the mid-second millennium brought new peoples, ideas, and products to these cultures but also contributed to the spy network. The travelers from the Hittite Empire in Anatolia and the Hurrian realm in north central Mesopotamia, as well as merchants from Arabia, Ethiopia, Yemen, and the Mediterranean island states, were available, for a price, as emissaries and agents.

Of course, alliances were formed and occasionally treaties were signed and witnessed to by kings, nobles, and gods. These documents, although swearing perpetual friendship and cooperation, generally reflected temporary agreements and were only binding as long as both states felt they were on a par with the other. Any perceived advantage could lead to an escalation of spying or outright military activity. Only the distances that armies had to travel and the costs of such operations placed a check on the ambitions of rulers.

Within the framework of this political situation, the smaller states and peoples of Syro-Palestine were faced with the necessity of accepting the condition of vassalage, subject to the political interests and economic demands of the superpowers. This placed them in a difficult position and probably did not contribute to the establishment of lasting loyalties or allegiances. For example, at the beginning of the fifteenth century, Egypt, under the strong rule of Thutmosis III (1479–1425), was the dominant state, and its armies and political functionaries were in a very strong position to control Syro-Palestine. However, during the second quarter of the next century, the unstable pharaoh Akhenaton (ca. 1379–1362) virtually left Canaan to fend for itself. The El-Amarna letters sent from the vassal rulers of Jerusalem, Shechem, and other cities in the area reflect a near anarchic situation. They describe attacks on caravans by outlaw bands called *habiru* and open rebellion on the part of some Egyptian-appointed rulers. The Hittites, from their kingdom in Anatolia, under their ruler Suppiluliumas (1377–1335), were quick to take advantage of this instability (Kitchen 1961). They managed in a series of swift campaigns to incorporate most of northern Syria, including the Mitannian principalities further to the east of the Tigris, into their realm. However, still wary of Egypt's potential to retaliate, a treaty establishing a contiguous boundary with Egyptian-controlled territories was negotiated. The opportunity to strike a decisive blow against Egypt came in the mid-1360s when Niqmaddu II of Ugarit abandoned his former allegiance to the pharaoh and accepted Hittite vassalage. He did this rather than join a coalition of Syrian states forming to oppose Hittite hegemony (Redford 1992, 174–76). Hittite ambitions to gain full control over Syro-Palestine, however, were thwarted by the geographical distances involved, the difficulty of holding all of the various petty kings and vassal rulers in check, and a plague spread by prisoners of war that killed a significant number of their soldiers as well as the king.

Plague Prayer of Mursilis, son of Suppiluliumas: "What is this that ye have done? A plague ye have let into the land. . . . For twenty years now men have been dying in my father's days, in my brother's days, and in mine own since I have become the priest of the gods. When men are dying in the Hatti land like this, the plague is in no wise over." (*ANET* 394–95)

The mid to late thirteenth century saw a resumption of the conflict between the Egyptians and the Hittites. The latter, under their king Hattusilis III, had been striving to challenge Egyptian control over the region comprised of northern Syria and Canaan. This was in fact part of a power struggle that had lasted for over two centuries. It culminated in 1275 with the battle of Kadesh in Syria, an inconclusive event that left both sides weakened and therefore open to negotiation of a nonaggression treaty, allowing them each, they hoped, the time to restore their forces before the conflict began again.

At the beginning of the twentieth century, archaeologists recovered both Egyptian and Hittite versions of the treaty. In the Egyptian version, Ramesses II elaborates on the role he played in negotiating the treaty. He had one copy carved in hieroglyphics on the walls of the temple of Amon in Karnak and another on the walls of the Ramesseum, his funeral chapel in the Valley of the Kings. The Hittite edition is a more sober legal document written on clay tablets in Akkadian cuneiform, which was the diplomatic language of the ancient Near East. Archaeologists recovered the tablets from the archives of Hattusas, the Hittite capital.

In what may be a face-saving bit of political rhetoric (Papyrus Harris), Ramesses III describes how he defeats contingents of Sea Peoples and other tribes while allowing some of them to settle in Canaan:
"I slew the Denyen in their islands, while the Tjeker and the Philistines [Peleset] were made ashes. The Sherden and the Weshesh of the Sea were made nonexistent. . . . I settled them in strongholds, bound in my name" (*ANET* 262)

What neither side had counted on, however, was the strength of the incursions at the end of the thirteenth century of large groups of mercenary troops and Aegean pirates known collectively as the Sea Peoples. These warlike bands were well organized and had for generations served the armies of the Mediterranean region. Eventually they chose to attack their employers, successfully invading Cyprus and defeating the Hittite army, which also had had to deal with military pressure from the Assyrians on its eastern and southern border (Moor 1996, 234). This extinguished the power of that Anatolian empire forever. The seaport city of Ugarit in northern Syria, an ally of the Hittites', was also destroyed, ending its grip on the carrying trade in the Mediterranean Sea and making way for successor states in Phoenicia, namely, the ports of Tyre and Sidon. Finally, the Sea Peoples, allied with the Libyan tribal groups who had troubled Egypt's borders for decades, nearly defeated the naval and land forces of the pharaoh Ramesses III. In 1174, he barely salvaged a costly victory, but it left Egypt licking its wounds and unable to effectively control its former holdings in Canaan (Singer 1992, 1060). This disruption of the political situation created a two-century window of opportunity in Syro-Palestine that saw the emergence of a number of new kingdoms: the Philistine city-states, Ammon, Moab, Edom, Phoenicia, Syria, and Israel.

The withdrawal of the Egyptians and the Hittites from Syro-Palestine was not an unqualified blessing for its indigenous peoples. Population, for example, dropped dramatically. Cities and towns collapsed, trade caravans vanished, and the Late Bronze period (1500–1250) came to an end (Coote and Whitelam 1987, 122, 129). By 1250 perhaps sixty percent of the people of Syro-Palestine had died from starvation due to crop failures, which followed subtle changes in climate and the exhaustion of natural resources. Famine led inevitably to the outbreak of regional wars and endemic diseases aggravated by shifting populations. These disasters were not isolated, but ongoing. Some of Egypt's and Hatti's former villagers and slaves in Syro-Palestine took advantage of their freedom and tried to ensure their households against an uncertain future by migrating into the hills, where they reestablished abandoned villages or founded new ones of their own. Among these refugees were the ancestors of biblical Israel.

Aids to Chronology and Historical Reconstruction

One way that scholars have attempted to reconstruct the period associated with the exodus narrative is through the use of comparative ancient Near Eastern texts. This data seldom makes reference to Israel, but it does help our understanding of some of the literary themes employed by the biblical writers and can be used to draw some conclusions about the sequence of events described in the biblical text.

Figure 6: Ancient Near Eastern Texts and the Exodus Account	
Tomb Biography of Ahmose of Nekheb: Ahmose I (1550–1525 B.C.E.) expels the Hyksos from Egypt, capturing Avaris (*COS*-2 5).	A pharaoh arises in Egypt who does not know Joseph, and the Israelites are enslaved (Exod. 1:8–14).
Birth Story of Sargon of Akkad: Describes a "baby in a basket" survival story for a future king of Akkad (*OTP* 85).	Moses miraculously survives Pharaoh's order to kill Hebrew babies and grows up in the royal court (Exod. 2:1–22).
Merneptah Stele: Contains a list of conquests by the pharaoh (ca. 1208 B.C.E.), including the "people of Israel" (*OTP* 91).	New villages begin to appear in the Judean hill country after 1200 B.C.E. that may include Israelites and reflect their presence in Canaan (Joshua 3).
Annals of Ramesses III: Describes conflict with the Sea Peoples between 1200–1180, indicating loss of Egypt's control over Canaan (*OTP* 143).	Archaeological evidence of destroyed cities in Canaan in the twelfth century B.C.E. and the appearance of the Philistine city-states (Judg. 13–16).

Below is an annotated discussion of several individual texts as well as formal archives that provide useful information in the reconstruction of events in the period from 2000 to 1100 B.C.E.

Egyptian texts mention Semites living and working in Egypt

The Tenth Dynasty's "Instruction of Merikare," the Twelfth Dynasty's "Prophecy of Neferti," and the "Tale of Sinuhe" from the reign of Senwosret I (1971–1926) contain citations of peoples from Canaan (Semitic or "Asiatic"). In addition, archaeological investigation of sites in the eastern delta region of Egypt and the Wadi Tumilat, including Tell ed-Dabʻa (Avaris), the Hyksos capital, increase the probability that these non-Egyptian groups were indeed housed in the Egyptian delta region (Hoffmeier 1997, 54–68). They may have both benefited from and later suffered for their connections with the Hyksos rulers of Egypt (1674–1550).

Merikare: "The east (Delta) abounds with foreigners. . . . As for the miserable Asiatic, wretched is the place where he is. . . . He has not settled in one place. . . . He fights since the time of Horus. He does not conquer nor is he conquered" (Hoffmeier 1997, 54–55).

Neferti: "Egypt bows under the weight of invaders from Syria-Palestine. Enemies arise in the east, Asia ravages Egypt" (*OTP* 314).

Sinuhe: "I collapsed on an island in the Bitter Lakes. . . . I heard the sounds of livestock. . . . Some Asiatic Bedouin were approaching. The head of their household, who had come to Egypt before, recognized me" (*OTP* 129–30).

Despite this credible research and historical reconstruction, the reader of the biblical account must still contend with the various strands or layers of tradition, some of which contain a well-crafted narrative, while in others subsidiary tales cloud the picture or simply highlight certain characters to give credence to the authority of later groups such as the Levites. It is this reality that causes some historians to become minimalists, accepting little of the biblical narrative at face value. They can appreciate a good story, but find this material extremely **ethnocentric** and full of gaps. Others will give more credence to the possible historicity of the accounts, considering the wealth of details and the indication of a strong cultural memory. It is essential for us to examine these texts, giving them an opportunity to tell their story while at the same time analyzing them in the light of existing material remains.

El-Amarna archive

Reflective of the "cuneiform culture" that existed throughout the ancient Near East during the latter half of the second millennium, the El-Amarna texts represent an archive of invaluable importance for the reconstruction of Egyptian and Syro-Palestinian history and culture. Egyptian natives first discovered these clay tablets among the ruins of the ancient capital city of Akhetaten in the late nineteenth century. Eventually 382 tablets and fragments found their way to museums and private collections and have been published. All but thirty-two are letters or inventories dealing with issues of administration in Egyptian-

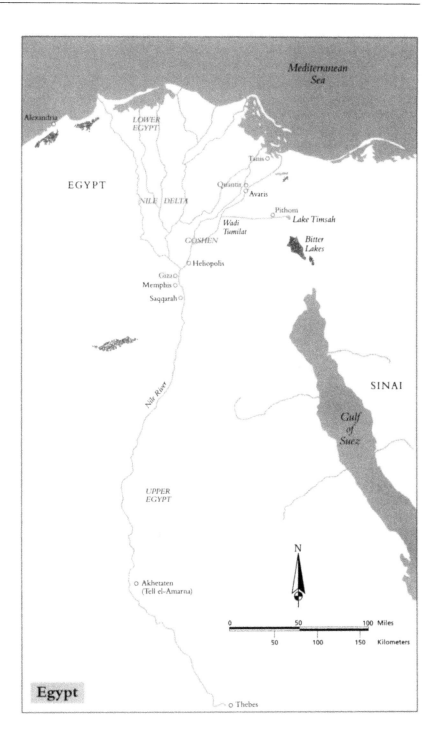

Egypt

controlled Syro-Palestine during the fourteenth century (Moran 1992, xv-xxxix). The Egyptian government received nearly all of them from its political representatives and vassals in that territory. The texts represent approximately a thirty-year span during the reigns of Amenophis III and Amenophis IV (later known as Akhenaton).

The site of Akhetaten is 190 miles south of Cairo on a plain on the east bank of the Nile River. It was briefly the capital of Egypt (starting ca. 1356) and was abandoned after the death of its founder, Akhenaton. The social and artistic revolution represented by the changes in architecture, sculpture, and religious activity during this brief period took Egypt's eyes off its possessions in Syro-Palestine. The result, as reflected in the El-Amarna tablets, is the practice of political opportunism by many of Egypt's vassals and a much greater degree of unrest in the form of banditry and civil disturbance.

With four exceptions (EA 15, 24, 31–32), the language used in the El-Amarna tablets is Babylonian, a *lingua franca* for international and diplomatic correspondence throughout the ancient Near East at this time. It has a provincial character, with the retention of obsolete vocabulary from an earlier period as well as the introduction of local forms and transliterations from native languages.

As is typical of the Old Babylonian letter form (see especially the eighteenth-century Mari texts), there is a general standardization of style, with the text usually beginning, "Speak to [personal name]. Thus says [personal name]." The body of the letters also contains conventional and diplomatic phrases. This is particularly evident in the international correspondence from the rulers of the Hittite Empire and from the Hurrian kings. There is a stylized character to phrases addressing the pharaoh's power or attributes and when the writer uses treaty language to point out a longstanding pattern of peace with Egypt or of the reciprocal receipt of gifts and assistance (see figure 1 on ancient Near Eastern treaties in chapter 1).

There are also set forms in the letters from Egyptian vassals and local rulers in Syro-Palestine, such as the prostration formula: "I bow myself seven times and seven times." One can get from these letters a sense of how the territory was supposed to be administered and what Egyptian expectations were in the way of tribute payments, the conscription of workers, and the maintenance of a peaceful, productive, subject people. As might be expected, the subordinates emphasize as much of the positive aspects of their activities as possible, and they are quick to remind the pharaoh of their loyalty and past accomplishments. However, in this troubled period they also must report on very practical concerns and make demands for assistance.

All of the demands of the pharaoh on his administrators cannot be met, and some of these officials are quite pointed in their reactions to orders that they find unrealistic or to charges of incompetence or disloyalty (see Lab'ayu's letters, EA 252–54). Among the officials most often represented in the archive is Rib-Hadda of Byblos. He is that most irritating of correspondents who constantly complains of conditions in his area, constantly makes requests of the pharaoh, and always has an excuse for why he cannot fulfill the pharaoh's demands (see EA 112, 117, 119, 121–26, 130).

The principal crisis addressed in the correspondence is the creation of the new kingdom of Amurru in Syria, on the northern reaches of Egyptian control, and the reemergence of the Hittite Empire in Anatolia. This latter event also occasions a struggle for control of northern Mesopotamia and Syria between the Hittites and the Hurrian kingdom of Mitanni. During this period of unrest, some of the Egyptian vassals took advantage of the situation to promote their own aims. Since Shechem and Jerusalem were the most prominent seats of local rulers (Na'aman 1996, 20), the correspondence from them gives the best sense of how independently they could operate and how far they could go in exercising independent action before the pharaoh took notice. Among these local "kings" were Lab'ayu of Shechem and his sons. They are accused in the texts of hiring habiru mercenaries to attack neighboring cities and towns and of forming an alliance with other city-states against Egyptian control. While the Egyptians and their Canaanite allies at Beth-Shean and elsewhere were strong enough to quell this attempt at state building, the area was never quiet for long.

The El-Amarna tablets represent a unique archive of historical materials that provide our only substantial information on the otherwise amorphous period of the fourteenth century. While they, like all royal correspondence, are filled with propaganda and formalized statements, they are also a source of data on the formation of new states in the region and the role of stateless peoples such as the habiru. The habiru appear in Egyptian and Mesopotamian texts as generic terms for groups of people who have been either forced or have chosen to leave their lands and cities. They served as mercenaries, temporary workers, and also plagued many areas as roving bandits, attacking caravans and small towns (Rainey 1995; compare Jephthah's activities in Judg. 11:1–3).

Linguistically the El-Amarna texts are important for the study of dialect and the use of an international language by non-Akkadian-speaking people. The relationship between these documents and the biblical narrative, however, is tenuous. Those who would attempt to establish a link between the habiru and the Hebrew people have not been able to make a strong case (Na'aman 1986). It may only be said that the itinerant nature of these stateless people, their apparent loyalty only to their own group, and their disruptive activities may be considered similar to some aspects of the ancestral narratives. They certainly contributed to the general instability of that period and may in that way have contributed to the breakup of the political order in the thirteenth century.

Leiden Papyrus 348

The very long reign of Ramesses II (1279–1212) generated a huge quantity of administrative reports. This papyrus is a ration list describing the distribution of grain to soldiers and to the 'Apiru (habiru in Mesopotamian texts) "who transport stones to the great pylon of Ramesses" (Malamat 1965, 64). Since this text is describing construction work at the storehouse city of Pi-Rameses, a case could be made for its correlation to Exodus 1:11 and the participation of the Israelites in similar building projects. The problem of course is whether the *'Apiru* have any relation to the Hebrews. Egypt employed itinerant laborers to complete its many monumental and mundane construction projects. It is quite possible that Hebrews, *'Apiru,* and any other unoccupied persons would have been put to work.

Merneptah Stele

This monumental inscription detailing a campaign by the pharaoh Merneptah (1212–1202) into Canaan provides for some historians a terminus date for the exodus event. It consists of a list of places (Ashkelon, Gezer, Yanoam) and peoples defeated and destroyed by the pharaoh's army. Most importantly, it contains the first mention of the name Israel outside the Bible. A determinative sign in the hieroglyphic writing indicates that Israel is an ethnic term—designating a people, not a place-name—and therefore serves as an indicator of the presence of that named group in Canaan at the end of the thirteenth century (but see Ahlström 1991, 22, for cautions on Egyptian scribal usage and possible errors).

"I have plundered Canaan from one end to the other, taken slaves from the city of Ashkelon, and conquered the city of Gezer. I have razed Yanoam to the ground. I have decimated the people of Israel and put their children to death" (*OTP* 91).

The argument would therefore go that the exodus would have had to occur prior to 1208 so that the Israelites would have had time to arrive in Canaan. Recently published battle scenes from the Karnak temple may provide corroboration of Merneptah's campaign and its four-part itinerary of victories (Yurco 1997). If this is correct, then the territory occupied by Israel, most likely the hill country of central Canaan, would be considered as important to Egyptian control of the region as Ashkelon or Gezer along the coastal plain. (Compare the description of Joshua's victories over different segments of Canaan in Joshua 6–11.)

In fact, no exodus event is required for Israelites to exist in Canaan at this time. It is possible that the group of people listed in the Merneptah inscription was simply one among many such tribal groups who inhabited Canaan and the Sinai region during this time period (Moor 1996, 216). For instance, Papyrus Anastasi I, dating to the reign of Ramesses II, describes the hill country of Canaan ("in the mountains of Shechem" [Weinstein 1981, 17–21]) as sparsely inhabited except for Shasu nomads. These people may have been enough of a nuisance to Egyptian trade and hegemony over the area to warrant being swept aside by the invading army. The official account would then have included them because this provided the pharaoh with one more people to add to his roster of victims, even if they were not on a par with the groups associated with walled cities.

What value is this inscription to the question of the origin of Israel? The answer may simply be that it provides the desired corroboration that Israel, as a people, inhabited an area of Canaan as early as the thirteenth century. No more need be drawn from this than that fact, although that by no means defines who or what "Israel" consisted of at that time (Guest 1998, 50; Stiebing 1989, 50–52). However, for those looking for a chronology for the exodus and conquest, the Merneptah Stele is crucial. It is the strongest argument against the traditional date supplied in 1 Kings 6:1 of 480 years prior to the construction of Solomon's temple in Jerusalem (960 B.C.E. + 480 years = 1440 B.C.E.). Egyptian control of Canaan in the fifteenth century, under the strong pharaoh Thutmosis III, was nearly absolute. His royal annals, carved into the walls of the temple of Karnak, describe campaigns into Canaan in which he captures Gaza and Megiddo and defeats all those who dared to oppose him (*ANET* 234–38). Such an active Egyptian foreign policy makes that time period an unlikely one for the exodus and conquest. During the thirteenth century, Canaan was held under the political sway of another strong pharaoh, Ramesses II (1279–1212). However, toward the end of his reign, the Egyptian empire in Canaan experienced a time of flux and disruption as the Sea Peoples began to emerge as a significant threat. This is therefore a much more likely scenario for the entrance of new peoples into the land of Canaan.

As a result of the invasion of the Near East by the Sea Peoples about 1200, a new political and ethnic situation was created in Syro-Palestine. For instance, one group of invaders, later known as the Philistines, established five city-states (Ashdod, Ashkelon, Ekron, Gath, Gaza) in the coastal and Shephelah region of southern Canaan. It is quite likely that the Philistines were not the only new people to enter the area. However, the invaders would have also driven existing Canaanite inhabitants from their homes and into less desirable places such as the central hill country, where archaeologists have found evidence of hundreds of new village sites founded in the twelfth century. As a result, the people known as Israel in the Merneptah inscription may be either (1) a distinctive people occupying a particular unspecified area in Canaan, (2) a pastoral nomadic group whose "territory" was claimed by the Egyptian invaders, or (3) an emerging mixture of peoples made up of displaced Canaanites and other groups who are, in a form of bureaucratic shorthand and for political convenience, referred to by the Egyptian scribe as "Israel."

One recent hypothesis (Noll 2000, 270–73) has suggested that the exodus story may even be a composite of several traditions, incorporating elements of historical events and the movement of ethnic groups. According to this view, these traditions might reflect in part the cultural memories of Merneptah's campaign and the possibility of the enslavement of the survivors of "Israel" in the construction gangs of the delta region during his reign. In addition, there may also be elements of the Late Bronze Shasu tribes (Redford 1992, 275–80), who could have migrated from the south into Canaan after the collapse of Egyptian power in the twelfth century to form an element of "nascent Israel" (see Exod.

15:10–18, 21). Finally, the suggestion has been made that the traditions were drawn together into a coherent story by the leaders of Jerusalem during the Israelite monarchy, who drew on earlier Egyptian traditions in Canaan, such as a priestly Moses figure and the Nehushtan (Num. 21:4–9; 2 Kgs. 18:4), as well as Canaanite El-worship to create the strong Yahwist movement in the eighth century Judah of King Hezekiah (Noll 2000). Whether or not this hypothesis is valid, it does speak to the diversity of the story and its roots in the cultural upheavals of the period from 1200 to 700 in Syro-Palestine.

ARCHAEOLOGICAL DATA

Piecing together the archaeological data that relates to the time period associated with the exodus and settlement (twelfth–eleventh centuries) is not an easy task. There are no extrabiblical written sources that can point to where the Israelites camped in the wilderness or which cities they may have captured. Archaeological excavations at Kadesh-Barnea, the oasis site said to be the staging point for the Israelites' wilderness experience (Num. 20:1), have shown no large-scale occupation levels prior to the tenth century. Moreover, there is no evidence of organized nation-states or large populations in Transjordan during the thirteenth to twelfth centuries. The cities of Dhiban and Hesban do not contain Late Bronze levels, nor are there significant Iron I remains at either of these sites, arguing against the account in Numbers 21:21–30 of the Israelites' victories over the Amorite kings there.

Figure 7: Archaeological Periods			
Middle Bronze II-A	ca. 2000–1800/1750	Iron Age I	ca. 1200–1000
Middle Bronze II-B/C	ca. 1800–1550	Iron Age II-A	ca. 1000–925
Late Bronze	ca. 1550–1200	Iron Age II-B/C	ca. 925–586

Archaeological surveys indicate that newly constructed villages began to appear in the hills or highlands of central Judah, west of the Jordan River and north of Jerusalem. Their initial growth took place in the period after 1250 (Dever 2001b, 71; 1995b, 72; Finkelstein 1989, 53–59). The more than three hundred unwalled village sites that have been examined in Canaan's central hill country, dating to the twelfth century, contain architecture and pottery types some have suggested are distinctive of new (i.e., Israelite) settlers. The inhabitants themselves have been identified as the Israelite tribes, or refugees from the Canaanite cities destroyed by Philistine or Egyptian armies, or a mixture of indigenous and newly arrived peoples following the Sea Peoples' conquest of Ugarit and the Hittite realm.

Some of the stories in the books of Joshua and Judges describe the arrival of these settlers as part of a conquest of the land of Canaan, but in others their arrival seems to be part of a mass migration from or a revolt against the cities on the plains along the Mediterranean coast (Isserlin 1983, 85–93). Throughout its history, herders migrated from the Sinai and other regions to settle in Syro-Palestine (Strange 1987, 18). Thus, some see these villages as evidence of the settlement of Middle Bronze Age pastoralists, who had moved into the hill country to escape the upheavals of the late thirteenth century (Finkelstein 1995; 1996b). One scholar has chosen to refer to them as "proto-Israelites" and argues that the continuity of material culture from Iron I to Iron II suggests that this emerging ethnic group was made up largely of the "indigenous peoples of Palestine, perhaps displaced Canaanites (Dever 1995a, 204–7; 1998, 46–47). This would mean that they would have tried to maintain an existence similar to what they had previously known. But it seems unlikely that *all* of these villages were founded by proto-Israelites, or by tribal groups who invaded Syro-Palestine such as the Sea Peoples, or by immigrants who filtered into previously unoccupied areas. The settlement picture is too complex to be ascribed to any one of these groups exclusively.

Furthermore, there is less and less archaeological evidence that the inhabitants of these newly established villages were outsiders or invaders. The material remains in their villages are neither foreign nor military in character. These people were plainly farmers and herders from civilization centers in the foothills and on the plains of Syro-Palestine, not nomads from the desert (Geus 1976, 159; Ahlström 1993, 350–70). Their economy was a mixture of agricultural and pastoral pursuits. Since they had little to protect, they built few walled towns or villages. And nothing in the ruins of these villages points to the inhabitants as warriors who had invaded Canaan, or as revolutionaries who overthrew it (Mendenhall 1973; Gottwald 1979). The writing, language, material culture, and religious traditions of the peoples who resettled or founded these villages link them to the Canaanite culture found throughout Syro-Palestine (M. S. Smith 1990, 1–40). However, given the disintegration in the previously heavily populated areas of the coastal plain and the foothills, these sites were not simply colonies founded by the cities of the plain (Frick 1989, 90).

Adding to this is the evidence that there does seem to be a basic continuity between Late Bronze II and Iron I ceramic repertoires, with variations, such as the collared rim jar, not being sufficiently unique to suggest the entrance of an entirely new ethnic group (Dever 1995a, 205). In fact, these frontier settlements tend, as might be expected, to produce utilitarian wares typical of a "cottage industry." Unlike the Canaanite and Philistine sites, there is an absence of luxury or imported products and little evidence of the type of finely made cultic vessels common in Late Bronze II sites. Where cultic objects have been found, such as at the "bull site" in the northern territory ascribed to Manasseh, this serves as strong evidence of the continuation of Canaanite religious practices rather than an innovation by new peoples (Bloch-Smith and Nakhai 1999, 76–77).

Furthermore, the pillared courtyard house that later evolved into the four-room house so common in Iron II Israelite contexts, simply can be defined as the type of building one would expect to find in an agriculturally based, village setting in the hill country (Stager 1985, 17). There is nothing so distinctive about this architectural design that it can be used unequivocally to tie these villagers specifically to the people of Israel mentioned in the Merneptah Stele or the biblical text. However, it does not discount the fact that eventually a new ethnic group, calling itself "Israelites," did appear in Canaan and became a distinct people.

In summary, an examination of the archaeological record related to the cities that are recorded as being conquered by Joshua and his forces shows that the evidence is still quite incomplete. The population shifts throughout Canaan, destruction levels, and construction of new villages in uninhabited areas or on the ruins of older sites seem more the result of the incursions of the Sea Peoples and the collapse of Egyptian hegemony. Extensive excavations at Jericho have yet to provide unequivocal evidence of a large Canaanite settlement during the late twelfth or early eleventh centuries. Ai, the second city said to be captured by Joshua (see Josh. 6:1–8:29) was in ruins at the end of the thirteenth century, despite evidence of massive wall systems associated with the Middle Bronze Age (ca. 2100). Both it and Jericho appear to have contained only small villages during this time period (see Dever 1992, 547–48). For those sites that do have destruction layers dated to the twelfth through the eleventh centuries, all we can say is that someone is responsible, but that may well be the Philistines or other groups of the Sea Peoples or even Egyptian armies (Ramesses VI campaigned here as late as the 1130s) attempting to restore order and control over the region (Redford 1992, 290).

What is clear from the archaeological excavations and surveys that have been conducted in Israel is that a major cultural disruption did occur at the end of the thirteenth century, which was followed by the rebuilding of cities by the Philistines in the Shephelah and coastal region and the establishment of many new villages in the less desirable hill country. Without written or more definitive ceramic or architectural evidence, this period of flux can only be defined as the cauldron out of which the tenth-to-eighth-century cultures emerged. One of these will ultimately be identified as the kingdom of Israel, but the ethnic origins of this people are most likely as mixed as the evidence associated with their cultural genesis.

When the exhausting international conflicts and the incursions of the Sea Peoples brought down the international empires of Hittites and Egyptians about 1200, the survivors in Syro-Palestine had neither the resources nor the desire to rebuild the social system that had previously controlled their lives. Therefore, the economy of early Israel became a subsistence economy. For a time at least, there would be no kings, no armies, no slaves, no taxes, and no disruptive wars. Eventually, however, this new society would require greater organization, and the process of state building in Syro-Palestine and the international intrigues of the ancient Near Eastern superpowers resumed after 1000.

PRECEDENTS IMPORTANT FOR LATER HISTORY

Like the ancestral narratives, the exodus account contains a number of episodes and events that will serve as precedents for later traditions and activities by the people of Israel (see figure 8). These episodes and events point to the way in which the exodus was viewed as a recurring phenomenon, allowing for Israel to be reminded of its covenant obligations and be reassured that Yahweh would continue to act in the face of its oppression. Although later editors may have injected some of these events into the story, the clarity and strength of many of these episodes suggest a long history within the transmitted oral tradition and must therefore be considered when piecing together an outline of the era.

Figure 8: Recurring Themes				
Contest between gods	Plague sequence vs. Pharaoh (Exod. 7–12)	Elijah vs. Baal prophets on Mount Carmel (1 Kgs. 18:20–40)	End of exile marks God's triumph over other gods (Isa. 40:12–31)	Daniel and three friends survive tests of faith (Dan. 1–6)
Covenant renewal ceremony	Moses reads the law on Mount Sinai (Exod. 24:1–8)	Joshua at Shechem (Josh. 24:1–28)	Josiah in Jerusalem (2 Kgs. 23:1–3)	Ezra in postexilic Jerusalem (Neh. 8:1–12)
Divine Warrior aids the people	Moses raises his arms to defeat Amalekites (Exod. 17:8–16)	Joshua marches around Jericho to capture city (Josh. 6:2–21)	Gideon's tiny army defeats Midianites (Judg. 7:2–23)	Judah's exiles are freed by Cyrus's capture of Babylon (Isa. 45:1–8)
Wilderness experience	Adult Israelites condemned to wilderness (Num. 14:1–35)	Elijah travels forty days to Mount Horeb (1 Kgs. 19:2–9)	Judah spends sixty years in exile (Isa. 40:1–5; Jer. 29:10–14)	Hasidim go to wilderness to escape Seleucid apostasy (1 Macc. 1:27–29)
Prophetic authority	Moses survives challenges (Num. 12:1–16; 16:1–35)	Elijah commands respect (2 Kgs. 1:2–16)	Amos responds to Amaziah (Amos 7:10–17)	Jeremiah duels with Hananiah (Jer. 28)

Perhaps the most important of these precedents is the development of the tradition of prophetic leadership and authority that transcends all other power sources. Moses, while clearly defined as a secular leader throughout the narrative (see Exod. 18:13–26), also functions as an intermediary figure separate from the role of the priesthood (Exod. 19:20–25; 24:2), which is exemplified by Aaron and his sons. In this way he serves as a unique divine representative, one to whom God speaks and a person who in turn voices God's commands to the people (see

Exod. 33:12–23). Moses' epitaph in Deuteronomy 34:10, "Never since has there arisen a prophet in Israel like Moses, whom the LORD knew face to face," creates a standard for prophetic behavior and authority that will later be found in the careers of the miracle working prophets Elijah and Elisha, and the Hebrew prophets of the eighth through the sixth centuries. Interestingly, each of these figures will function as opponents of the secular authority as well as what they perceive as a corrupt priestly community. Their arguments for a return to the Mosaic covenant (Mic. 6:4–8), the elimination or suppression of the powers of the unfaithful monarchy (1 Kgs. 18:18; Hos. 8:4) and the purification of the priesthood (Isa. 28:1–16; Jer. 6:13–15) all have their roots in the accounts of the exodus and wilderness wanderings.

Chapter 3

Early Monarchy Period
(ca. 1030–900 B.C.E.)

The emergence of Israel as a nation seems to have occurred during the tenth century B.C.E. Although we presently lack indisputable evidence for the various elements involved in this social and economic transition, there exists enough cultural and archaeological data to posit the course of events in the political development of ancient Israel. In addition, the biblical narrative introduces royal annals as a literary genre at this point, and they can be discussed and compared with those from Assyria and Babylonia. This section will include a systematic tracing of the monarchy's origins and its early political development, based on both the biblical text and comparative political theory.

JUDGES PERIOD AS A POLITICAL TRANSITION

Although the period of the Judges (ca. 1150–1000) can best be described as politically and socially chaotic, a number of important precedents occurred that would have an impact on the eventual establishment of the monarchy. These precedents are coupled with the governance process present in the village culture in which elders (landowners) presided over civil and criminal cases and made decisions based on consensus and tradition (Matthews and Benjamin 1993, 122–24; Willis 2001, 8). The elevation of a judge is portrayed in the biblical text as a divine decision, and in each case is in response to an immediate crisis. None of the judges ruled indefinitely or passed his or her office on to descendants. A judge functioned in ancient Israel as a temporary leader, most often as a war chief.

The text of the book of Judges contains a series of episodes that have been woven together using a framework device:

Israelites sin >>> God allows them to be oppressed by their neighbors >>> Israelites repent >>> God raises a judge to deal with the crisis >>> The oppression ends for a time >>> Israelites sin again, thereby restarting the cycle.

This device allowed disparate stories to be gathered together, but they should not be seen as a chronological account. All of the judges were local heroes, operating in small tribal territories, and only Deborah is portrayed as functioning as a legal official (Judg. 4:4–5). To display how the activities of the judges fit into the political development of ancient Israel, a series of events are listed in the box below. They serve as an indicator of the struggle within the villages to deal with immediate crises while holding back from full submission to centralized administration by a chief or king.

Figure 9: Formative Events prior to the Monarchy
• Deborah and Barak campaign against the Aramaean army of Sisera despite the failure of all of the tribes to assist them (Judg. 5:13–18).
• Gideon refuses elevation to kingship (Judg. 8:22–23).
• Jephthah the Gileadite defeats the Ammonites (Judg. 11:12–33) and faces intertribal war with the Ephraimites (Judg. 12:1–6).
• Samuel emerges as a "Moses-like" figure serving as priest, prophet, and judge in conflict with the Philistines (1 Sam. 7:3–17).

From the outset, the books of Judges and 1 Samuel portray the Israelite tribes as settled in Canaan and in portions of Transjordan (Gilead, east of the Jordan River), but in a weak condition in relation to their neighbors. The explanation for this situation is given both in terms of the material cultural ("the inhabitants of the plain . . . had chariots of iron," Judg. 1:19) as well as in a theological rationale, which suggests the Canaanites remained to provide the Israelites with practice in warfare (Judg. 3:1–2). What is revealed in Judges is the rather desperate condition of the Israelite tribes. They lack the weaponry, central leadership, and cooperative spirit needed to defeat the Philistines and other neighboring groups. There is no "Joshua" figure in the book of Judges. The tribes never fully cooperate with any of the judges, nor do they wish to unite into a single nation. Instead, local political enclaves, dominated by village elders, hold control of what land they claim as their territory. It is only during a crisis, such as the one described in Judges 4–5, that they are willing to relinquish their power, temporarily, to a judge. Even then, Deborah and Barak only convince a few tribes to rally to their banner, while others, such as Reuben, Dan, and Asher, tarry among their sheepfolds or have "great searchings of heart" (Judg. 5:15b–17).

Current archaeological evidence indicates that between 1200 and 1000, in the wake of the political and cultural disruption at the end of the Late Bronze Age, there was an expansion of the population into the hill country. This was concentrated from the Galilee in the north to the Judean hills in the south (Finkelstein 1998, 15; Zertal 1998, 240–42). It has been suggested that this expansion of village sites was facilitated by the introduction of plastered cisterns and terraced hillsides (Callaway 1983, 49–50; Stager 1985, 5–11). However, in most cases there is no indication that these farming technologies were invented during this time. In fact, there is clear evidence that both existed elsewhere during the Middle and Late Bronze Ages (Finkelstein 1988, 309). One new factor, however, that may have had a telling effect on the ability of these villages to clear forests for the cultivation of crops and to plow into deeper and richer soils is the introduction of iron implements after 1200. Iron provided a harder metal for use in warfare (iron chariots in Judg. 1:19) and in labor (a more efficient plow tip, ax, sickle or mattock; 1 Sam. 13:20–21).

The necessity for the shift from bronze to iron technology may be the result of shortages in the tin supply (an essential element in making bronze; Muhly 1982, 47), and thus a greater reliance on local resources and technology. However, the mixed character of the archaeological record may better indicate that the introduction of iron-working technology simply became available at that time (possibly brought by Hittite refugees or elements of the Sea Peoples such as the Philistines), and the benefits of iron made further advancements desirable in Palestine (McNutt 1990, 154–58). In fact, iron objects found in excavations in Palestine indicate that "by the late tenth century B.C.E. smiths in Palestine were able to produce carburized iron on a fairly consistent basis, and that iron was adopted as the primary material for manufacturing utilitarian metal objects" (McNutt 1990, 146). No other single innovation could have had such a great influence on the ability of villages to establish themselves in previously inhospitable areas and to expand in those areas where settlements had already been established (Muth 1997, 86–87).

One way of judging the success of the hill country villages may be found in their ability to produce agricultural surpluses and thus enhance the diet and the viability of the village population. To expand further upon their success and to protect themselves against ecological disasters such as drought, these villagers engaged in a mixed economy of farming and herding. In addition, to make maximum use of human and technological resources, it seems likely that a system was developed of staggering their planting and harvesting of crops (grains as well as horticultural products) that would provide a continuous supply of food for consumption and local trade (Hopkins 1985, 266). The Gezer Almanac, dating to the tenth century, provides graphic evidence of the agricultural calendar.

GEZER ALMANAC

August and September to pick the olives, October to sow the barley, December and January to sow the wheat, February to pull the flax,

March and April to harvest the barley, April to harvest the wheat and to feast, May and June to prune the vines, July to pick the fruit of summer. (*OTP* 146)

The problem with economic success, however, is that it cannot remain static forever. A dynamic society must find a way to continue to expand while at the same time staving off the predatory interest of its neighbors. For instance, agricultural surpluses would have made the new villages targets for taxation by the Philistine coastal city-states (Ashkelon, Ashdod, Gaza) and those in the Shephelah (Gezer, Ekron). In addition, the growth in population and the attendant need to increase both the agricultural surplus and the area under cultivation would have brought the Israelites into direct economic and territorial competition with the Canaanite and Philistine city-states, prompting raids by the Israelites on passing caravans. Once the Israelite population outgrew its hill country resources, the situation was forced to change. These communities became victims of inadequate space, what anthropologists call the process of **circumscription,** and they could no longer be contained.

Circumscription occurs when villages or states exhaust their natural resources and are cut off from any further development by either natural boundaries or hostile neighbors. What they need for survival at their accustomed level of prosperity is more than can be produced with their present resources (Carneiro 1981, 64–65). For the Israelites, the farms and herds around the hill country villages became too small to provide the expanding population with an adequate diet. The villagers had reached the limits of making any more efficient use of their land. And, according to the biblical account, they were unable to expand into the richer valleys and plains because of the superior military power of their Canaanite neighbors (Josh. 17:18; Judg. 1:19).

Typically, when a community is faced with a population explosion, a depletion of its natural resources, and the threat of war, it uses diplomacy to achieve social and political control (Earle 1989). As a consequence, some villages would have developed a **symbiotic,** or cooperative, relationship with their neighbors on the coastal plain and in upper Galilee (Coote and Whitelam 1987, 165–68; Gnuse 1991, 109–17). For instance, archaeological surveying has demonstrated a clustering of Iron I settlements in the vicinity of Tell el-Far'ah (Tirzah), an unfortified "Canaanite" town that has no break in its occupation from the Late

Bronze to the Iron I era (Bloch-Smith and Nakhai 1999, 71). Iron I hill country villagers and neighboring Canaanite city dwellers could have peacefully agreed by covenant to share water resources (Zertal 1998, 242) and exchange certain goods and services with one another. This would have benefited both, but it also would have given the villages time to organize into a more cohesive political unit.

In other areas, however, the friction between the hill country villages and outsiders was immediate and violent. Economic growth, population pressures, political threat, the raiding of caravans, and the encroaching settlements all contributed to the Philistines' desire to establish firm control over the Israelites and other hill country tribes (1 Sam. 4:1–11; Finkelstein 1985, 172–73). It may also explain the story of the migration of the tribe of Dan from close proximity to the Philistine territory to the area north of the Sea of Galilee (compare Josh. 19:40–47 and Judg. 18). The biblical narrative also mentions incursions into these hill country villages by the Midianites (Judg. 6:2–6), land disputes with the Ammonites (Judg. 11:4–33), Moabite taxes (Judg. 4:12–15), and the raids of the Amalekites (1 Sam. 15:2; 30:1–20). The villagers fought back with ingenious strategies such as grinding grain in a wine press to keep the raiders from knowing the grain harvest was completed (Judg. 6:11). These deceptions were designed to foil the encroaching people and to form the basis of resistance movements led by creative, local leaders such as Gideon.

SAUL AND THE ESTABLISHMENT OF A CHIEFDOM

The Bible does not report the exact order of events or the precise political climate that contributed to the transition from village to tribal leadership in Israel (Coote and Whitelam 1987, 143; Lemche 1988, 122). The contours of any particular tribe would have varied in response to the nature of the external crisis with which it was confronted (Earle 1989, 87; 1991, 10) and the internal opposition it faced (Johnson and Earle 1987, 313–14; Renfrew 1982, 3–6). It is certain, however, that one unresolved military crisis after the other would have provided strong support for the idea of appointing a single individual as a war "chief," whose responsibilities would have included marshaling the forces of the tribes and providing a political stepping stone to the establishment of a monarchy. Thus, Saul was able to build upon a central power base at Gibeon (Edelman 1996, 156–57), expanding his influence as he functioned in this role of chief while Israel moved toward unification (Finkelstein 1989, 63). Continuing clashes with the Philistines reinforced the necessity for a centralized leadership and made it less likely that Saul, once he had been proclaimed their chief (1 Sam. 11:17–24), could disband the tribes and return his power to the elders (Gottwald 1979, 415; 1983, 31). In order to protect their property and their households, the elders had been willing to relinquish a portion of their authority. Perhaps they believed it would be a temporary solution. However, the stakes were higher now. As can clearly be seen, "kingship will not arise until the increase in total output for a society under it is at least as great as the sum of" the costs of kingship (Muth 1997, 89). No longer could one judge or one group of Hebrew villages defend the people against the combined forces of their enemies (2 Sam. 10:6). A more powerful, central leader had proven to be necessary, and there was no going back to a decentralized model, despite concerns over possible abuses of power (1 Sam. 8:11–18; 12:13–15).

It is certainly not the case that there would have been a perfectly smooth political transition from village elders to chiefs as the leaders of the people. Even chiefs as powerful as Saul and David were subject to the counterbalance created by the elders during those periods when no crisis was evident (1 Sam. 10:27; 11:12; 13:10–15; 14:24–46). Regardless of how long a tribe existed, it was always possible that the villages could revolt to demand a new tribe and a new chief or to demand less centralization and a return to the village system (2 Sam. 20:1–3; 1 Kgs. 12:3–4). Nonetheless, statistically the state, more often than any other system, is the political form that replaces the tribe. The expansion of tribal power and the eventual collapse of the tribe's political autonomy carried within it the seeds for the development of states. Regional organization was established through alliance, force, and economic contacts as tribes were formed (1 Sam. 13:2–4). The competitive nature of neighboring chiefs, circumscription, aggressive incursion by the city-states, and the tenuous system of choosing tribal leaders all contributed to the dissolution of tribunal autonomy. However, consolidation of tribes into larger political units with bureaucratic levels of rule and centralized control over production and distribution was made easier by both the strengths and the weaknesses of tribes (Carneiro 1978, 208; Earle 1987, 281).

The Saul narrative (1 Sam. 9–31) graphically demonstrates the many crises in which a chief can be selected and the ease with which his tribal leadership can be supplanted or destroyed. Although the social institution of the chief was a practical strategy for protecting the villages in early Israel, the people and their leaders were repeatedly reminded that ultimately only Yahweh could feed and protect Israel (1 Sam. 12:16–25). For a remarkable period of almost 250 years, the Israelite villages maintained their commitment to a society without monarchs, without soldiers, and without slaves. Then they had to choose between accepting a monarch and becoming a state or facing annihilation altogether. It was a difficult choice with which Israel was never completely satisfied.

In reality, however, Israel in Saul's time was not yet formally a state. There was still no centralized administrative **bureaucracy,** no national cultic center and priesthood, and the roles of prophet, priest, and monarch were still not clearly defined (see 1 Sam. 13:8–14). The covenant that united the villages into a tribe was in continual danger of dissolution. Moreover, Saul himself was in danger of being supplanted by another chief who was able to marshal more support for his rule and complete the job of dealing with the Philistine threat (1 Sam. 15:28; 16:1; 18:7). As a result, Saul continued the pattern of tribal leadership as a military chief. David will step beyond this model and set the stage for the establishment of the monarchy (Edelman 1984, 208).

DAVID AND THE KINGDOM OF ISRAEL

According to the narrative of the **Deuteronomistic Historian** (or Deuterono-mist) in 1 and 2 Samuel, the Israelites finally broke out of their circumscription early in David's reign, and began to occupy, purchase, or conquer new land east, west, and south of their old land in the hills (2 Sam. 8; see Edelman 1988, 257). This narrative has in large part been shaped by the **apology** of David, a politi-cally motivated **disqualification story** for Saul's dynasty that highlights Saul's failures, justifies the accession of David's house and absolves him of any hint that he had betrayed Saul (McCarter 1980). It also magnifies the importance of Jeru-salem as the center of the kingdom (Hawk 1996, 20–25). Several scholars now see the demise of Saul's family as part of the Deuteronomist's "ideology of the founder," which, based on the sins of the founder, excludes the possibility of any later members of the ousted royal family from reviving their claim to the throne (Ash 1998, 16–17). This theme will be brought up again in the next chapter, which explores when the founder of the northern kingdom of Israel becomes a vilified model for unfaithfulness to Yahweh and thereby sets the standard for all "good" and "bad" kings in the future.

Turning back to the David narrative, it has been suggested that the emerging political fortunes of David's kingdom actually were aided by an alliance with the Egyptian pharaoh Siamun (Twenty-First Dynasty, ca. 979–959; see Kitchen 1997a, 117). The Egyptians were attempting to regain control over Philistia dur-ing this period (Ehrlich 1997, 201) and might well have seen David and later Solomon as helpful to their political aims. Portions of the lands David gained through his own political connivance and possible Egyptian links, along with those taken from Saul's family on his accession to the throne, would have pro-vided the wealth needed to support the construction of a palace. Other pieces would have been parceled out to friends (1 Sam. 8:14; 22:7–8; 2 Sam. 9:7; 14:30; 1 Kgs. 2:26; see Luria 1969–70, 16–18) and supporters of the new king to strengthen his political network in the country and establish control over the economy of the region (Earle 1987, 294). In doing this, David would have fol-lowed the pattern set by other ancient Near Eastern monarchs, including his for-mer Philistine patron, Achish of Gath, who had granted him the village of Ziklag (Mettinger 1971, 84). The fact that this practice continues into later periods is found in Sennacherib's account of his siege of Jerusalem in 701.

ANNALS OF SENNACHERIB (704–681 B.C.E.)

"As to Hezekiah, the Jew, he did not submit to my yoke. . . . His towns which I had plundered, I took away from him and gave them over to Mitinti, king of Ash-dod, Padi, king of Ekron, and Sillibel, king of Gaza" (*ANET* 288).

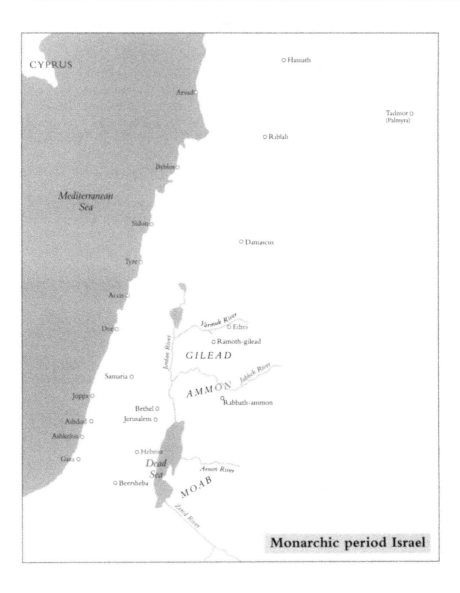

CYPRUS

Hamath ○

Arvad ○

Tadmor ○
(Palmyra)

○ Riblah

Byblos ○

*Mediterranean
Sea*

Sidon ○

○ Damascus

Tyre ○

Acco ○

Dor ○

Yarmuk River

○ Edrei

○ Ramoth-gilead

Jordan River

GILEAD

Samaria ○

Jabbok River

AMMON

Joppa ○

○ Rabbath-ammon

Bethel ○

Ashdod ○   Jerusalem ○

Ashkelon ○

Gaza ○

○ Hebron

*Dead
Sea*

Arnon River

○ Beersheba

MOAB

Zered River

Monarchic period Israel

Despite the detailed account provided by the Bible, the existence of David's "kingdom" has been brought into question because of a general lack of conclusive documentary and archaeological evidence. A discussion of some of these arguments will appear below. At this point, it is enough to point out that a recently excavated inscription from Tel Dan has provided a political tie between the tenth century and the late ninth century. In this document (Biran and Naveh 1993; 1995), the king of Judah is referred to as the representative of the "House of David." This indicates that there is a scribal as well as a political memory of the founding of the dynasty and a clear identification between David's ruling family and a territorial entity (Wesselius 1999, 184). The use of "House of David" rather than "king of Judah" has sparked some controversy among scholars. However, this form of address, using a dynast's name rather than the name of the country, does appear in the Mesha inscription from Moab (Kitchen 1997b, 33) as well as in the Assyrian Annals, which refer to Israel as "Omri-Land."

"I killed Jehoram, son of Ahab, king of Israel, and I killed Ahaziahu, son of Jeroham, king of the House of David, and I set their towns into ruins and turned their land into desolation" (Biran and Naveh 1995, 12–13, lines 7–9).

"Israel (lit.: "Omri-Land" *Bit Humria*) . . . all its inhabitants (and) their possessions I led to Assyria" (Annals of Tiglath-Pileser III [744–727]; *ANET* 284).

Even though the Tel Dan inscription provides a physical link to the founding of the Davidic dynasty, its chief value is found in its proximity in time to the events of the tenth century in Syro-Palestine. As with other extrabiblical texts, we are still forced to rely on the biblical account as a "prompt" to what might otherwise be disconnected or inexplicable references (J. M. Miller 1991, 94–95).

With this as a given, it may be said that the key to the successful operation of a state was its bureaucracy, whose makeup and complexity clearly distinguished it from a tribe (Whybray 1990, 133–39; Frick 1985, 203). Anthropologists have posited as many as ten different kinds of bureaucracies (Malamat 1965, 34–65; Earle 1989, 84–88). How sophisticated the scribes who made up the bureaucracy were prior to the eighth century is still in question (Jamieson-Drake 1991, 76–80). Still, one concrete sign of the activities of these royal bureaucrats may be the introduction of Egyptian **hieratic** numerals and signs in Israelite inscriptions, a level of sophistication indicating both cultural borrowing as well as a standardization of procedure by government officials. Although the earliest evidence we have of this dates to the eighth to seventh centuries, the scribal tradition and such usage most likely goes back at least a century (Glasswasser 1991). Thus, one contribution David and the other early kings of Israel would have chosen to make to facilitate the organization of a centralized state was the meticulous keeping of records of all types. If they indeed incorporated the Egyptian model, then scribes would have been ubiquitous, taking note of harvests, commercial transactions, and the use of labor in public works, as well as recording the activities of the various departments responsibility for the administration and protection of the state (see James 1984, 163–78).

The distribution of power from village to state is apparent in the contrast between the titles of the leaders in the tribe led by Saul (2 Sam. 2:9; see Edelman 1985, 88–89) and those in the state of David (1 Kgs. 4:1–19). The titles of Saul's officials are almost all kin-based, indicating his reliance on **nepotism**. He clearly depends on his son Jonathan (1 Sam. 13:2) and on Abner, who is the son of Saul's uncle (1 Sam. 14:50). In contrast, few of Solomon's officials (1 Kgs. 4:2–19) carry family titles, thereby demonstrating that by the end of the tenth century there was a maturing of the monarchy as an institution, with greater reliance on merit rather than family loyalties or kinship ties. It also indicates sufficient sharing of responsibility to ensure no one person within the bureaucracy could amass sufficient power to threaten the position of the king.

Another sign of the conversion from village to state appeared in the restructuring of the tribe into an army (Talmon 1980, 240–44). In the books of Samuel–Kings, David is pictured as courageous in battle, the master of cunning strategies, and is loyal to those who fought alongside him. He rises to power as a chief when he answers the call of the warriors who muster to defend their villages from the Philistines (1 Sam. 23:1–5). As a chief, he continues to be surrounded and supported by brothers, sons, and the sons of uncles (1 Chr. 2:16; 1 Sam. 22:1–2; 2 Sam. 8:16; 13:32; 17:25).

But David is also aware of the limitations of the tribe and the trap associated with kin-based administration. Without completely abandoning the old ways of defending the people, David begins to centralize the tribes and to move away from a heavy reliance on nepotism. He alters the way in which plunder is distributed, setting up new statutes for the various contingents within his army to demonstrate that all are equal who serve him (1 Sam. 30:21–25). In addition, he shares his wealth with the "elders of Judah," with whom he wishes to garner support (1 Sam. 30:26–31). He hires professional soldiers, and he borrows command patterns from the standing army of Egypt to create a cadre called the "Thirty," ready to counter the first Philistine threat. At one point, he distributes command between Joab and Abishai, who are Israelites and his cousins, and Ittai of Gath, who is a covenant partner (2 Sam. 18:2). Again, David makes his appointments from both Israelite and non-Israelite candidates (J. Rosenberg 1986, 165–68) when he names Benaiah, who is a covenant partner, the commander of the royal bodyguard while retaining Joab as the commander of the army (2 Sam. 20:23; see Ishida 1982, 185).

The biblical account indicates that the command structure of the army continued to be refined throughout the reigns of David and Solomon (Frick 1985, 79). Solomon's elimination of David's commander, Joab, sent a clear signal that he would not be restricted by former loyalties, as did the exile of Abiathar because of his association with Solomon's political rival Adonijah (1 Kgs. 2:13–35; Heaton 1974, 50–51; Ishida 1982, 186). Undoubtedly, during this early period in matters of local defense, the tribes of old still mustered warriors to defend their villages. But once Israel became a full-fledged state, it was the monarch as commander-in-chief of the new nation's standing army who was charged with its defense and expansion.

SOLOMON AND THE ORGANIZATION OF A MONARCHY

If the list of departments and provincial officials in 1 Kings 4:7–19 is to be taken as representative of Solomon's time, and not just a reflection of the Deuteronomist's recreation of his political organization (Ash 1995), then it can be said that a true monarchy came into being during Solomon's reign. The king, through this network of officials and allied members of the local elite (Niemann 2000, 64), was able to exercise some direct influence over the districts of his state but was dependent on allies in the border areas. This is not to say that Israel was a major power or that it had the international economic connections that are portrayed in the narrative. These are most likely part of the "golden age" legend that has been woven around Solomon (J. M. Miller 1997, 13–14; Garbini 1988, 22–25). However, in terms of political development, once the state is able to maintain itself militarily, construct monumental buildings as a reflection of its power and identity (Whitelam 1986), draw on the people for financial support, and extend its rule over a defined area including more than just surrounding villages, then it has crossed the line from a **chiefdom** to a kingdom (Na'aman 1996, 23–24; Ben Tor and Ben-Ami 1998, 36).

The major accomplishments of Solomon's rule, as listed in the biblical account, point to an influential and wealthy kingdom. Certainly, there was political opportunity for the expansion of a small state such as Israel during the tenth through ninth centuries, but this would have had to occur amidst the familiar jockeying for position by more powerful nations and peoples such as the Egyptians, Philistines, and Phoenicians. For instance, Phoenician control over maritime trade in the Mediterranean resulted from the destruction of Ugarit and the incursions of the Sea Peoples after 1200. It seems unlikely that this very wealthy region, with its powerful port cities of Tyre and Sidon, would have been controlled by or subsidiary to Solomon's kingdom as is claimed by 1 Kings 4:20–21 (Niemann 2000, 67). In fact, Solomon was required to transfer control of twenty cities along his northern border to the Phoenicians in payment for materials to build the temple in Jerusalem (1 Kgs. 9:11–14).

It has been suggested that this exchange of territory was justifiable considering the lack of available wealth other than grain and other raw materials in Israel. In fact, a case has been made, concluding that Hiram of Tyre became Solomon's political ally because he needed a buffer between his own territory and the reviving Egyptian kingdom under Shishak/Shoshenq, the new Libyan-born pharaoh of the Twenty-Second Dynasty (ca. 945–924; see Handy 1997, 166). If that was the case, it is interesting to note the marriage between Solomon and an Egyptian princess recorded in 1 Kings 3:1. Such a marriage alliance would have been unthinkable in earlier Egyptian history when pharaohs refused to send their daughters to foreign lands. Apparently that was no longer the case in the Twenty-First and Twenty-Second Dynasties (Kitchen 1997a, 118). Thus, in his attempt to recapture control over Philistia, Siamun might well have sent Solomon a bride and even presented Gezer as a dowry payment (1 Kgs. 9:16) to cement their alliance. If this reconstruction is correct, then Solomon would have been working both sides of the political street, aiding both Phoenician and Egyptian interests.

A reconstruction such as this must still be considered tentative, since we lack direct documentary evidence outside the biblical text. It is plausible (Redford 1992, 310–11) but not completely verifiable. Caution should also be exercised regarding Solomon's construction projects. For instance, a strong consensus developed in the 1970s regarding Solomon's rebuilding of the fortress cities of Hazor, Gezer, and Megiddo (1 Kgs. 9:15) as proof of standardized city planning by his administration. This was based on the appearance of six-chambered city gates, dating to the Iron I period, at each of these sites as well as at Lachish, Ashdod, and Tel Ira (Ussishkin 1990, 82–88). It was further bolstered by the excavations and arguments made by Yadin (1972) and Y. Aharoni (1974, 13–16). However, more recently these conclusions have come under heavy scrutiny. Although some scholars continue to make the case for Solomonic origin (Dever 1997a, 226–27), a number of archaeologists now dispute the claim for uniformity of construction of the gate systems and have withdrawn their support for this position (Knoppers 1997, 27–28). Many prefer either to dismiss any connection with Solomon or argue that such a widespread use of architectural style (both in Israel and in the Philistine/Canaanite cities) cannot serve as an argument for state-sponsored design (Knauf 1997, 92–93; Niemann 1997, 260–63; Finkelstein 1996a, 177–87). However, it can serve as evidence of population growth and increased urbanization during the tenth century (Master 2001, 120–21). In addition, the tenth and ninth-century pottery remains from both Megiddo and Jezreel may bolster the argument for cultural continuity and Solomonic presence in the area of the Jezreel Valley (Oredsson 1998, 98–99).

Caution is also necessary in any discussion of the construction of the Jerusalem temple as described in 1 Kings 5:16–6:38 and 2 Chronicles 4. It is quite likely that Solomon would have built a temple as part of his attempt to transform Jerusalem into a true capital city with several examples of monumental architecture (Hurowitz 1994). The exact size of the structure, however, given a more modest view of the actual wealth of Solomon's kingdom and his actual economic ventures, would more likely be smaller than that depicted in the biblical text. There is a continuity of temple worship described in the Bible throughout the history of Jerusalem from Solomon's time until the fall of the city to the army of Nebuchadnezzar in 587. This suggests that the Deuteronomist, writing at the end of this period, would be more likely to describe the temple of his own time, which had been expanded and embellished over the centuries, and ascribe it to Solomon (Na'aman 1997c, 47).

RECONSTRUCTION OF THE
TENTH-CENTURY MONARCHY

The lack of documentary evidence for the reigns of Saul, David, and Solomon handicaps any attempt at a full historical reconstruction. This is made even worse by the archaeological data from the eleventh and tenth centuries, which does not provide a consistent pattern of monumental construction at city sites and, in many cases, has been lost or badly damaged by erosion and later builders. Particularly difficult is the case of Jerusalem, which has remained in continuous occupation throughout the centuries and thus has not been open, like many other ancient cities, to widespread excavation. To this point very little of "David's city" has been uncovered other than the "stepped-structure" on the southeastern slope that has been identified by some with the *Millo* of 2 Samuel 5:9 (Shiloh 1984, 27). In addition, what has been uncovered is subject to dispute among historians and archaeologists (Stager 1982; Tarler and Cahill 1992, 55–56).

A number of historians currently dismiss even the possibility of the existence of a kingdom ruled by David and Solomon during the tenth century. Based on their survey of the political situation, the demographics of the hill country, and the contention that there is a complete lack of monumental architecture in this period, these scholars allow only for the creation of the kingdom of Judah during the time of the Assyrian hegemony of the eighth–seventh centuries (Thompson 1992: 412; Lemche and Thompson 1994, 19–20; Davies 1992, 69). One bases this same conclusion on a lack of evidence for sufficient "population, building, production, centralization and specialization" necessary to define a state's existence (Jamieson-Drake 1991, 38–39).

Faced with these arguments against the existence of a tenth-century Jerusalem as the center of an Israelite kingdom, other scholars have chosen to take a more positive view. A plausible argument is made that each successive city built on the site of Jerusalem demolished the foundations and robbed previous levels of their stones, making it unlikely that archaeologists would find a great deal of these earlier structures (Na'aman 1996, 19). Furthermore, the point is made that fourteenth-century El-Amarna texts describe Jerusalem as the "seat of a local king," with subsidiary towns and villages under its direct administration, and Late Bronze levels are almost nonexistent. Jerusalem's importance in the tenth century can therefore not be discounted simply on the basis of a current lack of archaeological remains.

EL-AMARNA LETTERS

EA 287: "As the king has placed his name in Jerusalem forever, he cannot abandon it—the land of Jerusalem" (Moran 1992, 328).

EA 290: "A town belonging to Jerusalem . . . a city of the king, has gone over to the side of the men of Qiltu. May the king give heed to 'Abdi-Ḫeba, your servant, and send archers to restore the land of the king to the king" (Moran 1992, 334).

Drawing this together, a more balanced view of events in the tenth century may be drawn from evidence that dates to the time after the breakup of the united kingdom following Solomon's death. Surveys in the hill country of Judah indicate at least thirty-four Judean sites were settled in the Iron Age IIA (Ofer 1994, 102–4). This would be sufficient to draw the conclusion that in the late tenth–ninth centuries Judah "was a peripheral small and powerless kingdom governed by its local dynasty from a highland stronghold of Jerusalem" (Na'aman 1996, 24). Although its rulers considered themselves to be kings and may well have been considered as such by their dependent villages, it would be better to define them as chiefs. In this way, it is possible to better distinguish this period from the time when a fully developed monarchy emerged.

Even with a diminished status, Jerusalem could still be portrayed as a regional power center in the tenth century (Knauf 2000). Reconstruction of the probable archaeological character of the Iron I period (1100–950 by Low Chronology) may also be based on economic assumptions as well as artifactual data. This approach posits the existence of a minor kingdom centered in Jerusalem but subsidiary to the Philistine core area along the southern coast. Such a scenario follows the biblical narrative, which identifies the Philistines as the principal adversary for both Saul and David. It is further corroborated by the shift of copper production and trade during the eleventh–tenth centuries from Cyprus and the Mediterranean coast to inland sources in the Jordan Rift Valley, especially in the area of Kinneret on the Sea of Galilee (Knauf 2000, 84–85). When Phoenicia gained control over the maritime trade in the period between 900 and 750, Jerusalem's fortunes would have declined along with those of the Philistine cities. In fact, excavations at Ekron indicate just such a pattern of prominence in the tenth century followed by a decline until the Assyrians restored the city as a major manufacturing and commercial center in the eighth century (Gitin 1997).

What makes this reconstruction difficult for some is the lack of archaeological remains from the tenth century in Jerusalem. It chooses to dismiss this concern by positing the likelihood that the bulk of David's Jerusalem is located beneath the Temple Mount, north of the Ophel (Knauf 2000, 76–77). Quite likely the Roman and Herodian architects who constructed the temple of Herod and refortified the city obliterated any remains of this settlement. This, of course, cannot be proven, but the economic assumptions of a core and periphery area are sound, based as they are on the changes that took place in the copper trade. The Sea Peoples had disrupted the Cypriot-based copper mining and distribution system that had favored Ugarit until 1200. During the period prior to the mid-tenth century, sources of copper in the Arabah region (from the Dead Sea south to the Gulf of Aqaba) were more extensively exploited, and an inland trade route was established that favored the Philistines and especially the city of Ekron. Then when Phoenicia gained ascendancy over the maritime carrying trade in the Mediterranean, the Cyprus copper mines were reopened, and the center of economic power and political hegemony was shifted north once again.

This scenario of shifting economic and political forces would therefore help to explain how Saul and David would have been able to establish a chiefdom centered on the region between Jerusalem and Shiloh. Just as the biblical narratives suggest, this early Israelite confederation was subsidiary to the Philistine overlords but independent enough to pull together the political loyalties of the Israelite tribes, who had previously depended on a patrimonial leadership model and could adapt them to a king when the situation made it necessary (Master 2001, 128–30). Thus, Jerusalem would have expanded in size and population during this period but would have shrunk temporarily during the mid-tenth century until Solomon was able to establish political and economic ties with the Phoenicians. Evidence of the expansion of Solomon's control, with construction of storehouse cities and chariot stations (1 Kgs. 9:15–19), may be found in pottery and architectural remains at Megiddo and Jezreel (Oredsson 1998, 99). Then, with the division of the kingdom after Solomon's death, a new political situation would have emerged, favoring the northern kingdom with its more abundant natural resources (arable land, grazing areas, moderate climate) and ties to international trade.

PRECEDENTS FORMED IN THE
EARLY MONARCHIC NARRATIVE

Like the ancestral and settlement narratives, the story of the establishment of Israel's monarchy also contains episodes or events that would have a lasting effect on later Israelite history. Admittedly, the Deuteronomistic Historian may have injected some of this data into the narrative at a later date. For example, the "king's call to justice" motif, found in at least five narratives in Samuel–Kings (see 1 Kgs. 21), is an artificial literary device designed to uphold the principle that the king, like every other member of the covenant community, is in fact not above the law (Matthews 1991). However, the select items listed in figure 10 below reflect long-standing traditions that may have been "enhanced" but are more likely to stand as part of the process of political development in the tenth–ninth centuries. Their focus on events and locales in Judah is again reflective of the Deuteronomistic Historian's viewpoint. There were corresponding political developments in the northern kingdom of Israel after the division of the kingdoms, and in fact that northern state evidenced greater maturity in terms of its international relations.

The long history of Jerusalem as a political center (Na'aman 1996, 19–21) and its physical attributes of defensibility and more centralized location made it a likely choice for David's capital city. In addition, since it had not been captured during the settlement period, it retained the character of a politically neutral site and thus one less likely to be a source of internal contention among David's tribal supporters. Finally, because David is said to have spared the Jebusite population, it is probable that he could have employed those who were trained as scribes and government bureaucrats to strengthen his fledging political organization.

Figure 10: Steps toward Monarchy				
Jerusalem becomes Israel's capital (2 Sam. 5:6–12)	Centralized location	Politically neutral city (Judg. 1:21)	Defensible location	Trained bureaucracy in place
Ark installed and the Jerusalem temple built (2 Sam. 6:1–19; 1 Kgs. 5–6)	Symbol of completion of settlement period	Aid in centralizing state religion	Identification of monarchy with divine right to rule	Submergence of potential rallying point vs. monarchy
Everlasting covenant (2 Sam. 7:5–16; 1 Kgs. 9:1–9)	Hereditary monarchy justified	Tie established between Yahweh and Davidic house	Prophet's role as divine messenger established	Potential conflict created with Mosaic covenant
Emergence of bureaucracy and standing army (1 Kgs. 4:1–19)	Reliance on nepotism ends (compare Saul's reliance on relatives)	Allows for expansion of government programs	Formalizes internal and external policy pathways	Kings control enforcement power and defense

When David transports the ark of the covenant to the newly conquered Jerusalem (2 Sam. 6:1–19), a political transformation is recorded. This sacred object connects David's rule to the leadership of Moses and Joshua. Both of these men are portrayed in the text as guardians of God's covenant, and both employ the ark to demonstrate God's direction of the people as well as the power of the Divine Warrior in battle (see Exod. 25:1–22; Num. 10:35; Josh. 6:6–7). While the strand of the ark narrative in 2 Samuel is most likely Deuteronomic in origin (i.e., ca. 600 B.C.E.; see Van der Toorn and Houtman 1994, 227–28), its portrayal of David's actions may well be based on an earlier tradition while at the same time providing a sense of origin for the ark and a justification for its placement in Jerusalem. Whatever the editorial history of the narrative may be, in this form it allows David to draw on the heritage of Israel's past association with the ark. He also garners a portion of the power attached to the ark as the physical symbol of God's presence (Miller and Roberts 1977, 9–17).

Interestingly, David clearly has no intention of using the ark as an object of power. In its previous "career," the ark had served as a focal point of the activities of the Divine Warrior in battle (Josh. 6:6–21; 1 Sam. 4:2–11, 19–22) or as the means of demonstrating Yahweh's control over nature (Josh. 3:5–17). However, David shows no interest in sharing the limelight with the ark. His person or his regime will now take the place of the ark in battle. As a result, David's actions can now be defined as an attempt to capture or contain the ark.

Once safely inside Jerusalem, the ark is submerged along with the other vestiges of the premonarchic, wilderness era (manna, the judges, the Divine Warrior). Clearly, for David's monarchy to be able to emerge and mature as an identifiable political entity, the person of the king and his "house" must take precedence or the monarchy will eventually succumb to nostalgia for the "old ways," as exemplified in Sheba's cry in 2 Samuel 20:1—"We have no portion in David, no share in the son of Jesse! Everyone to your tents, O Israel!"

David enhances the sense of the power of his regime by proving his ability to manipulate the ark and then placing it in the background. What is particularly interesting, however, is that David is unable to construct a temple to house the ark. He lacks complete control of the natural resources of the nation and a period of peace to devote to such a monumental project. It is left to his successor Solomon to complete this final step in subjugating the ark, transferring it from "the city of David" to its new home on Mount Zion (1 Kgs. 8:1–9). This once all-important object is forever hidden from public view and replaced in the minds and sight of the people with a piece of monumental architecture associated with the dynasty of David (Whitelam 1986, 66–73). Although the ark is given a place of ultimate sacred honor within the Holy of Holies, it has been effectively removed from the world of the living and is never heard of again. In fact, the final mention of the ark of the covenant is as a thing of the past, as an object that is no longer needed because Jerusalem has become the new "throne of the LORD" (Jer. 3:16–17). Hereafter, the temple, which serves as one means of centralizing the king's authority, becomes the focal point for worship as well as the symbol of God's designation of the house of David as the legitimate rulers of the state.

The "everlasting covenant" made with David begins by restating the promise of land for a chosen people (2 Sam. 7:8–11). David then is assured that his son will rule after him and that his descendants will continue to rule the kingdom "forever." At first glance, this statement sounds a good deal like the covenant promise made to Abraham that he would be the "father of many nations" (Gen. 17:4). The difference comes when David's descendants inevitably fail to be just and commit crimes that violate the Abrahamic covenant and the Ten Commandments. At that point, they, as individuals, are punished. However, the dynasty will live on and God's "steadfast love" or "faithfulness" will not be withdrawn (2 Sam. 7:12–16). The result is a lessening of the dangers over succession and a growing sense of a "divine right" to rule.

This relationship is to be everlasting, based on God's mercy and concern for Israel. In the context of the house of David, it is a reassurance of continual direction and a seal of divine approval for this dynasty's rule. What is curious about these two approaches to the monarchy is the way in which they appear to operate side by side throughout the history of the monarchy. Once the nation divides into two kingdoms, Israel and Judah, the idea of covenant is also divided. According to the official records contained in the book of Kings, Judah and Jerusalem continue to adhere to the Davidic dynasty, and presumably this four-hundred-year period of political stability is based on God's covenant with David. Assassination and the overthrow of kings occurs only a couple of times in Judah (2 Kgs. 14:19; 21:23).

On the other hand, the northern kingdom of Israel will be continually troubled by political turmoil. Since its leaders lack this understanding of "divine right" rule, there is more opportunity for adventurism. The rule in Israel becomes "succession by assassination," with one military coup d'etat after another. The only legitimating factor in this process is the occasional intervention by God's prophet, designating who should be the next king (see 2 Kgs. 9:1–13). The result is divine sanction for rebellion and civil war. A system such as this inevitably undermined the authority of the monarchy and was a prime factor in the conquest and destruction of the northern kingdom (Matthews 2000, 29).

Chapter 4

Period of the Divided Kingdom (ca. 925–586 B.C.E.)

During the late tenth to the end of the seventh centuries, the history of ancient Israel can be treated with more certainty. While it is not possible to reconstruct all aspects of the political climate of the divided monarchy, there are some things that can be said confidently about the forces that shaped the era. A combination of extrabiblical and biblical sources provides many insights into the workings of government, international affairs, trade, and the maturing of the states of Israel and Judah.

With this as a starting point, it is also necessary to state that the biblical narrative in the book of Kings continues to be dominated by the Deuteronomistic Historian's interpretation of history. Thus, the description of the period of the divided kingdom is a product of the Deuteronomistic Historian's attempt to increase the importance of the southern kingdom of Judah at the expense of the larger and more strategically placed northern kingdom of Israel. This can be explained, at least partially, by noting the Bible has an ethnocentric view of history. In other words, the writers and editors tell their history solely from their own point of view, and they choose to include only those details that match their understanding of their own history. It should also be noted, of course, that the southern kingdom will outlive the north by over a century and will thus be able to have the last word on many events recorded in the text and to make the editing decisions that will shape its message and story.

In addition, the repeated use of the term "all Israel" (1 Kgs. 12:20; 16:16–17, 2 Kgs. 11:17; 14:21; 23:2–3) in relation to the political upheavals in the northern kingdom of Israel tied the people to the fate of their leaders and provided a justification for the Deuteronomistic Historian to condemn them for their support of corrupt and non-Davidic kings (Knight 1995, 101–2). To add further weight to this version of the history of Israel and Judah, the Deuteronomistic Historian continuously refers to reference works, including "the Annals of the Kings of Israel" (1 Kgs. 14:19; 15:31; 16:14, 20; 22:39) and "the Annals of the Kings of Judah" (1 Kgs. 14:6; 15:23; 22:45). In this way, the reader is assured that the Deuteronomistic Historian is drawing on records of the time and that this account is indeed verifiable (Na'aman 1997b, 158).

Figure 11: What You Need to Know about the Divided Monarchy Period

- Solomon died ca. 925 B.C.E. and his successor could not maintain the consensus of rulership.
- Civil war divided Israel into two states: Judah (south) and Israel (north).
- Israel proved to be the stronger state and dominated Judah politically and economically.
- The house of David ruled Judah; various households (Jeroboam, Omri, Jehu) ruled Israel.
- In the midst of superpower conflicts over Syro-Palestine, Assyria destroyed Israel in 720.

In beginning the study of the period of the divided kingdom, it is best to keep in mind the relative differences between the two political areas of Israel (northern kingdom) and Judah (southern kingdom). What follows are thumbnail sketches for each:

Israel extended from Bethel in the south to Dan in the north (see map). It encompassed some of the most productive land in Canaan and also straddled the important trade routes that passed through the Jezreel Valley, guarded by Bethshean (eastern approach) and Megiddo (western approach) and along the coastal highway, the **Via Maris**. The climate is more moderate in this area as well, with annual rainfall of approximately thirty-two inches and large stretches of relatively level farmland and good pasturage for large numbers of sheep and cattle. Throughout much of its history, the northern and west central Transjordanian regions of Bashan and Gilead also were a part of the northern kingdom, and this added to its wealth and political importance. Bashan contained excellent pastureage for cattle, and Gilead provided needed farm acreage. These natural riches had their price, for Israel was a fairly desirable prize to the growing Mesopotamian and Egyptian empires. This eventually cost them their political existence. The capital city of Samaria fell to the Assyrians in 720.

Judah retained the important political/cultic center of Jerusalem, with its Solomonic temple and priestly community. However, in terms of arable land and natural resources, it was handicapped. The major Philistine city-states (Gaza,

Ashkelon, Ekron, Ashdod, and Gath) dominated the coastal region of the west and the fertile Shephelah plateau for most of Judah's existence. However, the Philistine cities were often under the political control of Egyptian, Assyrian, or Babylonian rulers during this period. Judah maintained a defensive frontier with Philistia, including the fortress city of Lachish. Much of the southeastern portion of Judah was minimally inhabited steppe and desert, especially around the Dead Sea. Only Beersheba, Arad, and Hebron functioned as relatively large population centers. In addition, the hill country inhibited travel and communication, making coordination of the economic resources in this village-based culture difficult. Thus, in nearly every respect Judah was a minor state, often dominated by its northern neighbor Israel, especially during the reigns of Omri and Ahab. Unlike Israel, which is often referenced in extrabiblical texts from the ninth century onward, Judah is not mentioned in extrabiblical texts until the late seventh century.

EXTRABIBLICAL SOURCES AND HISTORICITY

In contrast to the periods covered in the three previous chapters, the period that will be discussed below (ca. 925–587) has benefited from a wealth of extrabiblical data that helps to illumine the biblical record. There will still be some holes in our data, and a certain caution will have to be exercised in dealing with the official royal reports of events. These reports, known as annals, were written for the rulers of ancient Mesopotamia and by their nature are both exaggerated and filled with claims that can only be termed propaganda. Nevertheless, there is much more to work with here than is the case for earlier periods. In its coverage of the time period, this section will include the division of the nation into two separate political entities. It therefore will be necessary to make constant reference to which kingdom is under discussion. In addition, the fact that many of the kings of both kingdoms have the same name will require sorting out (see figure 17 listing kings for both nations). A number of chronological aids will be employed to help with this, but the student will also have to return frequently to the Bible to keep this material straight.

DIVISION OF THE KINGDOM

According to the biblical account, the forces that contributed to the division of the Israelite kingdom were both internal and external (1 Kgs. 11:14–25). A look at the map of the region graphically demonstrates the fragmented political character of the times. Neighboring kingdoms such as Edom and Aram to the south and east, as well as rival claimants to power such as Jeroboam, son of Nebat (1 Kgs. 11:26–40), put great pressure on Israel. With regard to external threats, some argue that the archaeological evidence cannot support a "kingdom" in either Seir (in the Negev highlands) or in Transjordanian Edom

(Edelman 1995, 176–77). If this is the case and only small clusters of village sites existed in Edom in this period, then this can only "indicate the emergence of a localized chiefdom—an unlikely threat to Solomon" (Edelman 1995, 177). Similarly, there are no tenth-century sources for a powerful kingdom in Aram (Syria) in Assyrian texts. The tradition that these regions were attempting to pressure Israel's borders during Solomon's reign may actually be dependent on later events that were projected by the biblical writers back into the early monarchy as well.

A more tangible sign of the approaching difficulties is seen in the activities of the Egyptians. They are said to have chosen to harbor at least two political ene-

Figure 12: Extrabiblical Parallels during the Monarchic Period	
TEXT	PARALLEL
Shishak/Shoshenq I Campaign Stele: Shishak campaigns in Palestine ca. 925.	**1 Kgs. 14:25–26:** Shishak loots temple of its golden shields
Annals of Shalmaneser III: Report of battle of Qarqar in 853 mentions Ahab	No direct parallel in Ahab narrative
Mesha Stele (ca. 840): Mentions Omri	**2 Kgs. 3:** Combined invasion of Moab
Black Obelisk of Shamaneser III (841): Mentions Jehu and depicts his tribute	No direct parallel in Jehu narrative
Tel Dan Inscription (ca. 805): Mentions Hazael of Aram, Joram (Israel), and Ahaziah (Judah)	**2 Kgs. 9:** Credits death of Joram and killing of Ahaziah to Jehu's revolt
Azekah Inscription (ca. 713): Mentions Sargon II's campaign and capture of a portion of Hezekiah's territory	**Isa. 20:** Describes the Ashdod revolt and the prophet's "naked circuit"
Siloam Inscription (ca. 705): Describes construction of Jerusalem water tunnel	**2 Kgs. 20:20:** Credits Hezekiah with bringing "water into the city"
Sennacherib's Annals (701): Describe the Assyrian siege of Jerusalem	**2 Kgs. 18:13–37:** Depicts the siege of Jerusalem and negotiations
Nebuchadnezzar II's Annals (598): Describe the fall of Jerusalem to the Neo-Babylonians and its plundering	**2 Kgs. 24:10, 13–17:** Narrates the capture of Jerusalem, its plundering, and the appointment of Zedekiah as king
Arad Letters (ca. 594): Warn against possible incursions by Edom against Judah's southern border	**Ps. 137:7–9:** Condemns Edom for taking Israelite territory after the Babylonians capture Jerusalem
Lachish Letters (ca. 587): Describe the last desperate days for Lachish	**Jer. 34:6–7:** Lists Lachish and Azekah as the only outposts remaining to Judah

mies of the Davidic dynasty—Hadad, ruler of Edom (1 Kgs. 11:17–22), and Jeroboam (1 Kgs. 11:40). The **Septuagint** (Greek) version of these passages suggests that the material about Hadad should actually be assigned to Jeroboam (Galpaz 1991, 13–15). This would then be an indication of the Deuteronomistic Historian's attempt to diminish Jeroboam as an important member of the pharaoh's court. It also calls into question whether Hadad was a historical contemporary of Solomon, and may remove him from the picture, providing Jeroboam sole claim to a position as a political exile in Egypt (Edelman 1995, 179).

In addition, the relative strength of Egypt under this Libyan-born pharaoh can be seen in the apparent ease with which Shishak/Shoshenq I was able to move his army through the Shephelah from southern Palestine toward the end of Solomon's reign. This suggests that Egypt had come to dominate relations with the Philistines (Clancy 1999, 7–8, 19). It also marked a return, after a period of nearly two centuries (since the end of the Late Bronze Age), of aggressive Egyptian military and economic activities in this area and much of the rest of the Levant (Weinstein 1998, 193–94).

Yet another factor in the coming crisis was the inherent problem of hereditary monarchy. As is often the case with newly emerged kingdoms, the consensus between Jerusalem and the tribal leaders that David and Solomon pulled together during their reigns proved to be too fragile to survive the forces of division that asserted themselves when Solomon's weak son, Rehoboam, came to the throne. It can be argued that when the new monarchs tried to expand their traditional role as judge/chief, "they failed to negotiate them successfully with the majority of the tribes" (Master 2001, 130). As a result, the tribal structures simply reverted to a revised and divided model, with kinship and political ties holding Judah to its allegiance to David's house and the newly recognized leadership of Jeroboam providing the glue needed to hold the northern tribes together. Thus, the cry for secession, first heard during Sheba's revolt in David's time (2 Sam. 20:1), was able to ring out again, spelling the demise of any further attempt to unite all of the Israelite tribes under a single leader.

What share do we have in David? We have no inheritance in the son of Jesse. To your tents, O Israel! Look now to your own house, O David. (1 Kgs. 12:16)

As tensions rose toward the end of Solomon's reign, it is not surprising that a rival leader such as Jeroboam would be chosen and authenticated through his designation by the prophet Ahijah (1 Kgs. 11:29–39). It is unlikely this **investiture** scene remained a secret, and since the text indicates that Solomon subsequently tried to kill Jeroboam, it must have been fairly well known (unlike what seems to be the case for Saul in 1 Sam. 10:1–8). Furthermore, it is not surprising that Jeroboam would have established a relationship with the Egyptian king Shishak/Shoshenq (1 Kgs. 11:40). The Egyptians, in sheltering a political enemy of Solomon, must have felt that they had much to gain from serving as a political haven. In addition, Solomon either did not have the power to demand extradition or did not have a formal treaty arrangement that would have required extradition by allies.

EXTRADITION CLAUSE: TREATY BETWEEN RAMESSES II AND HATTUSILIS III

"The great king of Hatti shall not grant asylum to any fugitive from Egypt. The great king of Hatti shall have fugitives extradited to Rameses. . . . The pharaoh of Egypt shall have fugitives extradited to the great king of Hatti" (*OTP* 89).

A case can be made that the smooth transition of power from Solomon to Rehoboam is evidence of the maturing of Israel's monarchy. Unlike the two previous generations, there is no struggle for power, no elimination of the previous dynasty (David's control over the Saulide survivors Mephibosheth and Michal) or of rival claimants from the Davidic ruling family (Solomon's execution of Adonijah). The narrative merely indicates that Rehoboam succeeded his father, but that simple statement (1 Kgs. 11:43) indicates that an orderly political transition had taken place. However, the forces of secession quickly drew Rehoboam into a confrontation that would provide the crisis leading to the division of the kingdoms.

The "summit meeting" at Shechem stands in stark contrast to a previous meeting of the tribal leaders and the king. In 2 Samuel 5:1–3, the elders came to David's stronghold at Hebron to anoint him their king and pledge their allegiance to him in place of Saul's family. However, Rehoboam is forced to go to the northern tribal center at Shechem to face what is apparently already a state of rebellion on the part of the northern tribes (Tadmor 1982, 252–54). There he will meet with the elders on their own terms (1 Kgs. 12:1). With Jeroboam standing in the wings ready to take power, the elders of the tribal groups ask for a lighter burden from the central government (1 Kgs. 2:3a, 12; 2 Chr. 10:2; Willis 1991, 42–43). If there is any historical character to Solomon's "district list" in 1 Kings 4:7–19 (Ash 1995), the various tribal areas had been heavily taxed by Solomon and closely managed from Jerusalem. Thus, it would not be unusual for them to make demands for more local autonomy in managing their affairs and territory and to ask that there be fewer demands for labor service. In fact, complaints over the continual drain of manpower to build roads and fortifications seems to be a common charge made against "tyrants" by their opponents.

CYRUS CYLINDER (CA. 540 B.C.E.)

As a political justification of his conquest of Babylon, the Persian king Cyrus charges that Nabonidus, the king of Babylon, "tormented its inhabitants with corvée-work (lit.: a yoke) without relief, he ruined them all" (*ANET* 315).

When, after three days, Rehoboam chose to listen to his younger advisors rather than the more mature men, who had more experience with the negotiation process that had lead to the establishment of David's and Solomon's kingdom, the northern tribal leaders had little choice. They were unwilling to bend to such a blatant attempt at intimidation by the blustering Rehoboam and voted with their feet. It is therefore possible to charge that Rehoboam's "evil deeds," also recorded in the Septuagint version, are the basis for the division of the kingdom (Shaw 1997, 61–63). To complete the Deuteronomistic Historian's case, the text then reinforces the divine intent behind these events, using an unusual technical term, *sibbâ* ("turn of affairs"), in both the Kings and Chronicles versions, thereby indicating that major policy shifts have their origin in the decisions made by God (Machinist 1995, 117–20).

(So) the king did not listen to the people, for it was a *sibbâ* [1 Kgs. 12:15]/ *nĕsibbâ* [2 Chr. 10:15] from Yahweh [Kgs.]/ God [Chr.] in order that he [Kgs.]/ Yahweh [Chr.] might confirm his work, which he [Kgs.]/ Yahweh [Chr.] spoke through Ahijah the Silonite to Jeroboam son of Nebat. (adapted from Machinist 1995, 106)

In summary, the Deuteronomistic Historian portrays the events that lead up to the secession of the northern tribes as a result of Solomon's apostasies (both religious and political) under the influence of his foreign wives, and the failure of Rehoboam to successfully negotiate with the tribal elders at Shechem (1 Kgs. 11–12:19). Ahijah's oracle (1 Kgs. 11:29–39) granting Jeroboam the right to rule and the subsequent accession of that "servant" of Solomon to power over the northern tribes can thus be seen as part of a pattern of prophecy and fulfillment (Knoppers 1990, 428). The **Chronicler's** account, however, never mentions Solomon's culpability in these events. Instead, the key to this later writer's version of events is found in Abijah's speech in 2 Chronicles 13:4–12. Here Rehoboam's son makes the case that the northern tribes and Jeroboam had no justification for their actions. They are ignoring the political rights of the house of David, granted to them by Yahweh in the everlasting covenant, and therefore have no choice, if they wish to remain a part of the covenantal community, but to return to Davidic rule and the supremacy of Jerusalem (Knoppers 1990, 437, 440).

One apparent result of the division is that Rehoboam builds a string of "cities of constraint" to help him protect and control that portion of the kingdom that remained to him (2 Chr. 11:5–10). This action may have prevented any further defections from the house of David, and it would have allowed Rehoboam the chance to build a political network among his family and supporters who would have been assigned to these cities (Hobbs 1994, 61).

On a wider scale, the division of the kingdoms led to the weakening of the two nations' defenses, allowing the Egyptian pharaoh Shishak/Shoshenq to campaign freely in Judah and Israel (Kitchen 1986, 296–300). His list of conquests, which includes fifty-five place-names, indicates that Rehoboam was unable to prevent this incursion. What the pharaoh may in fact have been doing is simply making a brief foray to reassert Egyptian claims in Canaan. The lack of major cities on the list and questions about his actual route, which seems to center primarily on the Judean Shephelah north to the Sharon Plain, may be an indicator of a fairly limited campaign strategy (Clancy 1999, 18–19). In addition, there is no mention in the Egyptian text of the city of Jerusalem, or a claim that matches the statement in 1 Kings 14:25–26 that the Jerusalem temple was looted. It is possible that Rehoboam paid a heavy tribute to the Egyptians, but apparently the capital city was not besieged or captured. The stele fragment discovered at Megiddo, which dates to this 925 B.C.E. campaign, does indicate the intent on the pharaoh's part to reestablish an Egyptian presence in Canaan, but Shishak's death a year later curtailed that plan (Ussishkin 1990, 73–74). Instead, it would be the Neo-Assyrians and Phoenicians who would dominate the political climate in Syro-Palestine for the next three centuries (Gitin 1998, 162–63).

JEROBOAM'S SIN AND THE PATTERN OF LEADERSHIP IN ISRAEL

The biblical text clearly sets an ideological tone in its recitation of the actions taken by Jeroboam after he becomes king. This section is crucial for an understanding of the Deuteronomistic Historian's conception of history and the monarchy. By making an extended case for Jeroboam's apostasy, an "ideology of the founder" is created, which will provide the explanation for Israel's eventual fall and Judah's survival (Ash 1998, 23). Because Jeroboam, the first king of the northern kingdom, was evil, then his dynasty must fail. His "sin" will in turn be the measuring stick for all subsequent kings. If they continue "Jeroboam's sin," then they are also evil and subject to the same condemnation that the founding dynast faced.

Interestingly, Jeroboam is not blamed in the book of Kings for the division of the kingdom and, like David, is given a prophetic promise that his dynasty will be successful if he keeps God's statutes (1 Kgs. 11:37–38). However, such bright prospects are quickly clouded by what the Deuteronomistic Historian considers unforgivable apostasy. "Jeroboam's sin" draws Israel away from Yahweh and Jerusalem and toward idolatry and cultic decentralization.

Figure 13: "Jeroboam's Sin" (1 Kgs. 12:26–32)

- Rival shrines are dedicated at Dan and Bethel, replacing Jerusalem as the sole cultic center
- Golden calves are placed in the shrines as substitutes for the ark of the covenant
- High places (*bamôt*) are tolerated in local village culture
- Non-Levites are appointed to serve as priests
- A revised religious calendar is mandated for the major festivals

---

Taken as a whole, it is possible to construe each of these politically based decisions as part of a systematic royal program to enhance Jeroboam's control over the northern tribes and to eliminate cultic ties to the south. These actions, which still included the worship of Yahweh, should be considered political, not moral, in tone. It is certain that Jeroboam would have had many advantages as well as some very real problems as the first king of the northern kingdom. Figure 14 below distinguishes the two nations:

Figure 14: Major Differences between Judah and Israel	
JUDAH	ISRAEL
- Smaller territory (two tribes)	- Larger territory (ten tribes)
- Smaller population	- Larger population
- Less wealth and natural resources	- More wealth and natural resources
- More isolated geographically but less conflict with neighbors	- Less isolated geographically but more conflict with neighbors
- Established dynastic succession and fairly stable government	- Strongman rule, many kings are murdered, government at times unstable
- Jerusalem as sole capital	- Capital moves from Tirzah to Shechem to Samaria
- Had administrative structures in place	- Had to create bureaucracy, army
- Had religious center in Jerusalem and an official cult	- Had no religious center, Dan and Bethel established as shrines
- Fell to Babylonians in 587 B.C.E.	- Fell to Assyrians in 720 B.C.E.
- Had more influence on editing of biblical account (e.g., Deuteronomistic Historian)	- Had less influence on biblical account
- Survived exile and returned to restore Jerusalem and the cult	- Exile ended political and social identity (ten lost tribes)

One of the first steps Jeroboam took in his program of reform was to sanction the establishment of royal shrines on the southern and northern borders of the newly formed state. This move to restore the importance of regional religious centers would have been seen as a betrayal by the religious centrists who wished to make Jerusalem the only place for cultic activity. Jeroboam's choice in this manner provided convenient religious centers for the Israelite people, allowing them an excuse to separate themselves from Jerusalem. Certainly, there is a long cultic history for Bethel (Gen. 28). It also is not surprising that Dan was chosen as the other royal shrine. The story in Judges 17–18 indicates long-standing cultic activity there at one of the sources of the Jordan River. In addition, like the pillar set up by Jacob and Laban (Gen. 31:44–54), these shrines functioned as political as well as cultic markers for the recognized limits of Israelite territory. One surprise in the narrative, however, is the omission of Shechem as a royal shrine. This was Jeroboam's capital city, and it might be expected that like David and Solomon he would have built or refurbished a shrine in that important city (Toews 1993, 109). This also is a place associated with sacrifice as far back as Abram's first entrance into Canaan (Gen. 12), and it would be natural for the capital city to also function as the chief religious center for the nation.

The placing of images of golden calves in each shrine is more problematic. It could be argued that Jeroboam was simply following the same pattern set by the ark of the covenant, whose lid featured the wings of the cherubim and functioned as a pedestal or throne for Yahweh. In the same way, the calves also could be seen as more generic divine pedestals, not as unique as the ark but still serving as substitutes. Furthermore, Jeroboam's actions also could be said to be a demonstration of a preexisting form of worship in Israel that accepted cult images and calf symbolism (Cross 1973, 73–75; Stern 2001b, 26–27). However, the Deuteronomistic Historian does not mean to give Jeroboam the benefit of the doubt. Instead, the king is condemned for promoting idolatry and leading the Israelites into false worship practices (Knoppers 1995, 101).

There are clear parallels between this story and Exodus 32, where Aaron shapes a golden calf for the frightened people at Mount Sinai. However, since the Exodus materials literarily predate the Deuteronomistic Historian, it is most likely that the late seventh-century editors of the Joshua–2 Kings text knew the story of Aaron. Furthermore, there is a real contrast between these two events. In Exodus 32, Moses quickly puts an end to the idolatry and employs the Levites to "cleanse" the camp by slaying three thousand offenders (32:27–28). In contrast, the Deuteronomistic Historian portrays Jeroboam as a leader who does not appear to have learned from these events (Knoppers 1995, 101–3). Jeroboam uses the same formula proclaimed by Aaron (Exod. 32:4), designating the images as "your gods . . . who brought you up out of the land of Egypt" (1 Kgs. 12:28). Furthermore, despite being given a sign of God's displeasure by a prophet (1 Kgs. 13:1–10), Jeroboam never repents his actions and makes no move either to remove the calves or to shut down the shrines at Dan and Bethel.

The inappropriateness of Jeroboam's use of golden calves is further highlighted in the text by the fact that all of his actions are motivated by his own thinking, not divine sanction or mandate. Some see this as a form of "original sin" on Jeroboam's part (Hoffmann 1980, 132). What it demonstrates is a king who is fearful of losing the support of the same people who had brought him to power, and who tries to forestall his own overthrow or assassination by "drawing them away" into idolatry rather than fulfilling the Deuteronomic ideal (Deut. 12, 16, 18) of "constraining them from idolatry" (Lasine 1992, 144–45).

The remainder of Jeroboam's reforms appear quite political in nature. His employing non-Levites in his shrines simply indicates that he valued political loyalty over cultic orthodoxy. The Levites had been bureaucrats in the service of the Davidic kings. These newly appointed men owed their jobs to King Jeroboam and therefore made decisions on ritual and the education of the people based on the government's position. Since there was no concern over separation of church and state in the ancient world, this should not be seen as an unusual perversion of royal power. Similarly, allowing local "high places" (*bamôt*) to continue to function and changing the religious calendar may be indications of political pandering and a practical understanding of people who will not have the time or money to go to major festivals at both the northern shrines as well as to Jerusalem. Still, the vast majority (80–90 percent) of the population continued to live in small villages and would have been more concerned with local issues than with the king's concern over Jerusalem's possible allure. If Jeroboam had not been overly aggressive in impinging upon their lives and their property, it is likely they would have supported him and his officials (Knight 1995, 105–7).

Whether these actions actually represented new reforms or whether they played upon already existing conditions in Israel cannot be readily proven. Some suggest that Jeroboam was simply taking advantage of religious traditions that already existed in Israel and shaping them to fit his political aims (Ash 1998, 24). Thus, the Deuteronomistic Historian is anachronistically condemning idolatrous and cultic practices in Jeroboam's day while actually aiming its vitriol at an audience in the eighth or seventh century. The argument is also made that the Deuteronomistic Historian "is waging a pre-exilic battle" (perhaps in defense of Hezekiah's reforms) in using Jeroboam as the exemplar of premeditated evil leadership (Knoppers 1995, 104). Whatever the case, the stamp that the editor has put on the royal annals displays a clear theological and political agenda.

DYNASTIC CHANGES IN THE NORTHERN KINGDOM

The royal annals contained in the biblical account make it clear that in the northern kingdom of Israel the stability of the government and the legitimacy of its rulers were based on a variety of sources. For example, the king needed to have the ability to marshal support from the elite groups (priests and large landowners) and maintain a modicum of popularity through a demonstration of personal competency, control of the military, and administration of economic forces

(Schulte 1995, 134). The text also indicates that the kings relied on bureaucrats to collect taxes and manage the forced labor service. In addition, military commanders took the field against the nation's enemies, protecting the borders and providing that show of force needed to prevent invasion or insurrection.

Despite these measures, it is evident that political takeovers did take place on a regular basis in the north. This is explained in the biblical text by repeated prophetic condemnations. Thus, Ahijah's prophecy calling for the destruction of Jeroboam's dynasty (1 Kgs. 14:7–14) is fulfilled in 1 Kings 15:25–31 when Baasha overthrows Jeroboam's son Nadab and a general purge of the royal family takes place. Similarly, the prophet Jehu, son of Hanani, condemns Baasha's dynasty (1 Kgs. 16:14), and subsequently the king's son Elah is overthrown by Zimri, a chariot commander. This is once again followed by a purge of the members of the royal house (1 Kgs. 16:8–13).

These violent changes of government would have created a sense of instability and would have undermined the loyalty of local leaders and the general population. It would not have been in anyone's best interests to place their entire faith in a particular dynasty if there was a regular sequence of palace revolts. As a result, there was probably less uniformity in the culture of the northern kingdom, leaving it open to the syncretistic influences and social injustices so often condemned by the eighth-century prophets Amos (2:6–12) and Hosea (4:12–19).

With the biblical writers concentrating on the failures of the kings of the northern kingdom, it is interesting to compare this with what we know from extrabiblical sources. For example, Omri, the rebellious chariot commander, who set himself up as king after overthrowing Zimri, purposely receives very little mention in the biblical account other than his construction of the new capital city at Samaria and the arranged marriage between his son Ahab and the Phoenician princess Jezebel (1 Kgs. 16:21–28). However, his name (i.e., his dynasty) becomes synonymous in Assyrian royal annals with the kingdom of Israel. Repeatedly, they refer to this region as *Bît Humria*, "Omri-Land."

Interestingly, the Assyrians also refer to Jehu as "the son of Omri" (Shalmaneser III's bull inscription in *ANET* 280), even after Jehu overthrew the family of Omri's son Ahab (2 Kgs. 9). It is possible that this is an indication that the Assyrians were aware of a kinship link between Jehu and Omri that the biblical writers chose not to include (Schneider 1996, 106–7). Whatever Jehu's paternity might be, it is clear that Omri was an important political figure but that the biblical writers chose not to give him due credit. In fact, Omri's designation as the founder of the dynasty is further submerged by the eighteen references to the "house of Ahab." The Deuteronomistic Historian as well as the prophetic writers chose to employ a formulaic designation to emphasize Ahab's house as "the most sinful royal house" in Israel's history (Ishida 1975, 135–37).

The decisions made by the biblical editors are a reflection of the ways in which "history" is shaped by an "insider" viewpoint and its religious and political biases. This is not unique to the Bible. It is quite likely that Mesopotamian and Egyptian royal annals were also selective in their treatment of events, and consciously chose not to include embarrassing items (Dion 1995, 486). The result of this editing process is an official version, with distinct biases, and a strict political and social agenda.

The Household of Omri

One of the most important international events to take place during the Omride Dynasty was the Battle of Qarqar in 853. The Assyrian Empire, under Ashurnasirpal II (883–859) and his successor Shalmaneser III (858–824), had steadily pushed westward toward the Mediterranean Sea during the ninth century in an attempt to establish a claim to hegemony over Syria and Palestine. Their continuous campaigning brought rich stores of luxury goods back to Assyria, and their territorial aspirations were bolstered by the establishment of colonial settlements in conquered regions (Tadmor 1975, 37–38). Fearing this approaching menace to their economic and political interests, the smaller states, led by the Syrian kingdoms of Damascus/Aram and Hamath, formed a coalition of twelve nations, pooling their military resources in an effort to take a stand at the Orontes River in Syria. According to the Assyrian Annals, among those rulers who contributed the most chariots and soldiers was Ahab, the king of Israel.

Based on this documentation, it is clear that Ahab was a significant treaty partner in this alliance (1 Kgs. 20:32–34), but again the biblical writers have chosen to totally ignore both this battle and Ahab's role in it. Curiously, neither the Assyrian inscription nor the biblical text mentions Judah as part of the alliance. This may be an indication that Judah was an ally of Israel at this time, an arrangement that may have been formalized by the marriage of Omri's granddaughter Athaliah to King Jehoshaphat's son Jehoram (2 Kgs. 8:26; 2 Chr. 22:2; Schulte 1995, 135). As a result, their troops and chariots would have been under Ahab's general command.

From this account, it is obvious that the allies had a larger chariot force than Shalmaneser. Although the Assyrian king does claim a victory at Qarqar, this was more likely a draw. He does not mention adding territory any further west, and

---

Figure 15: Shalmaneser III's Monolith Inscription

"I marched to Qarqar and laid siege to the city. Once it was captured, I set it on fire. Irhuleni, the ruler of Qarqar, mustered only 700 chariots, 700 cavalry and 10,000 soldiers, but his twelve covenant partners also fielded armies against me."

The most important of these allies were:
Ben-Hadad II, the ruler of Aram: 1,200 chariots; 1,200 calvary; 20,000 soldiers
Ahab, the ruler of Israel: 2,000 chariots; 10,000 soldiers
Irqanata, the ruler of an area northeast of Tripoli, Lebanon: 10 chariots; 10,000 soldiers
Adunu-ba'il, the ruler of Shian (Phoenicia): 30 chariots; 10,000 (?) soldiers
(*OTP* 168–69)

he was forced to fight the same coalition led by two kings, Ben-Hadad of Damascus and Irhuleni of Hamath, three more times in 849, 848, and 845 (Elat 1975, 28–29). Assyrian fortunes did change, however, following the deaths of Ahab (1 Kgs. 22:29–40) and Ben-Hadad. This was because when the usurper Hazael overthrew the Syrian king (see 2 Kgs. 8:7–15), all political ties with other states were dissolved until renegotiated.

Left in isolation, Iruleni of Hamath accepted Assyrian control, submitting to the usual imposition of tribute payments and forced labor demands (Dion 1995, 483). Hazael continued his open opposition to the Assyrians and forced Israel's king Jehoram to remain in the alliance after the Israelites failed to recapture Ramoth-Gilead from Aram (1 Kgs. 22:1–40; 2 Kgs. 6:24–7). A new Israelite political strategy did not occur until Jehu overthrew Jehoram and shifted his allegiance to the Assyrians. Subsequently, the entire alliance collapsed and Shalmaneser was able by 841 to invade Aram and at least temporarily defeat Hazael. Interestingly, evidence of subsequent Assyrian campaigns in the area indicates that Hazael and the Syrians continued to be a problem, and Hazael may have even crossed the Euphrates, raiding Shalmaneser's own territory (Dion 1995, 484–86).

It is possible that the Moabite king Mesha took advantage of Israel's participation in the alliance against Assyria to win Moab's freedom (Elat 1975, 31 n. 24). Certainly the military forces of Israel under King Jehoram would have been concentrated further north and east, supporting those of Aram, and no quick response would have been possible to a revolt. The Moabite Inscription, or Mesha Stele, was prepared to commemorate King Mesha's liberation of his country from Israelite control and dates to approximately 840. It is also an artful, political justification for Mesha's invasion of the land of Medeba, north of Moab's traditional border at the Wadi el-Mujib (River Arnon). Justifications such as this are a feature in ancient Near Eastern royal inscriptions, and in this case are the basis for the claim that Mesha had the right to reconquer previously captured Moabite territory (Na'aman 1997a, 83–84). The text describes how the Moabite king was able, over a period of at least a decade, to free his people from Israelite rule that had lasted nearly forty years. The reasons for this domination are couched in terms very similar to those found in the book of Judges, namely, that the national god was angry with his people and allowed a neighboring country to conquer them. In fact, these reasons represent further evidence of Omri's and Ahab's ability to extend their hegemony beyond the traditional boundaries of Israel during the ninth century.

Mesha Stele: "Omri was king of Israel, and he oppressed Moab for many days because Kemosh was angry with his country" (Jackson 1989, 97).

Judges 2:11–14: "Then the Israelites did what was evil in the sight of the LORD. . . . So the anger of the LORD was kindled against Israel, and he gave them over to plunderers . . . and sold them into the power of their enemies all around."

Omri had already established an alliance with the Phoenicians through his son Ahab's marriage to Jezebel (1 Kgs. 16:31), giving him an economic link to the Mediterranean and the coastal trade route, the Via Maris. By expanding eastward into the Moabite plateau north of the Arnon River, he would have gained some control over a portion of the important north-south trade route, the King's Highway, which linked Damascus to the Gulf of Aqaba in the south. A memory of this conquest perhaps may be found in the "Song of Heshbon" (Num. 21:27–30), which celebrates the struggles with the Amorite king Sihon and the conquest of Moabite territory (Na'aman 1997a, 90–91).

Omri's establishment of economic alliances and vassalage arrangements with neighboring states would have helped them to create a united front against their enemies. It can be surmised that these smaller states were strengthened in the face of increasing pressure from the Assyrian Empire. One direct result of this process was the anti-Assyrian coalition's ability to withstand the Assyrians at the battle of Qarqar in 853 (Tadmor 1975, 38–40; Dearman 1989, 158–59).

While Omri and Ahab were able to hold together political and economic agreements among the allied states, Jehoram was dominated by Aram, and as a result Israel lost it effective hegemony over Transjordan. Sensing this weakness, Mesha's actual break from Israelite control would have begun with his refusal to pay tribute and his subsequent military preparations following Ahab's death. When he saw that Ahab's successors made no moves to prevent the consolidation of his rule over the northern Moabite plateau, Mesha would have felt safe to take over the Gadite cities of Ataroth and Nebo and the Israelite outpost at Jahaz (J. M. Miller 1989, 39). In the process, he certainly would have reclaimed control over the King's Highway, thereby aiding the reconstruction of his country's cities as well as portions of the highway itself. An indication of this is found in line 26 of the inscription: "I built 'Aro'er and made the highway at the Arnon" (Jackson 1989, 98).

How these events are echoed in the biblical episodes found in 2 Kings 3:4–27 and 2 Chronicles 20 has been a source of debate among scholars (see Bartlett 1983). It is quite likely that these accounts were edited long after the events they purport to describe and thus contain erroneous information. For instance, the Chronicles narrative, which describes an alliance of Moabites and Ammonites fighting against King Jehoshaphat of Judah following Mesha's successes, may speak more to the postexilic Jewish community and its concerns with its neighbors than it does to Israel's past. Although it is also possible that it is an attempt by the fourth century Chronicler to balance the Deuteronomistic Historian's account in 2 Kings and provide more details on the "good Davidic king" Jehoshaphat (Rainey 2000, 176). In the 2 Kings 3 version, the coalition of kings is led by Ahab's son Jehoram, and there is no mention of Mesha's conquests. Furthermore, the description of Edom as an independent monarchy is anachronistic since this was not Edom's situation until the next generation (2 Kgs. 8:20–22). Moreover, Dibon, not Kir-Hareseth, was Mesha's capital (Na'aman 1999, 9).

The narrative describes an unusual itinerary, taking the combined armies of

Judah and Israel south around the Dead Sea, through Edom, and up into Moab. This mimics the route of the Israelites just prior to their entrance into Canaan in Joshua's day (Num. 21:10–22:3). It seems odd, given the likelihood that Israel in the ninth century would have had control of the territory north of the Arnon River, that its army would not have made a direct march east across the Jordan River. The story does, however, satisfy questions of the response made by Israel over Mesha's revolt, and it preserves a historical memory of Omride campaigns into Transjordan (Dearman 1989, 202–3).

Yet another extrabiblical text that speaks to this period of the latter half of the ninth century B.C.E. is the recently discovered Tel Dan Inscription (Biran and Naveh 1993; 1995). It was erected in the 830s to commemorate the victories of Hazael, the usurper king of Aram (2 Kgs. 8:7–15), sometime after the Assyrians had turned their military efforts north into Anatolia (Na'aman 2000, 100). The text indicates a history of conflict with Israelite rulers, and in the middle portion of the document Hazael claims to have killed both Joram/Jehoram, the king of Israel, as well as Ahaziah, king of the "house of David" (ca. 842). Finally, he describes his conquest of the city of Dan and, in a badly broken section, the erection of his stele there to mark his claim to this territory.

One controversy over this text has swirled around the designation "house of David" (Lemche and Thompson 1994; Schniedewind 1996; Kitchen 1997b), although a consensus is building for its authenticity. However, there remain some scholars who believe it is best to remain cautious in the light of continuing reinterpretation of the text (Becking 1999, 187–88; Lemaire 1998, 10–11). Yet another difficulty in the text is Hazael's claim that he was responsible for the death of the two kings, which contradicts the biblical account in which the Israelite usurper, Jehu, kills Ahaziah and Joram/Jehoram (2 Kgs. 9:14–28). In attempting to deal with this issue, some scholars (Schniedewind 1996, 82–85; Halpern 1996, 47) have suggested that Jehu slew them to demonstrate his good faith as Hazael's ally. The king of Aram could then take credit in his inscription for the actions of his vassal in much the same way that the Assyrian kings did in their royal annals (Schniedewind 1996, 84; see 1 Kgs. 19:17). However, the very prominence of Hazael's proud victory statement is an argument that he was in fact directly responsible for the deaths of these kings. In addition, Hazael continued to battle the Assyrians after 841, while Jehu was forced to pay tribute, again an argument against their working together as allies (Na'aman 2000, 102).

Disregarding Jehu's ties to the Syro-Palestinian alliance and his capitulation to the Assyrians, the biblical editors chose to highlight how he took advantage of the situation to seize control of Israel and purge the house of Ahab (2 Kgs. 10:1–25). It is possible that Jehu later did take credit or was given credit by later historians and prophets (Hos. 1:4) for this bloody deed (Irvine 1995). Whatever plans he might have had for additional territorial expansion, however, were quashed by Shalmaneser III's campaign in 841. Rather than rejoin the alliance of Syro-Palestinian states against the Assyrians, Jehu chose to submit and pay tribute. His mention by name in the Assyrian inscription may indicate the importance attached to solidifying control of their westernmost border (Schneider 1996, 106). Jehu's action is graphically depicted in the carved panels of Shalmaneser's "Black Obelisk." He is shown bowing at the feet of the Assyrian king, offering his obeisance as well as the ransom for his nation. This proved to be a smart move, since the Assyrians transferred their efforts away from Syro-Palestine after 838. Jehu was then left to consolidate his rule, although Hazael remained a local threat, apparently capturing Dan from the Israelites sometime in the 830s. In fact, Damascus, under Hazael's rule, was able to take advantage of the political weakness of the Assyrians after the death of Shalmaneser III, annexing Israelite territory from Bashan south to the Arnon River in Transjordan and creating sufficient ill will that Aram's activities are soundly condemned in prophetic writing as late as the mid-eighth century (Amos 1:3–5; Galil 2000, 36).

SHALMANESER III'S "BLACK OBELISK"

"My sixteenth campaign west of the Euphrates took place 18 years after I became the great king of Assyria. Hazael, king of Damascus, mustered a large army, and fortified Mt. Senir. I fought and defeated him. . . . He ran from the battle to save himself, and I besieged his capital city of Damascus. . . . Having demonstrated my power, I accepted the tribute of the people of Tyre and Sidon, and from Jehu, the son of Omri. . . . Jehu, king of Israel, ransomed his life with silver, with gold bowls, vases, cups and pitchers, with tin, and with hard wood for scepters and spears." (*OTP* 170–71)

With the establishment of Jehu's dynasty in Israel, relative stability returned to Israel for the next eighty years. Any plans he may have had for the reunification of Israel and Judah, however, were forestalled by the accession of Ahaziah's mother, Athaliah, to the throne in Jerusalem (2 Kgs. 11:1–3). She and her entourage had come to Judah as part of Omri's diplomatic efforts to establish economic and political ties throughout the region. It is quite likely that her marriage is evidence of Israelite **hegemony** over Judah and its kings. Although King Jehoshaphat of Judah generally receives positive treatment as a "righteous king" in the Elijah/Elisha narratives (1 Kgs. 22:1–38; 2 Kgs. 3:14; see Na'aman 1997b, 159) and in Chronicles (2 Chr. 20:31–37), he and his son Jehoram were forced to participate in Israelite military campaigns (1 Kgs. 22; 2 Kgs. 3) as the weaker member of a political alliance. In addition, Jehoram is tied to the "evil" Omrides through his wife Athaliah, and he, like Abimelech the son of Gideon (Judg. 9:5), is quick to commit fratricide, killing all of his brothers in order to eliminate all of his rivals (2 Kgs. 8:18; 2 Chr. 21:5–6). He reigns only eight years and is succeeded by his son Ahaziah, and the political tie to Israel remains intact until Jehu's revolt.

When Jehu kills King Ahaziah, Athaliah moves quickly to save herself and her nation, something that her mother-in-law (or perhaps sister-in-law) Jezebel had failed to do (2 Kgs. 9:30–37). Even though she is the last remnant of the Omrides and must have been seen by many in Judah as a foreigner, Athaliah apparently maintained sufficient control over the military after her son's death to rally them around her taking power (Spanier 1998, 143). Like her husband, Jehoram, she purges the royal house, murdering all of her grandchildren but one, and declares herself the ruler of the nation (2 Kgs. 11:1–3). Although her regency only lasts six years, it does provide Judah the time to rebuild its stability. When the priest Jehoiada and the supporters of her grandson Jehoash/Joash overthrow her, the direct hegemony of Israel and the Omrides seems to have been dissolved, and this is marked by the new king's religious reform and repair of the temple (2 Kgs. 12:1–16). Despite this newfound independence, the text indicates that Judah is still a relatively weak nation. For example, a ransom had to be paid to Hazael of Aram as he threatened Jerusalem during one of his raids against the Philistines toward the end of the ninth century (Cogan and Tadmor 1988, 141; 2 Kgs. 12:17–18).

The Eighth Century and the Mounting Assyrian Threat

During the first half of the eighth century, Israel and Judah enjoyed a period of economic prosperity and political autonomy unmatched since the establishment of the monarchy (King 1989). This was due to the defeat of Aram-Damascus by the Assyrian king Adad-narari III in 796. By eliminating Israel's chief political rival in the region, Assyria gave the smaller states in Syro-Palestine the opportunity to reclaim some lost territory, restore their control over the major trade routes, and establish new economic links with Phoenicia. Because of internal struggles and a major threat from the kingdom of Urartu in the Lake Van region of eastern Anatolia (Zimansky 1990, 8–9), Assyria did not interfere with this period of growth on the fringes of its western empire.

ANNALS OF ADAD-NARARI III (810–783 B.C.E.)

"I marched against the country. . . . I shut up Mari', king of Damascus in Damascus, his royal residence. The terror-inspiring glamour of Ashur, my lord, overwhelmed him and he seized my feet, assuming the position of a slave (of mine)" (*ANET* 281).

Despite the eclipse of Aram, the first part of the eighth century also was marked by continued conflict between Israel and Judah. The biblical account notes that Judah's king Amaziah (800–783) had attacked Edom with some success (2 Kgs. 14:7). However, he then overextended himself by challenging King Jehoash of Israel to a battle, perhaps over trading rights or over the control of the Jezreel Valley (Gray 1970, 608). Judah is soundly defeated at Beth-shemesh,

Amaziah is taken prisoner, and Jerusalem's northern defenses are destroyed and its temple looted (2 Kgs. 14:11–14). Amaziah is later assassinated when he flees to Lachish for sanctuary, and his young son Azariah/Uzziah is placed on the throne (2 Kgs. 14:19–21). It is possible that Azariah was already serving as coregent during the time his father was a hostage of the Israelites, and this may explain his long reign.

A temporary end of open hostilities between the two small states allows for the emergence of a near "golden age." Israel and Judah prosper under the strong leadership of Jeroboam II (793–753) and Azariah/Uzziah (790–739), respectively. Although the Deuteronomistic Historian is quick to condemn Jeroboam II for his continuing the earlier "Jeroboam's sin," it is still reported that the king was able to reassert Israel's control in Transjordan "from Lebohamath [central Syria] as far as the Sea of the Arabah [Dead Sea]" (2 Kgs. 14:25, 28).

Uzziah expanded both south to the Gulf of Elath and west into Philistine territory at Ashdod. There is also an indication in Hosea 5:10 that around 750 he may have tried to regain control over the territory of Benjamin, which had been lost to Israel for some time (Andersen and Freedman 1980, 34–36). If this northern prophet's complaint that "the princes of Judah have become like those who remove the landmark" is a reference to Uzziah, then apparently the periodic border clashes continued between the two nations. The growing hostility this generated eventually led both Israel and Judah to seek aid from either Assyria or Egypt against their rival. Such an arrangement with the more powerful states, however, came at the cost of foreign interference and heavy tribute payments.

The general tone of prosperity that had existed for several decades ended in the 730s, as the internal struggle for power heated up in the rivalry between Israel and Judah. The death of Jeroboam II also contributed an internal struggle in Israel. His immediate successors, Zechariah and Shallum, were assassinated after reigns of only six months and one month, respectively (2 Kgs. 15:8–14). Menahem, who paid tribute to the Assyrian monarch Tiglath-Pileser III in 738 to "help confirm his hold on the royal power," managed to rule for a decade (2 Kgs. 15:19–20). However, the bloody struggle resumed when the next king, Pekahiah, was assassinated after only two years by one of his military commanders, Pekah, whom Hosea condemns for his courting of Egypt's aid against the Assyrians (Hos. 7:11–16).

At this point, the Assyrian Annals provide a connection to the confusing struggle for power in Israel. In response to Pekah's apparent anti-Assyrian policies, Tiglath-Pileser III states that after Pekah was deposed, he confirmed the usurper Hoshea on the throne in Samaria (2 Kgs. 15:29–30). In examining the Assyrian texts related to this period, they appear at times to be a composite of actions, compressing campaigns against Philistia and Israel and arranging events geographically rather than chronologically (Tomes 1993, 64). Thus, the pacification of Menahem is mentioned right next to the overthrow of Pekah, despite the fact that several years separate these events.

ANNALS OF TIGLATH-PILESER III (744–727)

"As to Hanno of Gaza who had fled before my army and run away to Egypt, I conquered the town of Gaza . . . and I placed the images of my gods and my royal image in his own palace and declared them to be thenceforward the gods of their country. I imposed upon them tribute. As for Menahem I overwhelmed him like a snowstorm and he . . . fled like a bird, alone, and bowed to my feet. I returned him to his place and imposed tribute upon him. . . . Israel (lit. "Omri-Land") . . . and all its inhabitants and their possessions I led to Assyria. They overthrew their king Pekah and I placed Hoshea as king over them. I received from them 10 talents of gold, 1,000 talents of silver as their tribute and brought them to Assyria" (*ANET* 284).

The campaigns by the Assyrian rulers and the apparent involvement of Egypt in fomenting revolts in Syro-Palestine during the late eighth century have led some scholars to suggest that a new "grand coalition" of the smaller states was being formed to resist Assyrian advances (Soggin 1984, 225). Based on this supposition, the Syro-Ephraimite War, described in Isaiah 7:1–9 and 2 Kings 16:5–9, would be evidence of how Syria and Israel attempted to force Judah to join their coalition. When Judah's king Ahaz appealed for assistance from Tiglath-Pileser III, a subsequent Assyrian campaign against Damascus relieved the pressure on Judah. While this is one possible explanation for events, a recent study suggests that the conflict was only a continuation of the border disputes that extend back to the time of the division of the kingdoms (Tomes 1993, 70). Certainly the Assyrians wished to forestall any organized resistance by the smaller states in Syro-Palestine, but they make no mention of one during this period, unlike the well-documented alliances in the annals of Shalmaneser III and Sargon II.

The heavy tribute paid by Ahaz for Assyrian assistance saved his people from aggression from his neighbors and could therefore be termed an effective diplomatic maneuver (Parker 1996, 220). However, the biblical account suggests that the Edomites took advantage of the situation to regain control of Elath and the vital trade link to the Gulf of Aqaba (2 Kgs. 16:6). Meanwhile, Israel continued to sink into political chaos during the 720s, facing its ultimate destruction and the deportation of much of its population at the hands of the Assyrian kings Shalmaneser V and Sargon II.

The military campaigns that brought an end to the northern kingdom of Israel and its capital of Samaria are recorded in various Assyrian documents, the Babylonian Chronicle, and in 2 Kings 17:3–6 and 18:9–12. They demonstrate that the biblical account compresses a series of events and separate deportations into a single, devastating departure for the Israelites (Younger 1998, 215–19). While the reconstruction of events and their chronological order is difficult, the following is a plausible scenario:

Figure 16: Events in the Fall of Samaria (723–720 B.C.E.)

1. Hoshea was confirmed on Israel's throne by Tiglath-Pileser III about 732 and remained loyal until about 723 when the Egyptians convinced him to revolt (2 Kgs. 17:4). It is possible that difficulties in Assyria's prolonged siege of Tyre (Katzenstein 1997, 234–41) suggested an opening for other states to rebel.

2. Shalmaneser V responded in 722, as recorded in the Babylonian Chronicle, and "ravaged Samaria" (Grayson 1975, 73). The term "Samaria" should be considered generic for the country, not just the capital city (Galil 1995a, 54). There was only one campaign against Israel, not two (Tadmor 1958; Becking 1992) or three (Na'aman 1990, 212–25) as some scholars suggest. This date corresponds with 2 Kgs. 18:9, the fourth year of Hezekiah.

3. In 722, Hoshea was captured by the Assyrians and held hostage throughout the remainder of the siege of the city of Samaria that lasted for an additional two years. There is no record of a new king of Israel being crowned during the siege, and it is likely the Assyrians had already begun the administrative changes that would transform Israel from a vassal state into a province (Hayes and Kuan 1991, 164–66).

4. The length of the siege of Samaria was prolonged by the death of Shalmaneser V in 722 and the multiple revolts throughout the Assyrian Empire at the accession of Sargon II. For instance, Merodach-baladan quickly claimed the kingship of Babylon. As at Tyre, the Assyrians did not withdraw from their positions (contra Tadmor 1958, 33–40; Hayes and Kuan 1991, 162), but remained in place, blockading Samaria and slowly starving it until the defenders could no longer resist and the city fell in 720. Records of Sargon II's victory over Samaria are found in his royal annals, his "summary inscriptions" from Khorsabad, and the bull inscriptions, as well as on pavement inscriptions, naming him "the conqueror of Samaria and all the land of the house of Omri" (Galil 1995a, 54–55). The fall of Samaria corresponds with Hezekiah's sixth year (2 Kgs. 18:10).

5. A substantial portion of the population of the northern kingdom was deported, according to established Assyrian policy, creating the mystery of the fate of the "ten lost tribes of Israel," and the newly established Assyrian province of Samaria was repeopled with groups from elsewhere in the empire (Oded 1979, 66; 2 Kgs. 17:24).

The value of the above reconstruction is that it provides a less complicated solution to the question of which Assyrian king actually captured the city of Samaria and deported its inhabitants. However, there remains the question of why Shalmaneser is listed as the conqueror of Israel in 2 Kings 17:3–6 instead of Sargon II. This may be due to the likelihood that deportation of the Israelites began after the arrest of Hoshea and continued during the siege (Hayes and Kuan 1991, 169), or that the gap of 150 years between the events and the work of the biblical writer may have contributed to subsequent confusion in the records. A third possibility is that the name of Sargon II has been deliberately removed from the biblical account here and in 2 Kings 18:13 as part of the "hoped-for proscription of a tyrant" found in Isaiah 14:20 (Goldberg 1999, 363). Such a practice could also be compared to the omission of the pharaoh's name in the story of the exodus.

As for the Israelites who were deported by the Assyrian king, they were scattered throughout the empire in both urban and rural settings. They were resettled as part of imperial policy to reopen arable land in previously devastated areas and to bolster the population in cities crucial to the protection of Assyrian borders (Oded 1979, 67–74). Thus, their presence in Mesopotamia, including in those places listed in 2 Kings 17:6 (Halah, Habor, Gozan), is confirmed by lists of West Semitic names found in Neo-Assyrian documents (Becking 1992, 80–83; Oded 2000, 92–99). For instance, Israelite names continue to appear in Assyrian economic documents throughout the seventh century (Zadok 1988, 304), and in some cases they are listed as "Samarian" members of the Assyrian army during the time of Sargon II (Younger 1998, 219–21; Dalley 1985, 41). Two conclusions can therefore be drawn from this evidence. First, Assyrian offi-

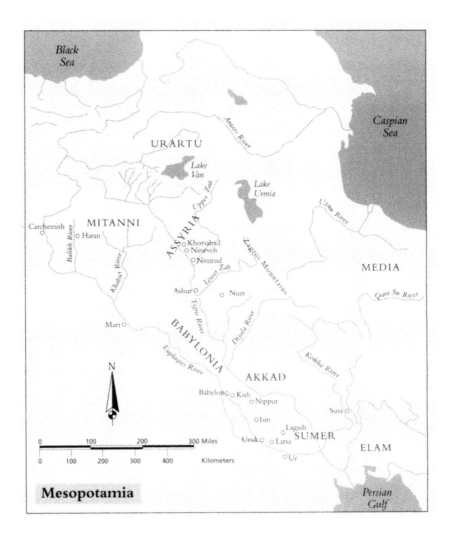

cials continued to identify minority peoples in their records according to their ethnic origin. Second, whether they chose to assimilate to the Mesopotamian culture in which they found themselves, the Israelite and post-701 Judean deportees retained their West Semitic personal names and may in fact have held on to other aspects of their culture while in exile.

With the demise of the northern kingdom, our attention will now shift to events in Judah. During much of the eighth century, Judah was either subsidiary or in conflict with Israel. At the end of the century, and later under the leadership of a dynamic monarch, Hezekiah (726–697/696), the southern kingdom would emerge onto the historical stage. Unfortunately, its newfound notoriety would also bring it to the attention of the superpowers, which ultimately would lead to its conquest and destruction.

Figure 17: Kings of the Divided Kingdom	
JUDAH	ISRAEL
Rehoboam (930–914)	Jeroboam I (930–909)
Abijam (914–911)	Nadab (909–908)
Asa (911–870)	Baasha (908–885)
Jehoshaphat (870–845)	Elah (885–884)
Jehoram (851–843)	Zimri (884)
Ahaziah (843–842)	Tibni (884–880)
Athaliah (842–835)	Omri (884–873)
Jehoash (842–802)	Ahab (873–852)
Amaziah (805–776)	Ahaziah (852–851)
Azariah/Uzziah (788–736)	Joram/Jehoram (851–842)
Jotham (758–742)	Jehu (842–815)
Ahaz (742–726)	Jehoahaz (819–804)
Hezekiah (726–697/696)	Joash (805–790)
Manasseh (696–642)	Jeroboam II (790–750)
Amon (642–640)	Zechariah (750–749)
Josiah (640–609)	Shallum (749)
Jehoahaz (609)	Menahem (749–738)
Jehoiakim (609–598)	Pekahiah (738–736)
Jehoiachin (598–597)	Pekah (750–732)
Jerusalem falls to Babylonians (598)	Hoshea (732–722)
Zedekiah (597–586)	
	Samaria falls to Assyria
Monarchy in Judah ends,	and monarchy ends (720)
Jerusalem destroyed and	
Babylonian exile begins (587/586)	

Note that there are overlapping dates in some reigns since there are occasional examples of coregencies when a king shared the throne for a time with his successor, and also examples of usurpers or dual claimants who reigned during the same period of time.

The dates above are based on those found in Galil 1996, appendix A.

Chapter 5

Judah Stands Alone
(ca. 720–586 B.C.E.)

There is no way to actually gauge the effect on Judah of the destruction of Israel and Samaria. However, at least two items should be noted. First, the Assyrian presence in what had been northern Israel and Philistia is well documented by archaeological discoveries. For instance, four stone stelae that were erected by Assyrian kings have been found at Samaria, Ashdod, Ben-Shemen, and Kakun. Mesopotamian architectural forms such as the open-court house and Assyrian-style gates are evident at several sites, and changes in burial customs (including the use of clay coffins) are clear from finds at Megiddo, Dor, and Jezreel (Stern 2000, 47–48). A second, undocumented factor would have been the tales told by fleeing refugees of the invincibility of the Assyrian troops (Broshi 1978, 12). These stories would have been confirmed by those who actually had seen the destruction wrought by these fierce plunderers, which must have impressed the people and rulers of the Judah and suggested that they were also in grave danger (Machinist 1983, 722). Some of the Hebrew prophets justified these events, referring to Assyrian aggression as the result of Israel's failure to maintain the covenant with Yahweh and pointing out that Assyria was therefore simply the "rod of God's anger" (Isa. 10:5). This is a fairly simple interpretation of very complex events on the political scene of the time. There were several "players" involved, and Judah and its king, Hezekiah, became embroiled in their various schemes.

Figure 18: Political Leaders in the Late Eighth and Seventh Centuries B.C.E.			
JUDAH	ASSYRIA	BABYLONIA	EGYPT
Hezekiah (726–697)	Sargon II (721–705) Sennacherib (704–681)	Merodach-baladan (721–710 and 703)	Osorkon IV (720–715) Shabaka (712–697)
The interaction between these Mesopotamian and Egyptian rulers dominated the political maneuvering throughout the Near East, offering an opportunity for Judah to briefly assert its independence and eventually be drawn back, forcefully, into the Assyrian Empire.			
Josiah (640–609)	Ashurbanipal (667–627)	Nebuchadnezzar (605–562)	Necho II (609–595)
The breakup of the Assyrian Empire after 605 led to conflicts between Egypt and the Chaldean rulers of Babylonia. Once again Judah was caught in the middle. Josiah attempted once again to restore the autonomy of Judah, but his death at Megiddo in 609 left his kingdom in the hands of three weak successors and ultimately led to the capture (597) and destruction of Jerusalem (587), the exile of many of the people to Mesopotamia, and the end of the monarchy.			

Undoubtedly, there were those who considered the last quarter of the eighth century to be filled with opportunity. It is otherwise quite difficult to explain why there were so many revolts by the vassal states and why Egypt and the Neo-Babylonian king Merodach-baladan made such blatant attempts to undermine Assyrian authority in Syro-Palestine. To be sure, Assyrian westward expansion in the past had been short-lived, tied as it was to the relative strength and determination of each king (Gallagher 1999, 263). This also may be one of the factors that led to the risk-taking activities of both local and international rulers.

Tracing events, it seems that after the fall of Samaria in 720 and the deportation of the people of Israel there were a few years of relative quiet in that area. Sargon II, who had fought the Elamite-Babylonian coalition to a stalemate in 720–719, turned his energies against the kingdom of Urartu to the north (Brinkman 1984, 48–49). This left both the southern and the western regions of his empire free of major incursions for several years. However, by 713 an Assyrian text from Sargon II's reign, known as the Azekah Inscription, describes new activity in Philistia. This included the suppression of a revolt lead by Iamani, who had seized the throne of the city of Ashdod (Tadmor 1958; Na'aman 1974). Apparently he was also successful in drawing the kings of Judah, Moab, Edom, and the rest of Philistia into his rebellion against the Assyrians. Overtures were also made to Pharaoh Osorkon IV, in order to seek Egyptian aid, but that weak ruler is better known for payment of tribute to the Assyrians than support for rebels (Redford 1992, 347).

AZEKAH INSCRIPTION OF SARGON II (712 B.C.E.)

"With the power and might of Anshar, my lord, I overwhelmed the district of Hezekiah of Judah. . . . Azekah, his stronghold, which is located between my land and the land of Judah . . . I besieged by means of beaten earth ramps, by great battering rams brought near its walls, and with the attack of foot soldiers. [. . .] They had seen the . . . of my cavalry and they had heard the roar of the mighty troops of the god Anshar, and their hearts became afraid. I captured this stronghold, I carried off its spoil, I destroyed, I devastated, I burned with fire. I approached Ekron, a royal city of the Philistines, which Hezekiah had captured and strengthened for himself. . . . His skillful battle warriors he caused to enter into it" (Galil 1995b, 323–24).

What is apparent from this text is that while Hezekiah was willing to provide some show of cooperation with Ashdod, he also took advantage of the situation in 713 to regain control of some of the cities in Philistia, such as Ekron, which his predecessor Ahaz had lost (Galil 1995b, 328). The mention of Sargon II's campaign against Judah can only describe events in 712 because after that date Ashdod lost its status as a vassal state. This in turn can be compared to the description of these events in Isaiah 20, which includes a strong condemnation against forging foreign alliances or relying on Egyptian assistance (see also Isa. 30:1–7). King Hezekiah, apparently, did not listen to all that Isaiah had to say, nor was he treated too harshly by the Assyrians if his display of wealth to the Neo-Babylonian embassy mentioned in 2 Kings 20:12–15 is any indicator (ca. 711). His entertaining of foreign ambassadors and his acceptance of these gifts from their king Merodach-baladan are an indication that this not so subtle strategy was two-sided and mutually agreeable (Gallagher 1999, 144 n. 5).

The period between 712 and 705 saw no further reports of rebellion in Canaan. Sargon II turned his attention after 710 to regaining control over southern Mesopotamia and was able to eventually oust Merodach-baladan from Babylon in 709 (Brinkman 1984, 50–52). Two factors then contributed to an abridgement of this activity. First, Sargon was consumed by the construction of his new capital at Dur-Sharrukin, which took vast resources in men and materials from the vassal states and weakened his control in southern Babylonia (Gallagher 1999, 265–68). In addition, an epidemic in 707 took a major toll on the Assyrians, making it difficult to respond to every request by local governors (Grayson 1975, 76; Parpola 1987, 188). The dedication of the new capital in 706 must have scored a major propaganda victory for the king as he displayed it to his vassals. However, Sargon's death in battle shortly afterward threw the new king, Sennacherib, into a period of uncertainty. He seems to have been absorbed over the possible "sin" committed by his predecessor that had led to his demise. This, in turn, caused Sennacherib to make a series of blunders during the transition of power (Tadmor, Landsberger, and Parpola 1989, 10–11).

Perhaps the most serious of these was his failure to go to Babylon in 704 to "take the hands of Bel," a ritual that was designed to tie his rule to divine sanction. Following established religious and political precedent would have made him more acceptable as the king of Babylon. The result, almost immediately, was the initiation of a struggle for power allowing his rival Merodach-baladan to seize the throne once again. In doing so he usurped the title that had been held by Sargon II and began to rally anti-Assyrian support (L. D. Levine 1982). In the face of this turmoil, Hezekiah began his economic revival of Judah and defensive preparations for the inevitable conflict with Assyria's king.

HEZEKIAH'S REFORM

There is disagreement among scholars over the dating of events in Hezekiah's reign. This is based on the problem raised by 2 Kings 18:13, which states that the siege of Jerusalem by Sennacherib began in Hezekiah's fourteenth year (see summary in Vaughn 1999, 8–14). Some reconcile this problem by positing a coregency for Ahaz and Hezekiah or a confusion on the part of the biblical editors over the date of Hezekiah's illness (2 Kgs. 20:1–11). However, a strong argument can be made that two campaigns were conducted against Hezekiah. The first was in 712 by Sargon II, which would have been Hezekiah's fourteenth year, and the second in 701 by Sennacherib. Thus, there may either be an unintentional conflation of events, or this could be another example of the intentional omission of Sargon's name by the biblical editors (see 2 Kgs. 17:3–6; Goldberg 1999, 387).

For the purposes of our reconstruction, the assumption is made that Hezekiah began to reign in 726, the same year that Ahaz and his nemesis, Tiglath-Pileser III, died (Isa. 14:28–29a). What followed was a turbulent period that would include the final destruction of the northern kingdom of Israel. The biblical chronology outlined in 2 Kings 18:1–10 places Hezekiah's accession in the third year of King Hoshea of Israel and notes that the siege of Samaria began in Hezekiah's fourth year. That drama was then completed in Hezekiah's sixth year (720), and thereafter Judah and its king were faced with the potential threat of a similar fate. From his first year on the throne, Hezekiah began a reform movement that was designed to restore Jerusalem as the religious center it had been under Solomon, and eventually to attempt to gain greater political and economic influence over a wider area (Borowski 1995). Toward the end of his reign, however, it appears that reform took a back seat to defensive preparations and consolidation of the economic resources of the nation.

The various reforms outlined in figure 19 from the Chronicler's account indicate that Hezekiah understood that the key to strengthening his own power and the influence of Jerusalem was in the complete control over the temple and its ability to collect and distribute food. He thus combined "purification" of religious practice with obtaining the support of the priesthood. Although local

Figure 19: Elements of Hezekiah's Reform in 2 Chronicles
1. A general refurbishing of the temple takes place, including repairing the doors, purifying the structure and its furnishings, and returning to the religious practices "prescribed by David, by Gad the king's seer, and Nathan the prophet" (29:25).
2. After the fall of Samaria, an invitation is extended to the remnant of Israel to join Judah in a celebration of the Passover (30:1–2).
3. The general fervor of the Passover in Jerusalem is transformed into a generalized destruction of all nontemple-based altars (30:13–14) and then a systematic destruction throughout the nation of sacred pillars and poles, shrines and altars (31:1; see also 2 Kgs. 18:4).
4. Subsequently, worship is centralized in Jerusalem, with the bringing of sacrificial offerings and tithes (31:5–7).
5. Having gained control of the economic surpluses of the nation, Hezekiah builds store chambers in the temple from which he makes "fair distribution" to the priests, Levites, and their families (31:15).
6. Local priests and Levites are then given the job of distributing the accumulated agricultural largess to the towns and cities (31:19) from the storehouses built by the king (32:28).

shrines would be shut down or have their activities curtailed, the priests would retain their status by tying them into the royal distribution system (Borowski 1995, 150). Once the economic reform was underway throughout the country, Hezekiah then could control the distribution of surpluses that were stored in his warehouses. Quite likely it was these storehouses that were located in the forty-six fortified cities targeted by Sennacherib's invading army in 701 and mentioned in his royal annals. His soldiers could both feed themselves from this larder and deprive the local areas of needed supplies in the process.

Some dispute the historical reliability of the Chronicles account, noting that any interference with the population or territory of the newly formed Assyrian province of Samaria would have brought swift and devastating consequences on Judah (Na'aman 1995, 180–81). The discovery of the remains of dismantled altars used as secondary building materials indicate to some scholars that Hezekiah attempted to extend his religious reforms throughout the kingdom of Judah (Rainey 1994). However, the ability to match conclusively what may be the remains of destroyed cultic installations at Beersheba and Arad has also been called into question, and a final determination will require additional investigation (Na'aman 1995, 185–89). The picture has become even more complex with the discovery at Tell Halif of what appears to be a private house shrine with incense altars and cultic figurines (Borowski 1995, 151–52). This, at least, indicates that if Hezekiah's religious reforms were instituted, then they were not always obeyed, or that the king may have allowed private worship that did not interfere with the activities of the official sacrificial cult.

However, the archaeological data does tend to support aspects of both the much shorter account in 2 Kings 18:4 as well as the 2 Chronicles 29–32 version, at least in terms of the economic buildup during the late eighth century. For example, there was a marked increase in settlements in the Shephelah region, with pottery types similar to that of Lachish III (the standard Judean ware for this period; Vaughn 1999, 22–23, 79). This matches the statement in 2 Kings 18:8 recording Hezekiah's recapture of territory in the Shephelah and portions of Philistia. The result of this expansion would have been the production of more agricultural products as well as increased political prestige.

Perhaps the single most important indicator of Hezekiah's policies is the widespread appearance of the so-called *lmlk* jars. These storage jars, which contained a distinctive seal impression on their handles indicating that they were the property of the king, were only manufactured during this time period (Ussishkin 1976, 1–3; Vaughn 1999, 94). Discussion of their possible use led initially to the consensus that the *lmlk* jars were part of Hezekiah's preparations for the invasion of his country by the Assyrians and that their contents were for the exclusive use of the military (Na'aman 1979, 75; Halpern 1991, 23). More recent examination of the distribution of the jars, however, demonstrates that they are found in many unfortified sites as well as towns that were not besieged and destroyed by the Assyrians. In addition, the jars are not unique in type, quality, or function, having their stylistic roots in an earlier period. They appear to be designed to transport and store liquids such as olive oil or wine, both commodities that Hezekiah would have wished to control and market. Therefore, it can be concluded that the *lmlk* jars were part of Hezekiah's economic reform measures and the buildup of trade, not just part of the preparations for siege warfare. They can be used to attest to the account in 2 Chronicles 29–32 that records the king's economic activities prior to the Assyrian invasion (Vaughn 1999, 152–57).

Given time, Hezekiah might well have been able to carry out even more widespread reforms. However, Sennacherib eventually was able to stabilize his control over the Assyrian throne, and after dealing with rebellious Babylon in 704 he began once again to look westward. It is probably during this time that Hezekiah began the efforts to refortify Jerusalem and other important military sites. One of these activities was the construction of a water tunnel that could ensure a continuous supply of water flowing from the Gihon Spring under Jerusalem's walls and into the city (2 Kgs. 20:20; 2 Chr. 32:30). This was made necessary by the likelihood of a long siege and the fact that Jerusalem's population would swell, as many of the people from the surrounding countryside would flee into the city for protection (Mic. 4:11–13; see R. L. Smith 1984, 42).

With two teams working from the south at the Gihon Spring and from the north at the pool of Siloam, they followed a circuitous route, making use of natural geological faults, cracks, and joint features to an eventual meeting point (Shaheen 1979; S. Rosenberg 1998; Gill 1994). Geological survey of the tunnel provides evidence of the work of these teams and the various adjustments that they had to make during the construction process (Lancaster and Long 1999, 16–23). In addition, an inscription was discovered, carved into the wall of the tunnel, that describes these events and thus provides a written chronicle of a major engineering feat of the late eighth century (Hendel 1996; contra Rogerson and Davies 1996).

SILOAM INSCRIPTION

The two teams working in opposite directions were digging toward one another with picks. The workers began shouting to each other when they realized they were four and one-half feet apart. Then, the teams turned toward one another following the sounds of their picks until they cut through the remaining rock and joined the tunnels. Thus, the water was able to flow through this tunnel 150 feet underground for some 1,800 feet from the Gihon spring outside the city wall to the Siloam reservoir. (*OTP* 181)

Ultimately, Hezekiah and the nation of Judah had to face the invading armies of Sennacherib. Massive devastation resulted, with many towns and villages destroyed and their people taken away as hostages. Among the most severely damaged major sites was the city of Lachish, which underwent an extended siege. Graphic images of its death throes are found on the walls of Sennacherib's palace in Nineveh. They show the siege ramps, the attacking soldiers, and the forlorn women and children led away with only what they could carry or throw onto wagons (Ussishkin 1980; Shanks 1984). The destruction was so massive that large numbers of houses were collapsed, leaving many storage jars and other implements in place. As a result, the ceramic remains from Level III, dated to the Assyrian capture of the city in 701, have become the diagnostic pottery types for this period throughout Judah (Ussishkin 1977).

Having captured the most significant of Judah's western fortresses, Sennacherib dispatched a diplomatic envoy, the Rabshakeh, to negotiate with Hezekiah for the surrender of Jerusalem and the rest of the nation. This was a rather strange choice since this official did not ordinarily engage in military activities. However, it is possible that he had an intimate knowledge either of Judean culture or language and could therefore speak without an interpreter (Chavalas 1995, 8).

Sennacherib's strategy in this case may be the result of the fact that Syro-Palestine had always functioned as a buffer zone between the great powers of Mesopotamia and Egypt. It had an allure to both sides, but overly aggressive actions or campaigns might well have led to an all-out war that neither side really wanted. Thus, when Sennacherib of Assyria began campaigning in Palestine, he seemed more intent on forcing rebellious Philistine vassals, such as the king of Gaza, back into the fold than totally devastating the area. This also seems to be the case with Judah. The Assyrian Annals describe the king's armies capturing and destroying many small towns and deporting thousands of the inhabitants. However, there is no mention of the capture of Jerusalem. The biblical account in 2 Kings 19:29–34 uses this fact to make the claim that Yahweh intervened to save the "place where his names dwells" (Deut. 16:2), but a more significant factor in the Assyrian strategy may have been superpower politics. If Sennacherib were to conquer Jerusalem, he would take, perhaps, one step too many in the direction of Egypt. Israel had already been invested into the empire, losing its vassal status and political identity. If Judah were also to be transformed into Assyrian territory rather than remaining a buffer state, then Egypt might have had to retaliate, leading to an escalation beyond the point that Assyria desired at the time (Na'aman 1991a, 96).

Thus, when the Rabshakeh presents himself before the walls of Jerusalem, his intent seems to be to frighten the populace into submission and thereby save Assyria the trouble of an extended siege or the possibility of Egyptian intervention (see 2 Kgs. 18). He warns Hezekiah's advisers of the consequences of further resistance. He belittles their reliance on Egyptian aid, calling that country a "broken reed," unable to fulfill its promises (2 Kgs. 18:21). In this case, he may be referring to the defeat of a group of Egyptian delta chiefs by the Assyrians at Eltekah (about seven miles northwest of Ekron in Philistia). Probably at the insistence of Pharaoh Shabaka, these chiefs had attempted to stop Assyrian incursion into an area they considered their province, but the Assyrian Annals record that they were badly defeated (*ANET* 287–88; Redford 1992, 353).

Having demoralized Hezekiah's advisors with this dashed hope, the Rabshakeh then taunts them by offering to "loan" them two thousand horses if they have the men to ride them. Finally, in a very telling remark, the envoy sketches out a theodicy, telling them that Judah's God is angry over Hezekiah's religious reforms and has summoned the Assyrians to punish Judah (2 Kgs. 18:22).

The Assyrian Annals contain other examples of this type of heraldic taunting. Elements of the Rabshakeh's speech are found in other Assyrian royal texts and can also be compared to the official document in Sennacherib's Annals of capitulation of Hezekiah and his payment of a huge fine to ransom the city of Jerusalem. For example, there are many instances in which the Assyrian rulers refer to their enemies as oath breakers, as ones who have "abandoned the gods," or who "lacked intelligence." In addition, rival nations or rebellious peoples are often said to be "broken like reeds of the canebrake." Egypt's failures as an ally are also mentioned in a number of texts, combining their unreliability with the allegory with a "broken reed" that pierces the hand of whoever relies on them for assistance (Cohen 1979, 41–43).

Certainly the Rabshakeh's words must have had a telling effect on Hezekiah's advisers, since they ask him to speak in Aramaic, the diplomatic language of the day, rather than in Hebrew. But his speech is directed to the defenders on the walls and thus he continues his harangue in the language of the common people (2 Kgs. 18:27–35). It must have been particularly frightening to hear that Yahweh had sent these ravaging armies to their land, especially in light of their prophet Isaiah's words that Assyria served as "the rod" of God's anger (Isa. 10:5). Apparently this is a common ploy in Assyrian texts, with a "plea for help" from local gods functioning as a typical justification for military campaigns (Chavalas 1995, 11; Oded 1992, 18–20, 97–98, 121–31). Again in this case, the arguments and the hardships of the military siege that followed worked. Hezekiah eventually agrees to a heavy tribute payment, but significantly the city of Jerusalem does not fall. As noted above, this may be due to Sennacherib's desire to minimize the possibility of a wider war, or he may in fact have been distracted by events back in Mesopotamia. Still, his claim to have taken 200,150 prisoners of war may have been a form of propagandistic "face saving," a boast that he had in essence taken control of the entire population of the nation of Judah while not actually completing its total conquest (Oded 1998, 424).

SENNACHERIB'S ANNALS (701 B.C.E.)

"Because Hezekiah of Judah did not submit to my yoke, I laid siege to 46 of his fortified cities, walled forts, and to the countless villages in their vicinity. I conquered them using earthen ramps and battering rams. . . . I took 200,150 prisoners of war. . . . I imprisoned Hezekiah in Jerusalem like a bird in a cage. I erected siege works to prevent anyone escaping through the city gates. The cities of Judah, which I captured I gave to Mitinti, ruler of Ashdod, and to Padi, ruler of Ekron, and to Sillibel, ruler of Gaza. . . . Hezekiah, who was overwhelmed by my terror-inspiring splendor, was deserted by his elite troops, which he had brought into Jerusalem. He was forced to send me 420 pounds of gold, 11,200 pounds of silver, precious stones, couches and chairs . . . his daughters, concubines. . . . He sent his personal messenger to deliver this tribute and bow down to me" (*OTP* 178–79).

The biblical writer of Kings attributes the survival of the city to divine intervention (2 Kgs. 19:7, 32–37), and the Chronicler does not even mention the Rabshakeh or the potential of Egyptian intervention, or even Hezekiah's surrender, choosing instead to emphasize the king's religious reforms and God's response to the prayers of Hezekiah and Isaiah (2 Chr. 32:20–23). Such an interpretation of events contributed to a myth of the inviolability of the city of Jerusalem and its temple to Yahweh. Events in the sixth century will explode this belief and require a new understanding of Judah's political and religious future.

THE LAST DAYS OF JUDAH

Although Hezekiah had attempted to assert a larger degree of sovereignty for his nation, the ultimate futility of that endeavor was punctuated by the mass destruction of much of Judah by Sennacherib's armies, and by the total subjugation of his successor, Manasseh, to the hegemony of the Assyrian kings. Although the writers of 2 Kings attempt to place a positive face on Hezekiah's "success" against the Assyrians, and do not even mention the activities of Assyria over the next sixty years, it is clear that Judah was sorely weakened, with its economy in shambles and many of its people killed or taken captive (Na'aman 1991b, 55).

Perhaps to further lionize Hezekiah's achievements, the Deuteronomistic Historian presents his successor, Manasseh, as a caricature of evil, the very antithesis of a "good king" (Ben Zvi 1991, 364). The description of Manasseh's reign in 2 Kings 21:1–17 gives no insight into the man. Instead there is simply a recital of all the sins a king might be capable of in that age, and there is no explicit mention of interaction with the people, the prophets, or any rival parties that might have sprung up to oppose his pro-Assyrian policies (Lasine 1993,163–65). What we have is a carefully crafted image by the Deuteronomistic Historian, who wishes both to provide a negative mirror image of the "good king" Josiah and also to justify the imposition of the exile on the nation of Judah (Eynikel 1997, 259–61). In contrast, the account in 2 Chronicles 33:1–20 begins with a list of Manasseh's crimes but concludes with a story of repentance and reform. It is difficult to determine the possible historicity of either of these accounts, but a reign of fifty-five years, longer than any other king of Judah, must have contained some activities of note and been marked by events other than simple homage to Assyria (Japhet 1993, 1002–4).

Since there are no existing extrabiblical historical records specifically mentioning the reign of Manasseh, it is necessary to turn to archaeological surveys of Judah to reconstruct a picture of the nation after the death of Hezekiah. Recent survey of sites in the Shephelah indicate that as many as 85 percent of the eighth-century settlements were not reoccupied during the remainder of the seventh century (Dagan 1992, 260–62). For instance, Lachish, utterly devastated by Sennacherib in 701, was not rebuilt until the mid-seventh century and was occupied by only a fraction of its former population (Ussishkin 1983: 133). This stands in stark contrast to the population growth and apparent prosperity of the area around Aijalon, immediately to the north of the Shephelah (Shavit 1992; Finkelstein 1994: 173). Philistia also benefited from the *pax Assyriaca*, with its increased economic interests and greater security for travel and trade. This seems to be especially the case for the olive oil trade centered in Ekron (Gitin 1989; 1997). Ekron's prosperity indicates that it took Judah's place in exploiting the resources and economy of the northern Shephelah in the seventh century (Na'aman 1993, 114).

There are indications of a shift of Judean population into the hill country, including an increase in the area around Jerusalem. In addition, several new or rebuilt settlements have been discovered in the Negev (Beit-Arieh and Cresson 1991) and the Judean Desert (Bar-Adon 1989). The Beersheba Valley was a center of population growth, indicating that those who were not deported fled from the Assyrians and established new, safer sites, away from the devastation (Finkelstein 1994, 177–78; Broshi 1974). In the Assyrian province of Samaria, some growth in population seems to be the result of deportations of Babylonians and Elamites into this region by Esarhaddon and Ashurbanipal during the mid-seventh century. Cuneiform documents found at Gezer contain many non-

Israelite names, demonstrating an infusion of new peoples into Samaria (Zadok 1985, 568–69; Na'aman 1993, 116–17).

Given the lack of human resources caused by the deportations, new construction and the expansion of agriculture must have strained the abilities of the remaining population during the first decades of the seventh century—a time when Assyria paid less attention to Judah (Na'aman 1993, 115). However, there is some evidence for a reopening or extension of trade links with Arabia during this period (Finkelstein 1994, 179), and it seems reasonable to suggest that Manasseh's administration had a hand in organizing and managing these efforts as well as some construction projects. Thus, by the 640s, the Chronicler's account of Manasseh's attempts to once again centralize authority from Jerusalem throughout the nation (2 Chr. 33:12–14) may have some real substance (Tatum 1991, 136–37).

Archaeological materials that relate to this period—such as stratum 10 at Jerusalem, dated to the latter half of the seventh century, as well as the establishment in the mid-seventh century of new forts at Tel Masos, Aroer, Beth Zur, and Tel 'Ira (all located in the Negev or hill country south of Jerusalem)—may be indicators of an attempt to protect trade and reassert the monarchy's political presence (Tatum 1991, 141–43). It is possible that Assyrian concerns over possible Egyptian incursions into this region by Pharaoh Psammeticus I after 650 also could have led to their construction (Redford 1992, 437–38).

Such activities, if they occurred during Manasseh's reign, would not have reflected major extensions of Judah's borders, and were at a relatively low level (Kletter 1999, 26). Given the reports of the destruction of the Phoenician city of Tyre by Ashurbanipal and repeated campaigns by the Assyrians against Egypt during the second quarter of the seventh century, Judah would have striven to stay below the radar of the Assyrians, forwarded its tribute payments, and shown no evidence of foreign alliances (Gane 1997). Thus, the account of Manasseh's revolt against Assyria in 2 Chronicles 33:11, based on a weakening of Assyrian control over its western empire during the 640s, is unlikely (Na'aman 1991b, 34–35; Williamson 1982, 391–93).

TRIBUTE LIST OF ASHURBANIPAL (668–627 B.C.E.)

"Two minas of gold from the inhabitants of Bit-Ammon; one mina of gold from the inhabitants of Moab; ten minas of silver from the inhabitants of Judah; . . . minas of silver from the inhabitants of Edom" (*ANET* 301).

The actual borders of Judah during the seventh century had shrunk as a result of Sennacherib's transfer of portions of the Shephelah to "more reliable" vassals, leaving a small "heartland" that included "the Judean mountains, Benjamin, the Judean desert, and the biblical Negev" (Kletter 1999, 28). During this period prior to the fall of Jerusalem to the Neo-Babylonians (Chaldeans), a distinct material culture helps to reinforce the geographical boundaries. Specifically, the distribution of pillar figurines, horse and rider figurines, inscribed scale weights, and rosette jar-handle impressions are indications of a distinct Judean polity within this defined geographic region (Kletter 1999, 28–40). They do not speak to the military strength of the nation, which can only be assumed to be capable of guarding its borders, not extending them.

JOSIAH, REFORM, AND DISASTER

The possibility that Judah sought a larger political role in Syro-Palestine in the latter half of the seventh century is suggested by some based on internal turmoil in Assyria (Cogan 1974, 70–71; Miller and Hayes 1986, 381–85). For instance, between 652 and 648 a struggle occurred within the royal family that pitted Ashurbanipal against the rebel Shamash-shum-ukin and his allies in Babylonia, Elam, and Arabia. This political stress, and possibly the incursions by the Scythian tribes from the steppes north and east of the Black Sea (Na'aman 1991b, 37–38), further divided the military resources of the empire. In this weakened state, it became more difficult to launch major campaigns after 640 (Brinkman 1984, 93). However, it should be noted that as late as 644 the Assyrian army campaigned against the northern Arabian tribes, and on their return journey suppressed a revolt by the Phoenician cities of Akko and Ushu (Katzenstein 1997, 293). In addition, with Ashurbanipal's appointment of Kandalanu as ruler of Babylon, peace was restored to that province, and there are no further references in the Assyrian Annals to any campaigns or revolts there during the period from 647 to 627 (Brinkman 1984, 105–6). It seems, therefore, that no change in Judah's political fortunes is possible prior to 640 and very likely a full pullout of Assyrian forces and political presence would not have taken place until after the death of Ashurbanipal in 627.

With this as background, it is possible to assert that the assassination of Manasseh's successor, Amon, in 638 (2 Kgs. 21:23–24) was an effort by an anti-Assyrian faction. However, it was quickly suppressed by the leaders of Judah, and the crowning of his eight-year-old son, Josiah, was an attempt on their part to prevent Assyrian intervention or displeasure. Additionally, Josiah's early reign would have been in the hands of a regency, which would have tried to maintain the economic policies of previous administrations and, where possible, annex towns or territory to expand Judah's tax rolls. For instance, the examination of bullae from Josiah's early reign indicate that Arubbot, a town just south of Taanach in what had been the northern kingdom, was paying taxes to Jerusalem in Josiah's tenth year (Heltzer 2000, 106).

These royal counselors would have been careful to gauge the current political climate and bide their time until a succession of revolts in Babylonia eventually proved to be fatal to the Assyrian grip on the Near East. The revolts between 626 and 623 and the outbreak of a civil war between Assyrian claimants to the throne serve as the prelude to Josiah's reform and any attempts on his part to expand Judah's territory and influence (Na'aman 1991b, 38–41). It is only after the Assyrians had withdrawn an active presence in Syro-Palestine and could no longer send punitive military expeditions against that area that such an attempt at restoring Judah's autonomy and territory could have been untaken with a likelihood of success. It should also be noted that Josiah might have been under at least nominal vassalage to the Egyptians during the period after 630 (Miller and Hayes 1986, 383–85). Jeremiah's cautionary word against too close a relationship with the Egyptians may have been a reflection of a more general opinion that Judah can only "be put to shame" when dealing with either Egypt or Assyria (Jer. 2:18, 36). In fact, any attempt at active subjugation of the area by Egyptian forces, especially in the hill country, seems unlikely at this time (Na'aman 1991b, 40–41).

Figure 20: Josiah's Reform

1. In his eighteenth year (621), Josiah orders the Jerusalem temple to be renovated (2 Kgs. 22:3–7; 2 Chr. 34:8–13).

2. After high priest Hilkiah "finds" the "book of the law" in the temple, Josiah orders that it be authenticated, and the prophet Huldah prophesies the coming destruction of the nation while declaring this book to contain God's words (2 Kgs. 22:8–20; 2 Chr. 34:14–28).

3. Josiah conducts a covenant renewal ceremony, which includes his reading the law to the assembled people and encouraging them to keep the commands of the covenant (2 Kgs. 23:1–3; 2 Chr. 34:29–32).

4. Josiah orders the destruction of the sacred vessels, images, and altars of foreign gods (including those built by Solomon, Ahaz, and Manasseh), the deposition of idolatrous priests, and the destruction of the houses of cult prostitutes (2 Kgs. 23:4–7, 10–14; 2 Chr. 34:3b–4 ascribes this cleansing of the temple and elimination of cult objects to Joshiah's twelfth year).

5. Josiah orders all priests of local high places from Geba to Beersheba to cease their activities (2 Kgs. 23:8–9).

6. Josiah pulls down the altar at Bethel erected by Jeroboam and burns the high place, its cult objects, and the exhumed bones of its priests. He then destroys the high places throughout Samaria and slaughters their priests (2 Kgs. 23:15–20; 2 Chr. 34:6–7 places this activity in the northern kingdom prior to the finding of the book of the law).

7. The Passover is reinstituted for the first time since the Judges period (2 Kgs. 23:21–23; 2 Chr. 35:1–19 provides a much more detailed account of the sacrifice and ceremony highlighting the role of the Levites).

In addition to the Kings and Chronicles versions of these events, the deuterocanonical book of 1 Esdras (chaps. 25–32) and the first-century C.E. Jewish historian Josephus (*Ant.* 10.74) also recount Josiah's reform movement. The question that arises from these multiple accounts is whether they can be treated in any way as historical or at least based on a strong historical tradition. Certainly each version is the product of a set of editors with their own political and religious agendas and a singular desire to present an ideological context for later law and practice. Some elements of the story are very similar to previous biblical narratives (covenant renewal also occurs in Exod. 24:4–8; Josh. 24:1–28; Neh. 8:1–12) as well as to public oath-taking ceremonies in Assyrian texts (Cogan and Tadmor 1988, 296). In addition, some of the geographic reference "from Geba to Beersheba" reflects a realistic set of boundaries for Judah during the late seventh century, stretching from just north of Jerusalem to the traditional border on the Negev. In fact, recent surveys and excavations seem to indicate that Jericho, Ein-gedi, and other eastern sites along Judah's border were reinforced and controlled by Josiah's government after the withdrawal of Assyrian influence (Stern 1994, 406–7).

Where difficulty begins to arise is in the lack of archaeological or extrabiblical evidence for the centralization of worship in Jerusalem, a systematic destruction of high places, and the expansion north into the former Assyrian province of Samaria. For example, the "pillar" figurines that are quite common in Judah, Israel, and Transjordan have been used as one possible indicator of Josiah's activity in eliminating Asherah worship (Dever 1990, 159–60; Holladay 1987, 278). However, it is not possible to conclusively make this identification with these simple clay statues since they are clearly not all of the same style or manufacture and may not even be sacred images (Kletter 1999, 29). Furthermore, the attempt to link the destruction of the sanctuary at Arad with Josiah's reform (M. Aharoni and Rainey 1987, 35; Mazar 1990, 496–98) apparently is dependent on uncertain dating of the strata and may actually correlate to Hezekiah's reign (Ussishkin 1988, 156).

There is also the matter of the "book of the law" (2 Kgs. 22:8). It has been assumed by some scholars to be at least a portion of the book of Deuteronomy, hidden away and rediscovered by Hilkiah's workmen as they renovated the temple chambers (Nicholson 1967, 2; Patrick 1985, 99–101). More recent studies point to the similarities between this "finding of a document" and other ancient documents. There is an obvious parallel, for instance, with Mesopotamian foundation inscriptions and royal annals describing temple renovations (Handy 1995, 264–69). References are also found in the sixth-century edition of the Egyptian "Book of the Dead" and even in Greek documents, such as Pausanias's "Guide to Greece" (Book IV, 26). According to this formula, there are several common steps that lead to the announcement of a reform (Romer 1997, 7–10).

If the Deuteronomist is simply employing this well-known literary pattern, designed to add authority to Josiah's actions, then the historicity of the event seems less certain (Handy 1995, 274–75). It is clear that the editors are making a transparent attempt to portray Josiah as a "new David" and thereby to sanction his reforms (2 Kgs. 23:25). Interestingly, this foundation for monarchic leadership is coupled with Huldah's prophecy of the coming exile and the end of the kingdom (2 Kgs. 22:15–20). It could be argued that this is actually an attempt by the Deuteronomistic Historian to explain and justify the end of the monar-

Figure 21: Discovery-Report Motif
1. An important person wants to change or to "restore" important features in society.
2. He is afraid of opposition.
3. He or one of his loyal servants is sent to a holy place.
4. There he discovers a book or written oracles that are of divine origin.
5. This discovery gives divine impulse to the projects of the hero.

chy (a physical reality at the time that the materials were edited together). Thus, in the Kings version, a "book" is found that will provide a foundation for later behavior and belief at just the point in Israel's history that all other institutions (monarchy and prophecy) are coming to an end (Romer 1997, 9–10). The Chronicler places less emphasis on the "book of the law," focusing instead on the greater efforts for reform by Josiah and a detailed portrayal of the revived Passover festival. The inevitability of destruction is less evident here, instead leaving it to each generation to create its own prosperity or punishment (Glatt-Gilad 1996, 29–31). In neither version is there a real attempt to tie the events of Josiah's reign to actual historical events. Their intent is ideological and theological, and their viewpoint, calling for a united Israel and Judah under Davidic rule, was seconded in some of the prophetic literature as well (Isa. 11; Jer. 30–31; Ezek. 37:24–28; see Sweeney 1991; 1996, 580–81).

A stronger historical foundation exists for the narrative about the battle of Megiddo and Josiah's death at the hands of the Egyptian pharaoh Necho II in 609 (2 Kgs. 23:28–30; 2 Chr. 35:20–24). The Babylonian Chronicle describes the siege of Harran by a combined army of Egyptian and Assyrian forces in 609, an event that could have only occurred after the Egyptians had traveled through Palestine north to the Euphrates. Their most likely route would have been through the Valley of Jezreel near Megiddo, following a path taken by previous Egyptian armies (Cline 2000, 90–91).

BABYLONIAN CHRONICLE

(17th year = 609 B.C.E.): "In the month of Du'uzu, Ashur-uballit, king of Assyria, (and) a large army of Egypt who had come to his aid crossed the river (Euphrates) and marched to conquer Harran" (*ANET* 305).

Unfortunately, there is no mention of Josiah in this text or any other ancient text from Mesopotamia or Egypt. In addition, the accounts in Kings and Chronicles of Josiah's encounter with Necho at Megiddo differ. In 2 Kings 23:29–30, a very terse narrative simply says that Necho killed Josiah during their meeting. Second Chronicles 35:20–24 offers a much more elaborate rendering of events, adding that Necho's ultimate destination was Carchemish in northern Syria and portraying Josiah as an intentional belligerent who challenged the Egyptians to battle. Josephus (*Ant.* 10.74) also describes Necho's march to "make war on the Medes and Babylonians" and the later battle at Carchemich in 605 (*Ant.* 10.84–86).

The question that arises from all of this is what exactly happened to Josiah at Megiddo? Some scholars attempt to reconstruct Josiah's motives as part of his efforts to unite Judah and Israel and obstruct Egyptian ambitions in the region (Malamat 1950, 219; 1973, 274; 1988, 121). Bolstering this argument is an interpretation of a fragmentary, late seventh-century text from Tel Arad (no. 88), which has been posited as a prophetic "call to arms" with language similar to that found in Psalm 47:9 and Ezekiel 30:22–26 (Malamat 1999, 37–38). This is taken as proof that Josiah had the backing of the prophetic community for resistance to Egyptian hegemony in Palestine.

"I reign over all the nations [or, over all the mountains of Judah]. Take strength [literally, arm] and . . . King of Egypt to . . ." (Arad text 88: Malamat 1999, 37).

"I am against Pharaoh king of Egypt, and will break his arms, both the strong arm and the one that was broken; and I will make the sword fall from his hand" (Ezek. 30:22).

Perhaps a more likely scenario of the events involved, however, is that Necho had summoned Josiah to a meeting at Megiddo in much the same way that Tiglath-Pileser III commanded that Ahaz of Judah attend on him at Damascus (2 Kgs. 16:10) to swear allegiance as his vassal (Talshir 1996, 217–18). Displeased over Josiah's moves to expand his territory into the former northern kingdom, he is "court-martialed" and executed by his overlord (Cogan and Tadmor 1988, 300–302). The more elaborate version of these events in Chronicles can be considered in this light as putting Josiah in a better position as a champion for his country rather than a rebellious vassal (Na'aman 1991b, 51–55). It also provides a closer approximation of Huldah's prophecy since Josiah will not have to physically witness the destruction of his nation (Talshir 1996, 220).

The death of Josiah ended any further hopes of a return to political independence for Judah. Although an anti-Egyptian faction was able to temporarily place Josiah's younger son, Jehoahaz, on the throne, he reigned only three months before being removed and taken as a hostage first to Riblah in central Syria and then to Egypt (2 Kgs. 23:31–34; Redford 1992, 448–49). Necho then installed Jehoahaz's brother Eliakim as a puppet ruler in Jerusalem and signaled his subservient status by changing his name to Jehoiakim and putting him in charge of collecting taxes in the province for the Egyptians (2 Kgs. 23:34–35). This political situation in Syria remained favorable to the Egyptians for the next several years, with a garrison installed in Carchemish and some military successes against the forces of the Babylonian king Nabopolassar in 606 (Wiseman 1956, 21, 65).

Figure 22: Judas's Last Days	
TEXT	BIBLICAL PARALLEL
Nebuchadnezzar II's Annals (598 B.C.E.) describe the fall of Jerusalem to the Neo-Babylonians and its plundering.	**2 Kgs. 24:10, 13–17** narrates the capture of Jerusalem, its plundering, and the appointment of Zedekiah as king.
Arad Letters (ca. 594) warn against possible incursions by Edom against Judah's southern border.	**Ps. 137:7–9** condemns Edom for taking Israelite territory after the Babylonians capture Jerusalem.
Lachish Letters (ca. 587) describe the last desperate days for Lachish.	**Jer. 34:6–7** lists Lachish and Azekah as the only outposts remaining to Judah.

The emergence of the crown prince Nebuchadnezzar (605–562) as the Neo-Babylonian ruler in 605 tips the balance of power and eventually leads to the decisive battle of Carchemish. Here the last contingents of the Assyrians are totally defeated along with their ally, Egypt. The latter's claims to Syro-Palestine as its territory now begin to waver in the face of the inevitable onslaught of the Neo-Babylonians (Saggs 1984, 120–21). One direct result of these changes in the political climate of the Near East is the eclipse of Josiah's political legacy. Still, the enhancement of Jerusalem as a religious center and the cultic reforms that may have been initiated or reintroduced during his reign will have an affect on the later cultural development of the people of Judah, both in Palestine and in the exile (Na'aman 1991b, 58–59).

BABYLONIAN CHRONICLE

"In the 21st year the king of Akkad [Nabopolassar] stayed in his own land, Nebuchadnezzar his eldest son, the crown-prince, mustered (the Babylonian army) and took command of his troops; he marched to Carchemish which is on the banks of the Euphrates, and crossed the river (to go) against the Egyptian army which lay in Carchemish. . . . He accomplished their defeat . . . and in the district of Hamath the Babylonian troops overtook and defeated them so that not a single man [escaped] to his own country" (Wiseman 1956, 68–69).

Therefore, to complete this chapter we will explore the shock of Josiah's death at Megiddo and the political turmoil as three of his sons successively were placed on the throne in Jerusalem but had no control over their own or their nation's destiny. These final rulers of Judah are ineffectual in their efforts to escape the political control of Egypt and Babylon, and ultimately their rebellions in 600–598 and again in 588–587 simply lead to the total destruction of Jerusalem and the end of the monarchy.

THE LAST KINGS OF JUDAH

Following the battle of Megiddo in 609, Jehoiakim (previously known as Eli-akim) was placed on the throne of Judah by Necho II and served his Egyptian master for several years. Egyptian control of Syro-Palestine was maintained through continuous campaigning and occasional victories such as the one at Kimuhu, south of Carchemish in 606. Their hegemony over the area, however, was short-lived since Egyptian control evaporated after their defeat at the battle of Carchemish in 605 (Jer. 46:2). While occupying Hamath in the summer of 605 (Grayson 1975, 99), Nebuchadnezzar had to return quickly to the capital after the death of his father. He consolidated his control over the Babylonian government, hastily accepting the traditional title of king of Sippar, and became ruler of the other cities of the empire's heartland in September (Wiseman 1956, 27). Subsequently, he campaigned in the west for the next several years, estab-lishing effective control, although it is unlikely that he ever actually visited Judah or Jerusalem.

The pharaoh's former allies and vassals did not easily accept the coming tran-sition of masters from Egypt to Babylon. One sign of this is found in an Aramaic papyrus from Saqqara, Egypt, which contains a plea from the ruler of Ekron. This loyal vassal in 604 or 603 advises Pharaoh Psammaticus II that the Babylonians are invading the region, and he asks for troop support (Porten 1981, 49). His continued good relations with Egypt are apparent in the description of Egypt's willingness to extradite the prophet Uriah ben Shemaiah (Jer. 26:20–23, and in Jehoiakim's public display of resistance to Babylon's influence when he burns Jeremiah's scroll (Jer. 36:20–26).

Jehoiakim, like the king of Ekron, eventually was forced to submit to Neb-uchadnezzar's control (2 Kgs. 24:1), and he endured it until about 600. Then, under the influence of the Egyptians, he and the Philistine states once again joined in a revolt that brought Nebuchadnezzar's armies into their territory and eventually led to the savage destruction of the Philistine cities in 598 (Stager 1996) and the surrender of Jerusalem in 587 on the second day of Adar, or March 16 (2 Kgs. 24:1–6). With regard to the fate of Jerusalem, the Babylon-ian Chronicle simply notes that the king placed a ruler on the throne in Jeru-salem "to his liking." However, this includes the fact of Jehoiakim's death during the siege and the surrender of the city by Jehoiakim's son Jehoiachin after a rule of only about a hundred days (Galil 1991, 377). With the fall of the city, Neb-uchadnezzar takes Jehoiachin and as many as ten thousand members of the royal family, priesthood, and others back to Mesopotamia (2 Kgs. 24:12; Malamat 1975, 134). He then installs Josiah's third son, Mattaniah, as the puppet ruler of Judah, perhaps hoping that he will be anti-Egyptian and therefore loyal to Babylon (Wiseman 1956, 33–34).

There seem to be mixed political signals regarding Jehoiachin's status. Both the biblical text (2 Kgs. 25:27–30) and a Babylonian ration list indicate that after he was taken to Mesopotamia as a hostage he retained the title of king of Judah

(Weidner 1939; *ANET* 308). He is said to have been accorded an honorable position, "eating at the king's table" in his Babylonian exile. Certainly Mattaniah, renamed Zedekiah by his new master, performed the administrative duties of king back in Judah, but there may have been some not so subtle pressure placed on him by continuing to honor Jehoiachin's legitimacy in exile. It may have also created tension among the people over which king represented the legitimate Davidic line, and ultimately served to force Zedekiah's rebellion against a master who chose not to give him clear title to the throne (Malamat 1975, 138).

Over the next decade, communication continued between the exiles and the Israelites who remained in Judah. While there is some uncertainty about the historicity of Jeremiah's "letter to the exiles" in Jeremiah 29 (Keown, Scalise, and Smothers 1995, 64–65), the sentiments expressing concern for the exiles and the apparent disagreements between the various voices of prophetic authority (see the conflict with Hananiah in Jer. 27–28) indicate a continuing dialogue. Additional intrigues were discussed among the leaders of the states of Syro-Palestine during this interim period in 594 at a sort of "mini-summit," but they had little chance of succeeding (Malamat 1999, 40). In fact, the list of delegates to a conference (Jer. 27:3) does not include any representatives from Philistia. That important group of city-states had been thoroughly pacified by the Babylonians in previous campaigns (Porten 1981, 50). Zedekiah himself or a representative was summoned to Babylon in 593, presumably to renew his allegiance and remind him of the dangers of rebellion (Jer. 51:59).

Taking heart from events swirling around his kingdom, Zedekiah of Judah eventually became embroiled in the political intrigues of Egypt and its aggressive pharaohs Psammaticus II (595–589) and Hophra (Greek: Apries; 589–570). Egypt had recently (593) been able to restore its control over the southern region of Kush and had once again sent expeditionary forces up the coast to Sidon. These militaristic efforts had put the Babylonians on notice that their own hold on Syro-Palestine might be in question soon (Redford 1992, 463–65). Perhaps hoping to take advantage of this unstable situation, Zedekiah joined a revolt in 588 against the Babylonians that brought the weight of foreign armies into his land once again. The Babylonian response is apparently a sign of a shift in foreign policy by Nebuchadnezzar. In the face of continuing problems in Syro-Palestine, he decided to move from allowing local autonomy of provinces to a much closer supervision of their affairs (Lipschits 1999, 158). This required active military intervention, including a thirteen–year siege of the Phoenician city of Tyre (Katzenstein 1997, 322–35) as well as campaigns to suppress revolts in Ammon and Moab (Bartlett 1989, 157–61).

One sign of just how chaotic things became in Judah during this period of Babylonian repression is a damaged inscription found at Arad. In it the commander of the garrison, Eliashib, is ordered to send fifty of his troops to Ramat-Negev (possibly Tel 'Ira just southwest of Arad) to prevent the incursions of Edomite forces into southern Judah (see Obad. 10; Ps. 137:7). The fact that Arad was destroyed shortly after this indicates Edom's success and heralds the end of Judah's control of the southern portion of its territory (Rainey 1987, 39).

A further signal of the end for Judah is found in the Lachish Letters, a group of short messages written to the border garrison at Lachish on broken shards of pottery and apparently stored by the commander of that garrison in a room attached to the city gate (Emerton 2001, 13–14; Smelik 1991, 119–20). Lachish (Level III) had been completely destroyed by the Assyrian army of Sennacherib in 701 and then rebuilt after a period of abandonment in the time of Josiah. This Level II city was smaller and not as heavily fortified as its predecessor (Ussishkin 1997, 321–22). While some of the documents found in the gatehouse contain the usual administrative details of a military outpost, such as ration lists, there is also a growing sense of urgency in them as Judah faced the wrath of the Neo-Babylonian army of Nebuchadnezzar starting in January of 588. The recitation of events in one letter (Lachish 3) includes a statement that indicates some expected support from Egypt would arrive soon. In this letter a report is made that Coniah, son of Elnathan, had passed through the area on his way to Egypt on a diplomatic mission (*ANET* 322). This same letter also points up the seriousness with which these local officials and the people took prophetic pronouncements (Parker 1994, 71). An outpost commander writes to his superior in Lachish to assure him that the communication link designed to forward military intelligence as well as all other relevant information is intact. Thus, it is reported that a man named Tobiah received the prophet's warning and he in turn passed it by official channels to Lachish. Presumably it would then have been sent on to Jerusalem for the benefit of the king and his advisers.

"With regard to the letter of Tobiah, a royal official, which was sent to Shallum, son of Jaddua, by the prophet, saying 'Beware!' I have already forwarded the prophecy to you" (Lachish 3; *OTP* 190).

Pharaoh Apries did send some of his Egyptian forces to the relief of Jerusalem and Judah in the fall of 588, and this resulted in a temporary end of the siege while the Neo-Babylonian army redeployed westward along the coastal plain where they could meet the Egyptians in open battle (Jer. 37:11). This quick response intimidated the limited Egyptian contingents and they swiftly withdrew, leaving Jerusalem to its fate (Malamat 1968, 151; Redford 1992, 466–67). The prophet Jeremiah confirms for Zedekiah that he cannot expect any further assistance from his fleeing allies: "Your trusted friends have seduced you and have overcome you; now that your feet are stuck in the mud, they desert you" (Jer. 38:22). It is also likely that during the siege many from Jerusalem chose to flee the city and go to the territory of Benjamin, where a group had already submitted to the "yoke of Babylon," and thus escape the destruction that would fall upon the capital city (Jer. 37:12–16; see Lipschits 1999, 160).

As the end approached, it is clear that the commander at Lachish held to his post guarding Judah's western border and serving as a haven for villagers from that area (Jer. 34:7). Just how loyal he proved to be might be seen in a report from one of his subordinate officers detailing his activities and determination to continue to carry out the orders of his commander. In this letter (Lachish 4), we learn of the transfer of a prisoner as well as the fact that the watch fires in Lachish at least are still lit, indicating the city remains as Judah's western fortress city. However, the devotion of Lachish and its outposts was in vain. The city of Lachish and, eventually, Jerusalem both fell and were destroyed by the Neo-Babylonian army in 587. The biblical account (2 Kgs. 25:1–25; Jer. 39:1–10; 52:1–30) is centered on the capture of Jerusalem and the destruction of the city along with the temple of Solomon. Archaeological surveys have confirmed a general destruction of the Jerusalem area as well as its western border region (Lipschits 1999, 158; 1997, 246–71). It is possible that some of this devastation occurred in the period after the fall of Jerusalem amidst the general chaos of the times, but the result is the same—most of Judah's urban centers and its economy were shattered.

"I have posted your orders in writing. Following your orders to make a reconnaissance of Beth-haraphid, I discovered that it had been abandoned. Semaiah has taken Semachiah into custody so that he can be transferred. . . . This letter certifies to the commanding officer that I remain on duty to carry out your orders. Judah's signal fire at Lachish still burns, even after the only other remaining signal fire at Azekah has gone out" (Lachish 4; *OTP* 190).

As for Zedekiah, the biblical narrative records that he was forced to watch the execution of his heirs and then was blinded before being led off into exile along with a large portion of his surviving people (2 Kgs. 25:6–7). A brief, caretaker government was installed by the Babylonians, headed by Gedaliah, a professional bureaucrat unrelated to the Davidic line (2 Kgs. 25:22; Jer. 40:5). His credentials, based on a seal impression found at Lachish, indicate that Gedaliah had served, as had his grandfather Shaphan (2 Kgs. 22:3), as chief minister to the king of Judah (Cogan and Tadmor 1988, 325). Such evidence must be treated carefully, however, since Gedaliah was a fairly common name during the sixth century (Becking 1997, 75–78), but the possibility remains that Nebuchadnezzar chose to appoint a man with proven administrative experience to assist the reconstruction of Judah (Oded 1977, 275).

Since Jerusalem could no longer serve as the seat of government, Gedaliah administered the remains of the province from Mizpah in the territory of Benjamin, an area that does not contain evidence of destruction by the Babylonians and may therefore have been a refuge for those in opposition to Zedekiah's policies (Malamat 1950, 226–27; Lipschits 1999, 158–59). Again, both 2 Kings (25:22–26) and the book of Jeremiah (40:7–41:15) contain accounts of Gedaliah's short period of administration. The events recorded in Jeremiah are more detailed and include the interesting note that many of the people of Judah who had fled to Transjordan to escape the violence were now beginning to return and assist in the vital task of harvesting the fields (Jer. 40:11–12). Both versions also recount Gedaliah's assassination by Ishmael ben Nethaniah, a member of the royal family. It seems likely that both accounts were written in the postexilic period, possibly as an attempt to maintain belief in the sanctity of the Davidic line (Becking 1997, 73; Begg 1987, 3–4). It is also probable that the postscript in which Ishmael took "all the people, high and low" with him to Egypt after the assassination (2 Kgs. 25:26) is part of a later writer's attempt to prove that the land of Judah was emptied of its people (Seitz 1989, 278–79). In this way, focus could then be placed on the exiles and reinforce their contention that they had the right to repossess the land after the exile had ended.

The reality of the situation is that portions of Judah continued to be fairly well populated after the Babylonian conquest in 586. As late as 581, in Nebuchad-nezzar's twenty-third regnal year, Jeremiah 42:7–12 reports a deportation of 745 persons from Judah, and this could not be connected with Babylonian repercussions over Gedaliah's death. Furthermore, archaeological surveys (see a general summary in Lipschits 1999, 165–78) of the region of Benjamin during the period of Babylonian control indicate:

Figure 23: Archaeological Surveys

Mizpah: Numerous storehouses as well as buildings suitable for administrative personnel bear evidence of continuous occupation at least until the mid-fifth century (Zorn 1993, 175–85).

Bethel: Pottery assemblage suggests continued occupation until the final third of the sixth century (Kelso 1968, 75–76).

Gibeon: Seal impressions employing Persian styles and a large cemetery indicate increased importance of the site during the sixth century (Zorn 1997, 37; Eshel 1987, 1–7).

Gibeah: Although partially destroyed by the Babylonians, sections of the town actually expanded during the sixth century beyond its Iron I boundaries (Lapp 1981, 39–46, 59).

While the material culture of this postdestruction era Judah, and in particular the region of Benjamin, is only now being revealed and identified, it may be expected to be well documented in the coming years. Clearly, Benjamin became a haven for the displaced people of Judah, and its cities prospered and grew during the Babylonian and Persian periods. The concentration of population in later towns, however, is an indication of security problems, especially on the borders with Samaria, that forced people off of small farms and out of the tiny villages that had previously existed in the Iron Age (Lipschits 1999, 182–84).

The destruction of Jerusalem along with its governmental apparatus had some significant ripple effects. This was a particularly major blow to those areas that depended upon the urban center for their livelihood. Most of the cities and towns in immediate proximity to Jerusalem—as well as its western and eastern border fortresses, which relied on trade and the protection of the military for their survival—could not continue to support their population. Still, in Judah proper, surveys also indicate that some of the smaller towns and villages continued to survive, at least as rebuilt, marginal population centers (Stern 2001a, 321–25). It should also be noted that the Babylonians would have had a vested interest in reviving, at least to some extent, the economy of Judah in order to extract tribute from those who remained in the land. One sign of this is a jar handle from Ein-gedi containing the inscription "belonging to the lord" (i.e., king). This would indicate that a standard system of taxation was in place and that the Babylonians expected a certain level of collection to be maintained (Graham 1984, 57).

Thus, the image of a land completely emptied of its people (2 Chr. 36:20–21) and left waiting for their return must be set aside. Certainly, it would have been to the advantage of the exiles to focus on their own plight and their manner of coping with the disaster of the fall of Judah, the destruction of Jerusalem and the temple, and their own displacement. It would only be natural for them to continue to portray Judah as the "promised land" as an inducement for their triumphant return (see Isa. 40:1–11). In this way they created a theodicy to explain the purpose of their exile and to set the stage for their place in the history of the nation. The next chapter will deal with the exilic experience as well as the construction of a postexilic existence in the **Diaspora** and in a restored Jerusalem community.

Chapter 6

From Exile to Alexander (ca. 597–322 B.C.E.)

As Judah lay on the brink of political annihilation at the beginning of the sixth century B.C.E., a social transformation began that ultimately would lead to the development of Judaism as both a religion and a social movement. One sign of this was the compilation during the last decades of the kingdom of Judah of historical, cultic, legal, and political documentation into what would later be referred to as the Deuteronomistic History. This editing of existing material and the addition of a very definite theological and political agenda (primarily a "southern" or Judean perspective) formed the "official" view of Israel's history from the time of the conquest until the end of the monarchy. It "created a useful past" for ancient Israel (Zevit 2001, 479), while providing a fairly rigid interpretation of events and, in particular, a condemnation of the abuse of political power by the kings of both Israel and Judah. While the Davidic dynasty is legitimized in the Deuteronomistic History through the declaration of the "everlasting covenant" and is put forward as the hope for the future of the nation (Isa. 11:1), there are some kings of Judah, such as Ahaz and Manasseh, who are singled out severely for their failures and apostasies. Such a judgmental tone may be a reflection of the frustration felt by the Deuteronomistic writers as they saw the end of the nation coming (Deut. 28:36–37).

In addition, the shock of the destruction of Jerusalem and the temple would have required a theological reaction, perhaps to be found in Deuteronomy 12:2–28, which requires the centralization of all cultic practice in "the place that the LORD your God will choose." Such an emphasis at a point when Jerusalem was no longer able to serve as the religious nexus point for the people was a signal that Babylon could not utterly destroy the sanctity of that place and that no other shrine could or should be allowed to replace it (Clements 1996, 8). This attitude resembles Jeremiah's daring act in Jeremiah 32:6–25 in which he purchases a field at the height of the siege of Jerusalem. By doing this, he too signals that the people will one day return to their land and it will once again be an expression of the covenant with Yahweh.

The Deuteronomistic writers' vision of the nation was based on the terms of the covenant agreement with Yahweh, which served as the basis for both correct behavior and national identity. They had hoped for a "just king," perhaps like Hezekiah or Josiah, who would finally fulfill their expectations and draw the kingdom into its proper adherence to God's commands. The ultimate failure of this hope led, in turn, to a reexamination of the value of political institutions within the larger world of the ancient Near East and the creation of a Jewish identity movement during the exilic and postexilic period (598–300). Since the people taken into exile and those left behind in Judah were no longer subject to a native dynasty, their social development took place during a time when they were dominated by foreign governments and therefore "alienated from all political power"(McEvenue 1981, 364). This allowed the people to free themselves from the "burden" of nationalism and to create an ethnic identity and philosophy of life that made their religion and their people capable of coping with social and political situations wherever they might live or work (see Jeremiah's "letter to the exiles" in Jer. 29). It also led to a division between those who went into the exile and those left behind. For instance, Jeremiah 24:2–10 refers to those not swept into the exile as the "bad figs," who are cursed for their continued resistance to the Babylonian conquerors.

Evidence of this process of transition can be found in the Priestly strand of the text that was composed in the eighth century by a group concerned with legitimizing the centralization of worship in Jerusalem under Hezekiah (Milgrom 1992, 459–60). They injected their viewpoint into such disparate narratives as creation (Gen. 1:1–2:4a), cultic legislation (Num. 28–29), the exodus drama, Aaron's role and the construction of the ark and tabernacle shrine (Exod. 25–31), and the religious restrictions placed on Nazirites (Num. 6:5–8). During the sixth century and during the exile, an additional redaction of the cultic legal practices was made, known as the Holiness Code (Lev. 17–26), which further refined the Priestly materials. Then, in the postexilic period, the restoration community chose to adopt this perspective on cultic practice and the central importance of Jerusalem after the temple in Jerusalem was rebuilt in 515. At that point the members of the priestly orders were able to restore their role as sacrificial offi-

ciants and arbiters of religious practice and law. Now they could couple their
desire to differentiate themselves from the non-Jews (defined by them as persons
who had not participated in the exile) by means of practice as well as the recog-
nition of sacred space (Coggins 1989, 166–67).

The solidification of this exclusivistic policy was furthered by the activities of
Ezra (who probably arrived about 458 in the reign of Artaxerxes I) and then by
the Persian-appointed governor, Nehemiah. Their efforts to annul mixed marriages must have created tension within the community in Yehud (the name for
the Persian province around Jerusalem), but because they had the administrative
and financial backing of the Persian government, they were able to impose their
ideology on the province (Williamson 1989, 158).

This is not to say that there were not minority voices, such as those of Second
and Third Isaiah, calling for a wider view of the exilic experience or at least compromise on the strict regulations being enforced on who could claim membership in the new "Israel." Certainly the prophets of the immediate return to
Palestine, Haggai and Zechariah (chaps. 1–8), concentrated their efforts and
message on the restoration of the temple in Jerusalem. But they saw it as a step
in the transition process out of the exile and into a new existence for the people
that would be more inclusive of the peoples who had remained in the land during the exile and also of Gentile nations (see Isa. 49:1–6 for this view). Chronicles (composed in the mid to late-fourth century) also attempted to form a
compromise position in order to prevent total polarization between the returnees
and the people of the land. The failure of this attempt, however, can be seen in
the establishment of a separate Samaritan cult center on Mount Gerizim at
Shechem and the development of total schism between these peoples within a
century (Williamson 1989, 156–57).

Figure 24: What You Need to Know about the Exilic and Postexilic Periods

- Jerusalem surrenders to Nebuchadnezzar in 597 and a group, including Jehoiachin, is taken hostage to Mesopotamia.
- Nebuchadnezzar captures and destroys Jerusalem in 587, deports another group from Judah, and leaves some of the population to cultivate the land.
- A Jewish identity movement is formed during the exile that creates a nontemple-based religion with strict legal traditions and ethnic identity for the exiles.
- Cyrus captures Babylon in 539 and issues a degree restoring images of gods to their people and making it possible for the Judean exiles to return to Jerusalem.
- Some of the exiles return to "Yehud" between 538–400, while the majority choose to remain in the Diasporic communities in the Persian Empire (Mesopotamia and Egypt).
- The Jerusalem temple is rebuilt in 515 and the priestly community restored, creating a temple-based group separate from the Samaritans and differing in its religious focus from the Diasporic community.
- The Persian administrators Ezra and Nehemiah represent in their policies the social control mechanisms of the Persian government as well as the differences between Jewish groups.
- The conquest of the Persian Empire by Alexander of Macedon in 331 brings both new political master and a new cultural tradition to Syro-Palestine (Hellenistic period begins).

AFTERMATH OF 587

Those Who Remained Behind

For those who remained in Judah after the destruction of Jerusalem and the elimination of the Davidic monarchy, the standard of living depended upon where they continued to dwell. The exact number of those who remained in the land is unclear. Estimates of the population of Jerusalem prior to 587 range from 25,000 (Broshi 1978, 12) to 250,000 (LaSor 1982, 1014). Even with the deaths of many due to war, famine, and disease (Jer. 21:9) and the removal of a portion of the population to Mesopotamia, the land would not have been emptied to the degree that is described in 2 Chronicles 36:20–21. It is possible that the Chronicler, writing in the late fourth century using the Deuteronomistic History and other sources in its compilation of events (Japhet 1993, 25–28; Hoglund 1997, 28–29), wished to minimize the importance or even existence of a Judean remnant left in the land during the exile. This was reflected in the later disputes between the returning exiles and the Samaritans and other "peoples of the land" (Smith-Christopher 1997, 20).

Excavations have shown that the towns and villages in the eastern, southern, and western sections of Judah, including Jericho, Lachish, and Beth-Shemesh, do have massive destruction levels and periods of abandonment after 587 (Stern 2001a, 324–25; Wiseman 1985, 36–38). However, the territory of Benjamin, north of Jerusalem, apparently was relatively untouched by the Babylonian armies. The people who dwelt there were able to plant and harvest their fields and continue commerce as before (Lipschits 1999, 159–64). With the seat of government moved to Mizpah, they would have also benefited from the maintenance of order supplied first by Gedaliah's administration and then, after his assassination, by a Babylonian appointee. Babylonian provincial governance, following the assassination of Gedaliah, was probably exercised from Samaria (Jer. 52:30; see Wiseman 1985, 38–39). It is quite likely that this political arrangement was also adopted by Persians, but once the exiles began to return to Jerusalem in larger numbers and the province of Yehud was established, that province would have been separated from Samaria and become an autonomous unit reporting directly to the satrap and the emperor (Weinberg 1992, 127–38).

One sign that the general makeup of the population of this region remained virtually the same can be found in the ceramic record and other evidence of the material culture (Carter 1994, 120–27). Surveys have been able to demonstrate that 70–80 percent of the pottery forms that had previously been used in Judah continued as a part of the basic assemblage (Stern 1982, 229). Presumably the Babylonians and later the Persians made some effort to restore the economic viability of this portion of their empire so that it could be both self-sustaining and also pay its taxes. This did not extend, however, to rebuilding Jerusalem. Much of it, outside the temple complex that was restored in 515, remained in ruins until the time of Nehemiah in the mid-fifth century.

There is no way to reconstruct the religious activities of those who remained in Judah and Samaria except in terms of what may be interpreted from the archaeological materials that have been recovered (Dever 1995c, 52–53). Rejections of indigenous groups—including the Samaritans, recorded in Ezra 4:1–5 and Josephus (*Ant.* 11.85–88)—by the returned exiles may have been based on political as well as religious bias and does not speak to the specific details of religious practice and belief (Freyne 1999, 41–44). The reference in Jeremiah 41:5 to a group of eighty men traveling from Shechem, Shiloh, and Samaria to Jerusalem to make a sacrifice also cannot be seen as a general expression of cultic practice. It is more likely, given their shaved beards, to be a delegation on pilgrimage to a sacred but destroyed site (Keown, Scalise, and Smothers 1995, 241). Without the monarchs to enforce ritual orthodoxy, without a temple and the priestly community to administer sacrificial activity, and with new peoples being brought into the area by the Assyrians and Babylonians, it is most likely that the people returned to their decentralized local shrines and traditional practices (Zevit 2001, 476–77). In addition, the polytheistic and syncretistic elements that had existed in their culture and religious activities would have continued to play a role in the development of their beliefs and their accommodation with their political masters (Margalith 1991, 316).

Those Taken into Exile

The exilic community that was formed in Mesopotamia was in great danger of cultural annihilation. When the Assyrians destroyed the northern kingdom of Israel in 720, much of its surviving population was deported. While reference to these "Samarians" does occur in the official annals of Sargon II (Younger 1998, 219–21) as well as in Neo-Assyrian economic and legal documents throughout the seventh century (Oded 2000, 94–99), the exact size of this exilic community and just how organized it may have been as a distinct minority group is unknown (Grabbe 1998, 82–84). A fictionalized account does exist in the deuterocanonical book of Tobit, but this cannot be relied upon to reconstruct life in the exile for the deported Israelites. Its knowledge of the fall of Nineveh and Jerusalem, and its religious focus on the home are more reflective on the Persian period, not the Assyrian era (Grabbe 1998, 91–92). Presumably, some of these people assimilated with the surrounding cultures and disappeared from history. Others may well have joined with the new exilic groups as they were brought to Mesopotamia during the late seventh century and throughout the sixth century by the Neo-Babylonians, and as they formed distinctive communities that survived and held onto their cultural heritage.

The conditions faced by this more recently arrived group now must be addressed. Some scholars, drawing on what appears to be a level of communal autonomy found in Ezekiel 8:1; 33:30–33, have suggested that life in the exile may have been relatively free of religious persecution and repressive policies (Oded 1977, 483). Others point to the traumatic effects of the deportation and

---

Figure 25: Neo-Babylonian Rulers

Nebuchadnezzar II (605–562 B.C.E.): Claimed Assyria's Mesopotamian empire after the battle of Carchemish in 605 and added Syro-Palestine to his domain shortly afterward. He captured Jerusalem and took Jehoiachin hostage after Jehoiakim's revolt in 597, and destroyed the city and deported a portion of the population in 587. The major source of information on the activities of his reign is the Babylonian Chronicle.

Amel-Marduk (= Evil-merodach of Jer. 52:31; 562–560 B.C.E.): 2 Kgs. 25:27–30 mentions his release of Jehoiachin from a thirty-seven-year imprisonment. No additional texts have been found to describe his reign.

Neriglissar (560–556 B.C.E.): Known as Nergal-sharezer in Jer. 39:3, he may have claimed the Babylonian throne by killing his brother-in-law Amel-Marduk. One campaign in western Asia Minor is mentioned in the Babylonian Chronicle (Wiseman 1956, 75–77). His son Lâbâši-Marduk was deposed after reigning two months (Beaulieu 1989, 88).

Nabonidus (556–539 B.C.E.): Son of Adad-guppi, priestess of the god Sin in Harran, and unrelated to the royal house, he seized the throne as an older man. He instituted a reorganization of the cult, placing emphasis on the moon god Sin of Harran and demoting the priesthood of Marduk. Much of his reign was spent on the Arabian border, perhaps protecting trade routes, and his son Belshazzar administered Babylon and the empire's affairs. He was deposed and stripped of his territory by the Persian king Cyrus in 539 (Beaulieu 1989, 89–91).

---

the likelihood that the Neo-Babylonians would have had specific plans for this newly arrived population (Smith-Christopher 1997, 23–25). The increase in the number of inhabited sites in Mesopotamia (from 143 to 221) that date to the Neo-Babylonian and Persian periods is one possible indicator that "large masses of people were involuntarily transferred as part of intensive Neo-Babylonian efforts to rehabilitate the central region" (Adams 1981,177). Evidence that Nebuchadnezzar made use of this new labor pool to engage in major building projects is found in texts from his reign. Interestingly, one of the charges that Cyrus made against Nabonidus, in his justification for taking Babylon and assuming command of the Neo-Babylonian Empire, is that the king engaged in "forced labor" practices that oppressed his people and presumably the exilic communities throughout Mesopotamia. This charge is apparently a standard feature of the royal inscriptions of Mesopotamian kings (Kuhrt 1983, 89).

NEO-BABYLONIAN FORCED LABOR PRACTICES

Texts from Nebuchadnezzar II's reign:

". . . the whole of the races, people from far places, whom Marduk my Lord delivered to me, I forced them to work on the building of Etemenanki. I imposed on them the brick basket" (Weissbach 1938, 46–47; trans. Smith-Christopher 1997, 24).

"I called into me the far dwelling peoples over whom Marduk my lord had appointed me . . . from all lands and of every inhabited place . . . that they should bear his yoke and also the subjects of Samas and Marduk I summoned to build Eteminanki" (Langdon 1912, 149; trans. Smith-Christopher 1997, 25).

Cyrus Cylinder:
"Nabonidus turned the worship of Marduk, ruler of the divine assembly in Babylon, into an abomination. . . .He also enslaved the people of Babylon to work for the state year round" (*OTP* 193).

The psychological trauma caused by their forced displacement and relocation far from their homeland and in the midst of a strange and intimidating society must have had an affect on many of them (D. L. Smith 1989, 49–56). It must have been quite a shock to the people of Judah that they too could be taken "far from the LORD" (Ezek. 11:15), a phrase that they had used for the exiles from the northern kingdom. Certainly, the laments found in Psalm 137 and the explicit language of despair over Nebuchadnezzar's triumph in Jeremiah 51:34–35 speak to the fear, despair, and hatred generated by the destruction of Jerusalem and the exile. If indeed the worship of Yahweh could only take place in Jerusalem, how could they now continue to practice their religion? One response may be Ezekiel's statement that Yahweh was to become a "sanctuary" to them in exile (11:16); thus, God would replace the temple as the focus of their worship activity (Joyce 1996, 52–58). Given the uncertainties of their situation, it is very likely therefore that some would choose to assimilate with their conquerors, accepting the notion that their God had failed them and disappearing as a distinctive people, while others moved toward a new identity within their understanding of the covenant.

One additional factor in the decision-making process for some of those in the "Gôlâh," or exilic community, was the possibility of opportunities that would allow them to become a part of the economy of their new region (i.e., farmers, herders, fishermen; see Coogan 1974, 10). Less likely was the chance to be appointed to government posts at any level. These positions would have gone to Babylonians, Persians, and Medes, with just a small minority from the exiled or expatriate groups (Zadok 1979b, 87). Other than the mention of Daniel, Mordecai, and Nehemiah in the Bible, there is no clear mention of Judean exiles rising to high office.

A body of economic documents from the Persian period may shed some light on the conditions of the exilic community after 539. The Murashu documents from Nippur on the alluvial plain of Lower Mesopotamia represent a portion of the correspondence of a major financial concern that made loans and provided business capital (Stolper 1985). They indicate that a number of Judean families engaged in a range of economic activities and also served as government officials. Opportunities such as this would have drawn some of them into an acceptance of assimilationist accommodations (Blenkinsopp

1991, 50–53). Approximately 3 percent of the people named in these published texts were Judean in origin (70 out of 2,500). Their names contained theophoric elements that are a form of the name Yahweh (Yahu, Yah, Yeho, Ia). While small, this is still one of the distinguishable minorities in the region, which also included Phoenicians, Philistines, and Moabites (Zadok 1979a). The process of redevelopment, which involved the redeployment of deported peoples in underpopulated or previously devastated areas served as a key feature of Babylonian policy's use of exiles (Yamauchi 1990, 243–44). This would have brought new capital into the region and opportunities for employment and economic advancement, which could have benefited these Judean families and given them an additional reason for remaining in the Diaspora (Eph'al 1978, 74–90; Blenkinsopp 1991, 52).

For those who chose not to assimilate, it became necessary for them to develop a theodicy of the exile. This required them to accept the statements of prophets such as Jeremiah and Ezekiel that they themselves were at fault for their current situation. They had broken the covenant agreement and forced Yahweh to abandon them to their enemies, in much the same way as in the Judges period when Yahweh allowed the Israelites to be oppressed by their neighbors. In this case, however, no judge or other divinely ordained leader would appear to serve as their champion. They would have to be realistic enough to know that their cultural survival would require a complete reformulation of their basic religious and social ideals. This group would also have to find some means of maintaining their identity while accommodating to the reality of their living situation in exile (Sparks 1998, 314–15; Ackroyd 1968, 31–38). The solution for them took the form of the Jewish identity movement.

The earliest development of the canon of Scripture probably began during the monarchy period, but it became essential to the exilic community since it provided the basis for their national identity and cultural survival (Sanders 1997, 39–46). The process included the compiling, editing, and arranging of previous documents, including primordial stories, ancestral narratives, legal codes, and royal annals. This was done with an eye to ensuring the survival of this cultural heritage and perhaps with a boost from the Persian government, which had a vested interest in creating identifiable political units within its empire (Balentine 1996, 139; Berquist 1995, 131–46).

Figure 26: Elements of the Jewish Identity Movement

1. Development of the canon of Scripture.
2. Use of Hebrew as a liturgical language for cultic practices and sacred texts.
3. An emphasis on Sabbath worship.
4. The practice of circumcision to distinguish Jews from other communities.
5. Formulation and enforcement of a Holiness Code to maintain ritual purity through personal hygiene and diet.
6. Strict adherence to endogamy (marrying only within their own group).

It seems likely that a formal attempt was made at this point to put a greater emphasis on theological matters that had previously been developed during the eighth century (the **Priestly source** in the text). This was coupled with the Holiness Code (Lev. 17–26) of the sixth century, which placed a greater emphasis on ritual purity and holy living. The key here is to provide a clear sense of the differentiation between what is clean and unclean, pure and impure (D. P. Wright 1992, 246–47). Scholarly discussion of this section of Leviticus includes the arguments that it is related to legislation in the Priestly and Deuteronomic sources but is a separate source altogether, and that it contains some preexilic speeches and legal traditions (Knohl 1987, 65–74; Sun 1990). Certainly it has redacted portions of the Priestly source to reflect changes in the cult and the condition of the nation brought on by the last days of Judah and the exile (Milgrom 2001, 2054–56). Whether or not it is in fact completely separate from the Priestly source, its style suggests it was designed to be read to the people and to serve as instruction for their lives as members of a distinct, covenantal community (Hartley 1992, 259). Once the temple had been rebuilt in Jerusalem, the power to determine and protect that which is defined as holy added greater authority to the priestly community.

Although the final form of the biblical text would not be set for several more centuries, the efforts of these preexilic and exilic redactors in compiling written and oral materials set the stage for a body of writings that were clearly identifiable by the Hellenistic period (second century) in the Prologue of Ben Sira as "the Law and the Prophets and the other books" (Sir. Prologue). The theme sustained by these writings was the understanding that (1) Yahweh is the sole, transcendent, creator God, (2) that as a result of the covenant with Abraham and the exodus event Israel is the chosen people, (3) that special legal obligations under the covenant have been placed upon them, (4) that failure to obey the covenant led to punishment and defeat, and (5) that ultimately they would regain their full status as the chosen people of Yahweh and be restored to their own land (Sanders 1997, 39–41).

The use of Hebrew as a liturgical language allowed the Israelites in exile—who most likely spoke Aramaic, the lingua franca of the Persian Empire—to retain a "family language" that set them aside from the surrounding cultures when engaged in religious activity and also maintained the belief that they were continuing to use and study the "original" words of Yahweh. There is precedent for this use of an essentially "dead" language in religious ritual in Mesopotamia, where Sumerian remained in use for thousands of years in cultic contexts after it ceased to be a spoken language. Latin has had a similar history in western European culture.

An emphasis on **Sabbath** worship is the direct result of the destruction of the Jerusalem temple and a shift away from a sacrificial-based cult administered by priests. This weekly celebration is the only holy day in the cultic calendar that could have been observed in the exile (Milgrom 1991, 28). Without a central shrine or designated "high place" in which to worship and make their sacrifices, the exiles and their families would have been most likely to withdraw into private, family-based devotions, including prayer, recitation of the history of their people, and perhaps the reading or study of written passages from legal or prophetic literature. By commemorating Yahweh's creative act and the injunction to cease work on the Sabbath, the exilic community was able to affirm Yahweh as the sole creative force and thereby make an argument for monotheism. The fact that the Sabbath provided an opportunity for the parents, who would otherwise be at work, to engage in simple rituals and explain to their children their theology strengthened the cultural foundation of the exilic community.

Presumably, this practice continued in the Diaspora and was formalized with the establishment of local synagogues, where prayer and study could be carried out every day of the week. For those who chose to return to Yehud, Sabbath remained an important aspect of their lives. However, when the temple was rebuilt in Jerusalem, the priests once again began the work of managing sacrificial practice and serving as the protectors and teachers of the traditions of the people. It also became their task to determine membership in the nation and thus who would be allowed to participate in the worship activities in the temple. This explains Third Isaiah's counterargument that all that is necessary to be a faithful Jew is Sabbath worship (Isa. 58:13–14). It should be noted that after the destruction of Herod's temple in 70 C.E., Sabbath worship once again became the center point of Judaism.

If circumcision had ceased to be widely practiced during the monarchy period, it was revived in the exile and emphasized as a necessary ritual act of initiation for all Jewish males, involving "more technical than cultic" significance (Zevit 2001, 665). While a precedent is found for this in Genesis 17:9–14 and Exodus 4:24–26, the origin of circumcision is unknown. It is possible that the Israelites borrowed it from the Egyptians or from other West Semites, but there is no conclusive evidence to demonstrate this (Sasson 1966). The emphasis it receives in the royal annals where the Philistines are labeled as the "uncircumcised" may suggest a possible date (Judg. 14:3; 1 Sam. 17:26; 31:4), but in the exilic and postexilic periods it was the Babylonians and Greeks who did not practice circumcision and thus served as the cultural enemies of the Jews.

To be sure, the exilic community did not invent **ritual purification practices.** The legislation found in the Priestly materials of Exodus and Numbers and in the Holiness Code in Leviticus 17–26 was part of the legal tradition developed during the monarchy period and then applied with some modification during the exile and the restoration period. There is evidence of these types of practices in Hittite texts (1500–1400), and it may be assumed that every religious tradition had its own forms of purificatory ritual to transform and dedicate altars, sacred precincts, and those who performed ritual acts. For the individual Israelite, ritual purity, at its heart, involved aspects of personal hygiene (ritual bathing) as well as attention to strict dietary practices. The endorsement of the actions in the Daniel 1–6 stories, which date to the Hellenistic period (300–100), suggests a formal acceptance by the Jews at least by the time of the postexilic period.

HITTITE PURIFICATION RITUAL FOR A TEMPLE

Afterwards they hand to him an onion, and while this is being done, she [the queen] speaks as follows: "If in the presence of the god anyone speaks as follows: 'Just as this onion consists of skins which are wrapped together, one being unable to get loose from another—as in an onion let evil, oath, curse and uncleanliness be wrapped around that temple!' See now, I have picked this onion apart and have now left only one wretched stem. Even so let him pick apart evil word, oath, curse and uncleanliness from the god's temple! Let god and sacrificer be free of that matter!" (*ANET* 346).

One of the greatest dangers to the existence of the exilic community was submersion into the surrounding culture through intermarriage. **Endogamy,** or marriage within a select, defined group, served as a social response to what may even be described as an "instinctive" struggle to protect Jewish culture from outside influences (Cerroni-Long 1984, 28). The mother is always the child's first teacher, and if she comes from a non-Jewish household, she will present mixed signals that could draw the child away from Judaism. The only other time in which endogamy is emphasized is in the ancestral narratives (Gen. 24:3–4; 26:34), and for the same reason—-cultural survival. Aside from this emphasis on cultural identity, endogamy makes little economic or political sense. Thus, it was not a factor during the monarchy period, and, as will be discussed below, it had to be enforced on the descendants of the returned exiles by the more stringent Diasporic Jews Ezra and Nehemiah (Ezra 9:1–4; Neh. 13:23–30). It is also likely that the Persian government supported this marriage practice as part of its attempt to maintain distinct ethnic units within its provinces (Hoglund 1991, 67–68; Matthews 1998, 10–11).

The formulation and enforcement of the Jewish identity movement would occupy the Diasporic community for the next several centuries. In the restoration period, it would eventually lead to the development of a new cultic community in Palestine and an exclusivistic attitude toward all those who did not share the experience of the exile. The "Israel" that this group would create as a part of its own identity would therefore be restricted to a much smaller group than that described in Isaiah 49:1–6 or 56:1–8. They would refer to the people who remained in Judah during the exile as "unclean" (Hag. 2:14) and refuse them the right to participate in worship or the rebuilding of the temple in Jerusalem (Ezra 4:3).

RESTORATION PERIOD

As had been the case throughout their history, the shifts in fortune for the Israelites would come as a result of their interaction with the superpowers of the ancient Near East. After the death of Nebuchadnezzar in 562, no strong successor emerged among the royal family, and eventually an older man, unrelated to the former king, with origins in the northern Syrian region of Harran rose to take the throne. His name was Nabonidus (556–539), and his career prior to taking the throne seems to have been as a court official, military leader, and diplomat. There is some textual evidence that suggests he owed his position to the influence exercised by his mother Adad-guppi, a priestess of the moon god Sin of Harran, who had been taken as a captive by Nebuchadnezzar when he suppressed a revolt in that city (Beaulieu 1989, 68–77). When Nebuchadnezzar's son Neriglissar died in 556, a palace coup deposed his successor Lābâši-Marduk, and the conspirators placed a somewhat reluctant Nabonidus on the throne. It is possible that Nabonidus's son Belshazzar was a prime mover in this plot, and his prominent role as his father's chief administrator in Babylon during much of his reign supports this reconstruction (Beaulieu 1989, 86–98).

The texts from Nabonidus's royal archives, like those of his predecessors, report on his campaigns, political exchanges with other nations and cities, grants of land and offices, and the ritual activities associated with the role of the king. From these early years of his reign it can be determined that he engaged in political reorganization, replacing officials whose loyalty was suspect and rebuilding temples in various parts of the kingdom (Beaulieu 1989, 104–37). Much of what is known about Nabonidus's later years comes from his enemies and as such is clouded by their political bias (Sack 1992, 973–75). If what they say is correct, however, he made some significant changes in the religious establishment in Babylon, removing Marduk as the city's patron deity and replacing him with the moon god Sin of Harran (Beaulieu 1989, 212–19; Kuhrt 1983, 90). This also involved politically deemphasizing the importance of the Marduk priesthood as well as that of many of the other deities of Babylonia (S. Smith 1924, 103–4). Their revenues would have dwindled as well and thereby turned them into the type of enemy that Akhenaton created when he staged his religious reform in Egypt in the mid-fourteenth century. In addition, Nabonidus seemed to be more concerned with protecting and maintaining the Arabian trade routes than governing Babylonia. He spent ten years (553–543) at Tema in northern Arabia, fortifying that city and delegating his duties in Babylon to his son Belshazzar, who dealt with the day-to-day details of office in the capital city (Millard 1985; Beaulieu 1989, 155–60; 169–85).

The political unrest created by Nabonidus's administration left an opening for Cyrus, the newly rising leader of Persia. He had already consolidated his control of the tribes of his own land as well as of Media. Starting in 550, he staged a series of military campaigns that added most of Anatolia, including the rich kingdom of Lydia, to his territory. Finally, in the autumn of 539 he marched on Babylon and called on Nabonidus's subjects to abandon their king in favor of the Persian monarch. His eventual victory and rebuilding of the Marduk temple in Babylon is recorded in a self-aggrandizing document known as the Cyrus Cylinder, which was written in the international diplomatic language of Mesopotamia so that it could receive a wider reading and reflect Cyrus's rule over the entire area. It was part of his official propaganda campaign and made light of what some other ancient sources (Herodotus 1.188–91; Xenophon, *Cyropaedia* 7.5.7–32, 58) describe as a much more serious level of resistance by the Neo-Babylonians (Haerinck 1997, 26–27). In any case, Nabonidus was captured by the Persians, the images of the gods that he had collected and stored in Babylon (perhaps in an attempt either to protect the city or enforce the loyalty of the cities whose images were held "hostage" by the king) were returned to their cities, and for a time Babylonia accepted, if not as graciously as Cyrus suggests, the role of Persian vassal state (Beaulieu 1989, 231–32).

CYRUS CYLINDER

"Nabonidus turned the worship of Marduk, ruler of the divine assembly in Babylon, into an abomination. . . . Marduk . . . heard the people of Babylon when they cried out and became angry. Therefore, he and the other members of the divine assembly left the sanctuaries, which had been built for them in Babylon. Marduk . . . chose Cyrus . . . and anointed him as ruler of all the earth. . . . He ordered him to march against Babylon. . . . Marduk allowed Cyrus to enter Babylon without a battle . . . and delivered Nabonidus . . . into the hands of Cyrus" (*OTP* 193–94).

There is a remarkable similarity between the language in Cyrus's victory proclamation and Second Isaiah's description of these events (figure 27). It is quite possible that the author of this exilic prophecy had seen or heard Cyrus's document and chose to substitute Yahweh's action for Marduk's. Although this would not have been "politically correct" in Babylonian circles, it effectively provided a theodicy for the exilic community that is sufficiently similar to the official version that no sanctions were likely to be felt. It also provided the historical basis for the beginning of the restoration period. In his inscription, Cyrus mandates that the images of the gods are to be restored to their "homes" and their cultic practices resumed. This would have also required the resettlement of formerly captive peoples. Some, like the Jewish exiles, would be allowed to return to their homelands, probably as a means of reinforcing Persian hegemony over that region by placing a loyal population on its border with Egypt (Kuhrt 1983, 93–95). It is also likely that funds were provided to help this returned community to rebuild the sanctuary of their God.

Those Who Returned

The vast majority of the Jewish Gôlâh community chose to remain in the Diasporic communities in Mesopotamia, Iran, and Egypt. They had established themselves

Figure 27: Isaiah and Cyrus	
ISAIAH 45:1–6	CYRUS CYLINDER ACCOUNT
Yahweh chose Cyrus and anointed him to be his champion.	Marduk chose Cyrus and anointed him to be his champion.
Yahweh promises victory, "open doors" and gates that are not closed.	Marduk orders the attack on Babylon and gives him a victory without a battle.
Yahweh arms Cyrus so that all will know, "from the rising of the sun and from the west, that there is no one besides me" (v. 6).	Cyrus claims the kingship of the "four rims of the earth" (*ANET* 316).

and their families and had created a cultural and religious identity that did not require them to return to Jerusalem. However, starting in 538, a minority of the Judean exiles began their return to what would for the next segment of their history be known as the Persian province of Yehud. Although the initial group of returnees could not be described as the glorious procession envisioned by Second Isaiah (40:3–5), undoubtedly their leader Sheshbazzar, a descendant of the royal house of Judah, expected to be able to quickly rebuild and restore Jerusalem and much of their old territorial holdings in Judah (Ezra 1:8–11). Although a myth of an "empty land" was formulated by the Chronicler to justify restoration of the land to this returned community of exiles (see the reference to "foreigners" in Ezra 4:2), they had to contend with the reality that not all Israelites had been taken into exile (Carroll 1992, 79–93; 1998, 65–66). In fact, most of what had been the territory of Israel and Judah was divided into small political units separate from Jerusalem and Yehud (see Carter 1994, 142, for a map).

Indications are that the returned exiles quickly expended the funds and resources provided by Cyrus's decree. They also were faced with staunch opposition from both those peoples who had remained in the land during the exile and their neighbors in Samaria and Transjordan (Ezra 4:1–16). This, plus international events occupying the attention of the Persian government, had sidetracked the construction of a new temple in Jerusalem for a generation. The prophet Haggai's complaint about 522 that the returned community had failed to complete the construction (Hag. 1:4) is an indication that economic and political conditions at that point were quite tenuous. They simply needed what resources they had to build their own houses, plant their fields, and make a new start in a land that had to be rehabilitated (Hoglund 1992, 57).

In addition, imperial Persian interests had turned first to additional conquests and then to determining the succession to the throne after Cyrus's death in battle in 530 and his son Cambyses II's death during his return from a successful campaign against Egypt in 522. Eventually, Darius I was able to build a political coalition among the Persian and Median nobility and ascend to the control of the empire in 522. Jerusalem and Yehud were of less real interest to an administrator who first needed to demonstrate his ability to command the respect of his bureaucracy and quell revolts by political rivals in Elam and Babylon (Stern 2001a, 354). In fact, the only event involving Darius in the biblical narrative is found in the dispute between the returned exiles, led by their governor Zerubbabel, and Tatenai, the governor of "the province Beyond the River," involving the rebuilding of the temple in Jerusalem (Ezra 5:1–6:15). According to the biblical account (Ezra 6:2–5), once Darius's bureaucrats had retrieved a copy of Cyrus's original decree and reaffirmed the Persian commitment to support of local temples, a royal order was given and funds supplied that quickly led to the completion of the project in 515. Zerubbabel's success is an indication that he and Jerusalem were being favored over the politically suspect rulers of Samaria, Ammon, and Philistia. However, after 515, when Darius had restored Persia's firm control over Egypt, he showed no more interest in his southwestern border and turned his attention to Greece. Any further signs of favor to one of the small provinces in Syro-Palestine would have unnecessarily destabilized the area (Margalith 1991, 320).

Figure 28: Persian Rulers

Cyrus (559–530 B.C.E.): Combined Persia with Media in 550, conquered Lydia in 547, and completed the conquest of the Neo-Babylonian Empire in 539 with the capture of Babylon. His decree allowed for the return of exiled peoples and the rebuilding of their temples. He was killed in battle in northeastern Iran in 530 and succeeded by his son Cambyses II.

Cambyses II (530–522 B.C.E.): During his short reign he completed the conquest of Egypt, but while hurrying back to Persia in 522 to forestall a revolt led by Gaumata, he was injured and died, leaving the succession in question.

Darius I (522–486 B.C.E.): After taking the Achaemenid throne by force, he quelled revolts throughout the empire and recorded his victories in an inscription carved into a cliff face at Behistun. He expanded the empire into northwest India and attempted to conquer the Greek city-states but was defeated at Marathon in 490. According to Ezra 6:1–12, Darius provided funds to complete the rebuilding of the Jerusalem temple in 515.

Xerxes (486–465 B.C.E.): After restructuring provincial boundaries, he attempted to complete Darius's campaign against the Greeks. However, the naval defeat at Salamis in 480 and the draining conflict on the Greek mainland depleted Persian resources and ended their attempt to control the west. He and his son were murdered in a palace uprising in 465.

Artaxerxes I (465–424 B.C.E.): After his father's assassination, he took the throne and responded to revolts in Egypt and along the coast that were sparked by the Athenians. He built a group of fortresses to protect trade routes and provide quick response to military threats. The activities of Ezra and Nehemiah are likely to be dated to his reign.

Darius II (423–405 B.C.E.): An illegitimate son of Artaxerxes I, he displaced two brothers to take the throne. While most of his activities were centered on Media and Asia Minor, he is mentioned in the Elephantine papyri (Cowley 21) in which he sends instructions for the staging of the Passover by the garrison of this Persia outpost in Egypt in 419.

Thus, Yehud became a very small part of an empire that was divided by Darius I into twenty provinces or satrapies administered by governors (satraps) appointed by the Persian emperor (Stern 2001a, 368; Herodotus 3.88–95). Population estimates for the early Persian period in Yehud are about 13,350 and about 20,650 for the later Persian period. Jerusalem during this time averaged about 1,500 persons, approximately 20 percent its size prior to its destruction by Nebuchadnezzar (Carter 1999, 200–201, 247). Like all of the political divisions in the empire, activities in Yehud would have been monitored, through a regular reporting system, by the royal bureaucracy based at the imperial capital of Susa. Yehud, as a small administrative unit within a larger province ("the province Beyond the River." Ezra 7:21), would have been governed by a local appointee (a *pehāh*) and would have had a certain measure of local autonomy to conduct its affairs (Balentine 1996, 138). Archaeological surveys have demonstrated that the majority of the people in Yehud lived in small, unwalled villages, and only Jerusalem, during the governorship of Nehemiah, was a walled city (Hoglund 1991, 57–58; Carter 1999, 215). It seems, based on a group of **bullae** impressions (Avigad 1976) and papyri from Wadi Daliyeh (Cross 1975), that there was a continuous line of administrators in Yehud from Sheshbazzar to Nehemiah, including Zerubbabel and Elnathan (Meyers and Meyers 1987, 8–15). They served as local governors and were not directly subservient to the governor in Samaria (Hoglund 1992, 78–86: Japhet 1983, 219–20). The primary expectations for Yehud's administrator would have been to collect taxes, ensure the economic well being of his unit, and demonstrate loyalty to the Persian government by maintaining the peace and preventing civil unrest (Berquist 1995, 132–33).

Naturally, bureaucratic systems such as this one would operate on the assumption that a quiet province is a loyal province. In other words, as long as there were no sign of trouble among the local population, these regions on the fringes of the empire would be allowed to develop culturally without too much interference from the central government. Of course, larger security concerns of the empire could bring the region into closer focus. After the Athenians defeated Darius's army in 490 at the battle of Marathon, foiling his designs on expending his hegemony into the Cyclades and the Greek mainland, portions of the empire became unstable. One sign of this occurred in the fall of 486 when, after Darius's death, an Egyptian revolt took advantage of the transition of power that brought Xerxes to the Persian throne. Despite a vicious suppression of this uprising by Xerxes (Dandamaev 1989, 182), his successor, Artaxerxes I, was forced to deal with yet another revolt in 460 led by the Libyan leader Inarus. Initial successes by the Egyptians and their Greek allies were squandered when Greece became embroiled in the Peloponnesian War between Athens and Sparta beginning in 458. By 454, the Persian general Megabyzus had defeated the remaining rebel forces and restored Egypt as a Persian province (Dandamaev 1989, 238–41). As a result of these conflicts, a series of Persian fortresses were constructed along major trade routes throughout the Levant. Presumably, this also indicates a greater appreciation for the importance of the provinces in Syro-Palestine as a buffer against additional unrest from Egypt or incursions by the Greeks. Although this was not a purely local issue (Hoglund 1991, 203; Carter 1999, 88–89), it did have an effect on Yehud. The increased military presence would have drained some resources from the local economy to supply these garrisons. Although many of the soldiers would have been drawn from local villages, there would have been enough foreign troops to ensure that new ideas and customs would also have been introduced to the area.

In order to manage an empire that encompassed thousands of square miles from India to Egypt and north to Ionia in western Anatolia, and that included many different ethnic groups with widely divergent cultures, Persian imperial policy had to find common denominators with which to identify, classify, and categorize all of these peoples and places. The ultimate goal would be to make them both identifiable to the royal bureaucracy and compliant with the basic imperial aims (Hoglund 1991, 57–68). Among the social and economic control mechanisms that were employed in Yehud were the following:

Figure 29: Persian Imperial Policies That Shaped Provincial Activities in Yehud

Rural settlement: Many new rural villages were established in the last quarter of the sixth century. Archaeological surveys (Kochavi 1972, 23; Carter 1994, 129–33; 1999, 233–48) suggests that in Yehud there was an intentional policy to disperse the returned population of exiles. This policy ensured continuous agricultural production that could be siphoned off in tribute as well as feed the local population. It would also help to reduce the number of land disputes with current inhabitants, since many of these were new villages in sparsely inhabited areas (Hoglund 1991, 57–60).

Commercial interaction: Widespread evidence of Greek pottery at sites throughout the eastern Mediterranean, including in Phoenicia, Philistia, and Yehud, indicate an upsurge in international commercial activity during the Persian period (Stern 1982, 137–41; 2001a, 383, 410–11). Although what impact Persian economic policies (including encouragement of specific products for exchange and taxes on transport) had on Yehud is not known, it likely resulted in some changes or conformity to imperial goals (Hoglund 1991, 60–62).

Regulation of taxation: Persia was able to control the flow of available capital into its provinces by regulating taxation levels, providing funds for construction projects and cultural activities, and using the governor and temple leaders as mediators between province and empire (Berquist 1995, 134–35). Taxation reduced the income of temples by siphoning off agricultural and other products that might have otherwise gone to temples in tithes or fees (Dandamaev and Lukonin 1989, 362–66). In the fourth century, the appearance of locally minted coins containing the name Yehud demonstrates that Persia allowed some political autonomy while promoting a regulated economy (Stern 2001a, 565–70).

Military presence: During the mid-fifth century, a system of fortresses was constructed by the Persians to protect their trade routes and possibly to defend against Athenian incursions into the eastern Mediterranean and as a reaction to a revolt in Egypt (Hoglund 1992, 88–91). The forts were garrisoned by local troops and paid for with taxes imposed on the local area in which they were built. Nehemiah's mission (Neh. 2:1–10) can be seen in the light of these concerns to maintain control of Yehud and other outlying districts (Hoglund 1991, 62–64). It also points to the ability of the Persians to make quick military responses in times of crisis.

> **Ethnic identification:** Persian policy, like that of the Assyrians and Babylonians, included resettlement of dependent peoples to new areas and their assignment as distinct communities whose produce would be considered an imperial asset and heavily taxed by the state (Briant 1975, 176–77). It is possible to interpret the Yehud community in terms of Persian resettlement of a distinct ethnic group, in this case in their former homeland, with the expectation that a portion of their grain and other products would be taxed (Neh. 5:1–4) to pay for their protection and to support imperial policy. To prevent confusion over who belonged to this defined "collective" community, Persian policy, as reflected in the actions of Nehemiah (Neh. 13:23–31) and Ezra (Ezra 10:6–12), may have restricted intermarriage (Hoglund 1991, 65–68).
>
> **Codification of law:** Persia encouraged the standardization of local law codes throughout its empire (Blenkinsopp 1987). By becoming a part of this process, the empire could ensure that legal structures did not conflict with imperial policy, that they legitimized the authority of those given the task to canonize law (Artaxerxes' commission for Ezra in Ezra 7:26), and that they maintained a sense of local autonomy and identity while ensuring ultimate support of Persian authorities and policies (Balentine 1996, 138–39).
>
> **Maintenance of regional temples:** Starting with Cyrus's decree, successive Persian rulers promoted the maintenance of regional temples and provided patronage to local cults that proved loyal to the state (Blenkinsopp 1991, 24–26). By lending their support to local priests and leaders, Persia strengthened its network of support. The Jerusalem temple, rebuilt in part with Persian funds (Ezra 6:4–5; 7:14–15, 20; 8:25), represented a Persian presence while functioning as a local cult center. By turning the flow of funds on and off, the Persian government controlled the relative influence of the temple and its priesthood (Balentine 1996, 141–42; Berquist 1995, 60–63, 94–101). Emphasis on the temple and obedience to religious law, rather than traditional (i.e., Davidic) leaders, also defused the potential for political unrest. The postexilic wisdom tradition (Pss. 37; 49; 52; 73) that contrasts the "wicked man" and the "pious man" bolstered obedience to the authority of the priestly community and promoted a tranquil society loyal to Persian government (Albertz 1994, 500–503).

Ultimately, this set of administrative policies combined imperial aims with the establishment of stable local elites whose positions were created and maintained by the Persian government. It would be expected that these individuals would therefore pledge their loyalty and support to their patron. For instance, it was to the advantage of the priestly community in Jerusalem to tie its authority to that of the emperor. In that way, the priests could combine their power as religious practitioners with their recognized position within the Persian bureaucratic structure. They could also forestall opponents with the threat that unrest or dissent would bring swift military or economic reprisals from the empire (Berquist 1995, 135). The transformation of the administrative apparatus and the emergence, with Persian support, of a dominant priestly authority in Palestine at the end of the exile set a new tone for legal interpretation and social practice. Later, following the conquests of Alexander of Macedon, the reaction to many aspects of Hellenization, which is evident in Sirach (Collins 1997, 29–32), suggests that law and its social context continued to evolve.

The Role of Ezra and Nehemiah

There is a break in the biblical narrative following the restoration of the Jerusalem temple. While this event had been one goal of the returnees (as expressed
in Hag. 1:2–11), it could not have been more than a visible symbol of their newly
restored political condition. Presumably, for the community in Yehud to be successful, they would have had to continue to develop their social identity and their
local economy as one small portion of the Persian Empire. For instance, recent
surveys by the Israel Antiquities Authority have discovered many small agricultural installations (wine presses, cisterns, grain storage facilities) that would have
served to provision Jerusalem and contribute to the economy of the province
(Carter 1999, 250–52). As was the case in the monarchic period, these villages
were taxed fairly heavily. They made "in-kind" contributions even after the
introduction of coined money in large part because there would not have been
wide distribution of coins and because the system of collecting agricultural products was so long-standing and efficient. Their taxes were used to support the
provincial elite (both the temple community and the governor's bureaucracy) and
to meet the tribute quota set by the imperial government. That left the average
citizen at a subsistence level and did not allow for the creation of a middle class
except among those merchants who participated in trade (Carter 1999, 281;
Horsley 1991, 166).

Some sense of at least an idealized view of their cultural development immediately after the return of the exiles can be seen in the visions of Zechariah 1–8
in which the prophet describes the proper ethical system for the returned community. Based in Jerusalem, but not yet tied to a temple-based system (Zech.
1:16 is the only mention of the temple), this group was urged to rebuild its community as a "house of Yahweh" that was committed to just dealings, mercy, and
concern for obedience to the law. This would ensure that they were restored to
their relationship with Yahweh (Marinkovic 1994, 95–103). While this was
undoubtedly part of the effort made by prophets and other leaders to restore a
sense of identity and cooperation among the returned exiles, it does not provide
concrete ties to historical events of the time. Without direct contact with the Persians, there is no chronology of events described in the biblical text until the mid-
fifth century and the mission of Ezra to Jerusalem about 458.

What is known about the period between 515 and 458 comes from Persian
and Greek sources, including Herodotus. Both Darius I and Xerxes attempted to
expand Persian hegemony into Greece, and in doing so they drained the empire
of men for their armies and a great deal of their wealth to support campaigns that
extended over a period of thirty years. The defeat in 490 at the battle of Marathon
stalled Persian hopes, and the death of Darius in 486, followed by revolts in Egypt
and Babylon, kept his successor, Xerxes, busy shoring up his control over the
empire. He was not able to resume his campaign against the Greek city-states until
480, when he put together a huge army that marched from Thrace in northern
Greece south to Athens, taking and burning that city. However, Themistocles and

the Athenian fleet at the battle of Salamis defeated Persia's navy, and the Persian army was subsequently defeated in 479 at the battle of Plataea by an alliance of Greek city-states. Although hostilities continued until 448, when the Peace of Callias was signed, Persia's aims in Europe were brought to an end and were never seriously resumed (Briant 1992, 240–41; Cook 1983, 113–25).

With the emperors concentrating their efforts on events outside of the empire, it is not surprising, therefore, that the biblical narrative of events does not resume until the mid-fifth century. At that point, Persia had had to deal with a serious revolt in Egypt (560–554) and had begun once again to concern itself with its internal security as well as external security along the borders to the east and along the coastline where Greek incursions had been occurring. Given this situation, it is difficult to determine exactly what Ezra's mission in 458 was supposed to accomplish (Grabbe 1994). In some respects it takes on the character of a political fact-finding trip for a man referred to as "the scribe of the law of the God of heaven" (Ezra 7:12; see Williamson 1985, 100). His efforts, as a "lower level bureaucrat" (Berquist 1995, 112), may have been tied to the Egyptian crisis or more generally to the restoration of some aspects of the empire's bureaucratic identity for that province that may have come "unraveled" during the past several decades. For instance, the commission given to Ezra by Artaxerxes I in 458 is "to make inquiry concerning Yehud and Jerusalem with the law of your god that is in your hand" (Ezra 7:14). This seems very open ended and is nonspecific regarding what portion of the Jewish law is intended here. To be sure, there were some very specific tasks given to Ezra by the Persian emperor, including the return of sacred vessels to the temple (7:19), the appointment of magistrates and judges, and the teaching of "the laws of your God" (7:25). However, the authenticity of the document is still in question and must therefore be treated carefully as a source for reconstruction of the events of this period (Grabbe 1991, 98–106; Becking 1998, 52–54).

The fact that the biblical account (Ezra 7:12–24; 8:15–34; 9:1–10:44) does not describe Ezra as a governor or as a high priest, and that he is not required to report to the satrap of the "province Beyond the River" may suggest that he was working directly for the Persian government (Margalith 1991, 312). However, his activities while in Jerusalem centered on enforcing marriage customs (Ezra 9–10), staging a **covenant renewal ceremony** (Neh. 8:1–12), and reintroducing major religious festivals (Neh. 8:13–18). This concentration on religious matters and priestly activity seems to take Ezra's mission out of the political sphere. It is possible, however, that by dealing with disputes within the priestly community, formalizing religious practice, and stabilizing social customs, Ezra was indeed doing the work of the Persian government and also forwarding any agenda he may have had himself with regard to the preservation of the "true Israel" in Yehud (Grabbe 1992, 136–37).

Similar administrative interest in provincial religious practices by vassal peoples can be found in the Aramaic papyri found at the site of a Persian outpost on the island of Elephantine in southern Egypt. These documents, which deal with personal and communal issues of its Jewish garrison, including legal matters, are dated throughout the fifth century. The soldiers and their families were probably descendants of mercenaries who had served in the Egyptian army during the sixth century and may have also included some descendants of the Judeans who fled to Egypt following Nebuchadnezzar's destruction of Jerusalem in 587. One, dated to 419, the fifth year of Darius II, contains a directive from the emperor allowing the garrison to conduct its annual Passover celebration. Since the community faced problems with its Egyptian neighbors, which would later include the destruction of its temple by an angry mob in 408 (Cowley 30), such a document was necessary to ensure that religious and civic unrest did not spring up again during their festival (Grabbe 1992, 54–55).

PASSOVER PAPYRUS FROM ELEPHANTINE (419 B.C.E.)

"To my brothers Jedaniah and his colleagues [of] the Jewish garrison, [from] your brother Hananiah. May God seek after the welfare of my brothers at all times. And now, this year, year 5 of King Darius, it has been sent from the king to Arsames [satrap of Egypt]. . . . Now, do you count fourteen days in Nisan and on the 14th at twilight observe the Passover and from the 15th day until the 21st day of Nisan the festival of Unleavened Bread observe. Seven days eat unleavened bread. Now, be pure and take heed. Do not do work on the 15th day and on the 21st day. And do not drink anything of leaven. And do not eat anything of leaven" (Cowley 21; Porten 1979, 91).

Somewhat more straightforward is the role that Nehemiah played. He was appointed as the Persian governor of Yehud and he carried out a series of building projects and administrative reforms that were very much in character for such a professional bureaucrat. His overall mission can be described against the backdrop of the Inarus revolt in Egypt and the threat of intervention in the Near East by the allied Greek forces of the Delian league. Persia in the mid-fifth century would have been more conscious of the need to shore up its borders with Egypt, and thus the security and loyalty of Jerusalem, as well as the other small provinces in Syro-Palestine, would have to be assured (M. Smith 1971, 127–28). The revenues needed to support these new garrisons would have put a strain on the local economy and could have led to some abuses by members of the local elite (Yamauchi 1980a, 285–91). When famine occurred (Neh. 5:1–4), adding to this burden, some flexibility exercised by the local governor could have prevented problems or unrest from getting out of hand (Hoglund 1992, 225).

Nehemiah, as the representative of the Persian government, would have been expected to carry out this mission as well as deal with local issues as they arose. In order to accomplish this, he also would have had to deal with local political tensions brought on by the enhanced role now being played by Jerusalem. This included confrontations between Yehud and Samaria, and its

---

Figure 30: Nehemiah's Mission and Activities

- Build a garrisoned fortress adjacent to the Jerusalem temple (Neh. 2:5–8)
- Repair the wall system of Jerusalem (Neh. 3–5)
- Provide economic reform in the face of famine and taxes to support Persian garrisons (Neh. 5:4–10)
- Establish a security system for Jerusalem and appoint Hananiah fortress commander (Neh. 7:1–4)
- Clearly define the ethnic identity of the people of Yehud by enforcing laws related to the Levites, observing the Sabbath ban on work/commerce, and banning intermarriage (Neh. 13:4–31)

---

governor, Sanballat, over the rebuilding of Jerusalem's wall system (Neh. 6:6–7). Other problems included dealing with the political influence of Tobiah, a local Ammonite leader who opposed Nehemiah's reforms (Neh. 2:19). Difficulties such as these can be compared to those faced by the Jewish community housed in the Persian garrison at Elephantine in Egypt. In 410, local Egyptian priests of the god Khnum destroyed the temple of these Jews, which they claimed to have constructed in the time of Cambyses with the support of the Persian governor Vidranga. Subsequently, the community wrote to Bagoas, the governor in Yehud, offering him payment for his support and asking for permission to rebuild their temple and, significantly, not asking to be able to resume sacrificial worship there (Porten 1992, 449).

ELEPHANTINE PETITION TO REBUILD THE TEMPLE (408 B.C.E.)

Memorandum of Bagohi and Delaiah. They said to me: "Let this indeed be a memorandum for you in Egypt to say before Arsames [satrap of Egypt] about the altar-house of the God of Heaven which was built in Elephantine-the-fortress formerly, before Cambyses, which that wicked Vidranga demolished in year 14 of King Darius: to rebuild it on its site as it was formerly and the meal-offerings and the incense they shall offer upon that altar as formerly was done" (Cowley 30; Porten 1979, 100).

Although the people of Yehud were not always enthusiastic in their response to his methods, Nehemiah chose to employ some of the social mechanisms mentioned above and presumably had the military backing needed to enforce them. These policies were designed to solidify the ethnic identity of the population of Yehud by excluding "foreigners" and the "peoples of the land" (Neh. 10:30), who had not experienced the exile and thus were not to be counted as part of the Yehud community. In doing this, Nehemiah was able to more clearly define the religious observances of the people and role of the temple community, whose charge was to care for the "house of God," which included both the temple structure and the worship community (Hoglund 1992, 220; Eskenazi 1988, 101–4).

The emphasis that Ezra and Nehemiah place on endogamy as a means of preserving the ethnic identity of the Yehud community suggests that this practice had not been enforced for some time among the returned exiles. This likelihood is more reflective either of immigrants who wish to marry into propertied families and thus gain a greater hold on territories they otherwise might not possess, or a community whose demographic factors (lack of females) require it to accept marriage arrangements out of necessity (see the fairly common evidence of intermarriage in the Jewish garrison on the Egyptian island of Elephantine; Porten 1968, 249–50). The first scenario is based on the immigrants' desire to "marry up" in order to more quickly make their community viable and welcome in the area (Smith-Christopher 1994, 249–50; Mayer 1961). Furthermore, it is likely that some of the "foreigners" involved were actually Israelites who had not gone into exile and thus had not undergone the "purification" experienced by the exiles.

One argument suggests that Ezra's marriage crisis actually may reflect a later time period when "denominations" within Judaism may have been the issue and the "foreigners" may have been nonnormative sects (Smith-Christopher 1994, 257). Although that is a possibility, it is more likely that Ezra's attitude (which is most likely a reflection of a postexilic priestly attitude) was based on his perception that the Yehud community was in danger of losing its Jewish identity. Thus, to establish a means of social "boundary maintenance," he issued the decree against mixed marriages.

Another way of looking at this is in terms of the community's desire to purify itself of "foreign" influences (Eskenazi 1988, 190–91). The constancy of ritual and adherence to the rule of "law," advocated by Ezra and Nehemiah, would thus replace the dangers of social evolution and assimilation that were manifested, in part, by the mixed marriages and the concern over the ability to speak Hebrew (Neh. 13:23–24), another "ingredient of national identity" (Blenkinsopp 1988, 363). It would also lead to the redefining of proper marriage partners. Those matches that had been deemed acceptable previously, due to a lack of females among the returnees or some other demographic factor, would, under this new social order, be forbidden (Eskenazi and Judd 1994, 274–77; Merton 1941, 361–63).

As a career bureaucrat, however, Nehemiah especially would not have been able to satisfy his personal religious concerns at the expense of his royal duties (Hoglund 1992, 223). As representatives of the Persian government and, in Nehemiah's case, a former "cupbearer" of the king (Neh. 1:11; Yamauchi 1980b, 133), Ezra and Nehemiah would have promoted reforms that necessarily reflected the official policies of the empire. If it was Persian strategy (1) to use Yehud as a military buffer against Egyptian or Edomite expansion (signaled by the rebuilding of Jerusalem's walls and its revived status as an urban center), and (2) to reinforce ethnic identity among those peoples who had been resettled or had been returned to former homelands, then royal governors, judges, and magistrates would have been required to set forth proclamations and procedures to get this done (Neh. 13 and Ezra 9). What is a bit ironic here is that both the enhanced status of Jerusalem and the policy of endogamy, which may serve the purposes of empire, also served the desires of exclusivist voices among the Jewish community. Ezra and Nehemiah, adherents of what is called the "Yahweh-alone party" (M. Smith 1971, 127–28), would have been able to use the backing of the empire to engineer their reforms to purify Palestinian Judaism and restore it to the model of Jewish identity that they, as representatives of Diasporic Judaism, advocated.

There is also an ideological aspect to the marriage policies of Ezra and Nehemiah, namely, their intention to create an identifiable people who adheres to a particular set of cultural and religious values. They found that the best way to do this was through a policy of exclusion, which in turn required a genealogical foundation to prove who was actually a member of that community. They required members to adhere to and publicly advocate this policy of purification and cultural identity as the only true means of gaining God's support and as the manifestation of their acceptance of the covenant.

The fact that they were not entirely successful in universalizing this social doctrine can be found in the book of Ruth. Although the author(s) had to set the story in the premonarchic period, it would not have been lost on the audience that it concludes with a genealogy clearly pointing to a mixed origin for King David (Ruth 4:13–22). What better argument could the critics of Ezra and Nehemiah make than one that demonstrates the value of mixed marriage?

For such an ideological change to take place, however, it was necessary to draw upon previously held traditions or to create authentic-sounding precedents for social custom. Thus, Ezra and Nehemiah's insistence on endogamy is reinforced by the mandate given to the covenantal community to keep itself separate from the "peoples of the land" (Exod. 34:12–16; Deut. 7:1–11) and by the custom of the ancestors to marry only within their own social group for the first two generations (Gen. 24:3–4; 28:1–5). The result was an acceptance of a custom, irrespective of the possible fictitious nature of the precedents drawn from saga, because it was identified as socially and legally valid (see Japhet 1992, 83–84 for another example of this type of socio-legal rationale).

Overall, the role played by Ezra and Nehemiah seems to have consisted of efforts to ensure the loyalty of Yehud to the Persian Empire. This is especially clear with regard to Nehemiah's building projects and his attempts to strengthen the economic condition of the province. In those instances where their policies shape religious practice or enforce laws associated with the Sabbath, maintain the resources of the Levites and the priestly community, and enforce marriage customs, they can be seen as part of the Persian policy to create definable ethnic groups within the empire. Since the biblical narrative does not describe either man's full career or the aftermath of his activities, the reader is left with the impression, irregardless of the actual demographics of the region (Ahlström 1993, 900), that hereafter the community in Yehud had been prepared for their future. They alone had become "Israel" restored, defined as the community that had experienced the exile, and were tied to Yahweh by covenant relationship and by acceptance of the law of the "God of heaven."

ALEXANDER OF MACEDON AND THE BEGINNING OF THE HELLENISTIC AGE

The political shift that marked the end of the era for the history of the ancient Near East took place as a result of the conquest of the Persian Empire by the Macedonian army of Alexander the Great. His father, Philip, had planned the initial campaign against the Persians, pulling together an army primarily from Macedonia in 338, but he was assassinated in 336 before the expedition could begin. The task fell to his young son and heir, Alexander, and initially he simply followed his father's plan to master Greece and extend his influence into Asia Minor. However, by using the dynamic energy of the Macedonian aristocracy (his two thousand "Companions"), the well-organized cavalry and infantry forces of the Macedonian army (numbering about twelve thousand), and by exploiting the weaknesses of the Persian regime, Alexander achieved a military success far beyond what his father had envisioned (Tcherikover 1972, 8–10).

The pretext for the war against Persia, which began in 334, was revenge for the devastation that the Persians had inflicted on Greece during the previous century, and Alexander's army of thirty thousand infantry and five thousand cavalry did contain contingents from the Greek city-states under the alliance of the Corinthian League. These allies, however, were a minority, and it was the Macedonians who formed the core of his army (Dandamaev 1989, 319–25). Aided by his father's veteran commanders and leading the cavalry charges himself in several battles, Alexander was able to slice away first Asia Minor and then Syria from the Persians. When the ports of Tyre and Sidon were taken in 331 and the Egyptians proclaimed Alexander a pharaoh (Diodorus 17.49–51), the Persians were deprived of ports for their fleet and could no longer harass Alexander's forces by sea. Darius III (336–330) proved no match for Alexander in battle or as a strategist. Despite huge levies of troops that he raised from the empire, Darius was defeated at the crucial battle of Gaugamela on the northern Tigris River on October 31, 331, leaving Babylon open for conquest and allowing Alexander to move into Persia to take its capital (Cook 1983, 225–28).

When Alexander burned the Persian capital of Persepolis, he broke Persia's control over the Near East and set the stage for the introduction of an entirely new period in that region's history. Alexander hoped to create a new culture in his empire that would be a fusion of both east and west. This Hellenistic culture was then to be formed from the synthesis of Greek ideas and the customs and traditions of the areas into which it was introduced. To retain political stability, Alexander's successors retained those officials who proved loyal to the new regime. The local economy was then stimulated by the introduction of Greek marketing techniques and fresh operating capital taken from the plundering of the Persian imperial treasury. However, Alexander's untimely death in 323 and the division of the empire among his generals, later known as the **Diadochi,** meant that much of the administration of this vast domain would have to rely on Persian models and in many cases return to the inefficient and corrupt management that had facilitated Alexander's conquest (Tcherikover 1972, 14–15).

In the principal areas of the former Persian Empire, two of Alexander's generals eventually obtained mastery. Ptolemy ruled Egypt and Syro-Palestine, setting himself and his descendants up as successors to the pharaohs, while Seleucus gained control over the provinces of Asia (Mesopotamia and Persia) and Asia Minor. Their successors introduced typical forms of Greek culture: the gymnasium, the theater, and the social associations for professional, cultural, and religious groups. At the same time, these foreign rulers and their Greek subjects acclimated themselves to the patterns and traditions of their new home, forming the Hellenized culture that would dominate the area until the coming of Islam.

During the early years of Greek rule, Palestine saw no drastic cultural changes, nor were the people required to conform to Greek social customs. The Ptolemies introduced new coinage and broadly exploited the economic resources of that region, but they did not attempt to impose Hellenistic ideas on the Jews (Bickerman 1988, 69–80). Temple worship in Jerusalem continued unhindered, and the office of high priest still exercised great authority on matters of religion. Rival temples were constructed at Samaria and later at Mount Gerizim near Shechem, which allowed the people of the Galilee and the old territory of Israel to worship without the constraints or influence of Jerusalem (Ahlström 1993, 901–3).

Ultimately, the next stage of history for the Jews and other inhabitants of Syro-Palestine would involve the choices they would have to make with regard to the acceptance or rejection of Hellenization. Hellenization became popular among the new generation after Alexander's conquest and among those Jews who had contact with Jewish communities outside of Palestine, such as those in Antioch, Alexandria, and Damascus. There were also obvious advantages for merchants and administrators who adopted Greek language and manners, but their choice might eventually only have involved personal names, clothing styles, and material goods, not necessarily religious practice (Hengel 1974, 1.6–57). For those who chose a more traditional path, as represented by the writings of Ben Sira, which date to the last quarter of the second century B.C.E., the cosmopolitan character of the Hellenistic Age was considered a danger to their social ethics. They preferred an "ethic of caution" (Sanders 1979), which encouraged a healthy respect for traditional values and the "fear of the Lord" (Collins 1997, 31–33). They could embrace the good things that commercial prosperity brought, but they disdained a culture that seemed to lack humility or moderation.

The cultural dispute would take on a political aspect during the mid-third century B.C.E. as conflicts grew between the Selucid and Ptolemaic rulers. International intrigues, much like those of previous eras between Egypt and Mesopotamia, drew the smaller states and their leaders into alliances as each tried to destabilize the other's supporters. It is not possible, however, to determine to what extent Hellenism influenced the lives of the majority of the people of Syro-Palestine (L. I. Levine 1999, 234). As always, written sources concern themselves with the activities of the elites in society. Given the shape of Jewish culture as it developed in the next two centuries, it is fair to say that Judaism was influenced by Hellenistic ideas and customs. However, that story is the subject of a volume dealing with the world that the Romans would shape. The world of the ancient Israelites, marked by the period from the ancestors to the conquest of Alexander, concludes with the Jews scattered throughout the Near East and a community in Jerusalem striving to maintain its identity—both political and cultural—in the face of mounting international forces.

Major Events During the Monarchy Period

Ca. 1030: Saul becomes chief over a confederation of Israelite tribes

Ca. 1000: David becomes the first king of the twelve tribes of Israel
• Jerusalem becomes the capital city and the ark of the covenant is brought to Jerusalem
• Prophet: Nathan

Ca. 960: Solomon becomes king
• Temple is constructed and worship is centralized
• Economic alliance with Phoenicia brings riches and syncretism
• Prophet: Ahijah

Ca. 920: The kingdom divides
• Jeroboam becomes the first king of the northern kingdom of Israel
• Rehoboam continues as king of the southern kingdom of Judah
• Prophets: Ahijah; unnamed prophet from Judah (1 Kgs. 13)

885: Omri establishes dynasty in Israel
• Samaria becomes the capital of Israel and Transjordan is controlled
• Ahab and Jezebel; battle of Qarqar (845); Mesha Stele
• Prophets: Elijah, Elisha

841: Assyrian hegemony expands
• Shalmaneser III's Black Obelisk (Jehu pays tribute)
• Syro-Ephraimitic War (730s)
• Fall of northern kingdom to Sargon II (720)
• Jerusalem besieged by Sennacherib (701 and 688)
• Prophets: Amos, Hosea, Isaiah, Micah

627: Assyrian Empire collapses and new empires are born
• Egyptian hegemony over Palestine (Necho II until 601)
• Nebuchadnezzar begins Babylonian hegemony (601–540)
• Jerusalem captured (597) and destroyed (587)
• Babylonian exile (597–538)
• Prophets: Nahum, Zephaniah, Habakkuk, Jeremiah, Huldah, Ezekiel

535: Postexilic period
• Persian Empire rises under Cyrus and Darius (550–480) and exiles return
  to Jerusalem
• Temple rebuilt, tension develops between Diasporic and Jerusalem com-
  munities (Nehemiah, Ezra)
• Hellenistic period begins with Alexander's conquests (336–322)
• Prophets: Second and Third Isaiah, Malachi, Joel, Haggai, Zechariah,
  Daniel

Glossary

assimilation. The submergence of a people and their culture into that of another people through close contact.

anachronism. A detail in a story that does not fit the time period of the story.

anthropomorphism. The attribution of human characteristics to a god.

apology. A literary device used to defend a character or to provide a political background for a leader's rise to power.

apostasy. Any action that allows or condones false worship.

archaeology. The scientific process of examining the ancient remains of human settlements and the artifacts produced by their inhabitants.

ark of the covenant. The gold-covered box created to house the Ten Commandments. It was carried by the Levites and was kept in the Holy of Holies of the tabernacle during the wilderness period.

artifact. Anything human beings have modified. In an archaeological excavation, artifacts are those objects found within each stratum or occupation layer that are used to clarify and date the site.

B.C.E. "Before the Common Era"; used in this book in place of B.C., but the dates are the same.

bullae. Small clay seals that were attached to string that bound papyrus documents. Each contained a stamp seal of the owner, often with the name of the scribe or the author of the document.

bureaucracy. A system of nonelected government officials who facilitate the operation of the various departments and functions of governing a state through the issuance and enforcement of rules.

call narrative. The story of a person's call to become a prophet.

canon. The collection of books designated by a faith community as authoritative and as the standard for faith and practice.

C.E. "Common Era"; used in this book in place of A.D., but the dates are the same.

chiefdom. A loose confederation of villages and tribes held together by a war chief and a crisis situation. Although this is a possible step toward statehood, it does not necessarily ensure a state will be established.

Chronicler. The writer(s) who created the revisionist history of Israel found in 1 and 2 Chronicles some time in the fourth century B.C.E.

circumscription. A process that occurs when villages or states exhaust their natural resources and are cut off from any further development.

city-state. A political unit comprising an urban center and its immediate environs and villages.

corporate identity. A legal principle that rewards or punishes an entire household for the righteousness or the sins of the head of the household.

cosmopolitan. Demonstrating an attitude of cultural openness and sophistication.

covenant. The contractual agreement between Yahweh and the chosen people that promised land and children in exchange for exclusive worship and obedience.

covenant renewal ceremony. A ritual used several times by Israelite leaders to reinforce the importance of the covenant with Yahweh.

cultic. Anything having to do with religious activity.

D-source. The Deuteronomistic History, which, according to the Documentary Hypothesis, is the layer of editing of the biblical text found primarily in the books of Joshua–2 Kings, dated to ca. 600 B.C.E. This source reflects a view of history in which the Israelites are punished for their failure to obey the covenant.

Dead Sea Scrolls. The scrolls discovered in 1947 in the caves near Qumran on the northern shore of the Dead Sea that contain the oldest copies of the books in the Hebrew Bible that have been found to date. They date to the second–first centuries B.C.E.

Decalogue. The Ten Commandments.

demythologize. To interpret a myth from a culture without ascribing any supernatural powers to the gods or humans in those stories.

deuterocanon. Also known as the Apocrypha, these books were composed during the intertestamental period (400–60 B.C.E.) and contain accounts of the history, literature, and wisdom of the Hellenistic era. They were not included in the Hebrew canon but are part of the Septuagint (Greek) and the Latin Bible (Vulgate) of the Roman Catholic Church.

Deuteronomistic Historian. The name given to the editor(s) of the D-source in the documentary hypothesis and generally dated to post-600 B.C.E. This source is characterized by a strict moralism and a view of Israelite history in which the people continually fail to obey the covenant and therefore deserve Yahweh's punishment.

Diadochi. The generals of Alexander the Great who succeeded him in ruling the Near Eastern territories they had conquered together.

Diasporic Judaism. A conservative strand of Judaism that evolved during the exile and is characteristic of the Jews who remained in the lands of the exile.

disqualification story. A story designed to eliminate a person or a family from succession to the throne of Israel or from inheriting the covenantal promise.

divination. A set of practices, including casting lots and examining animal entrails and natural phenomena, that attempt to determine the future and the will of the gods.

divine assembly. The divine company that serves Yahweh in the form of messengers and is portrayed surrounding Yahweh enthroned.

Divine Warrior. The role of Yahweh in warfare.

E-source. The Elohist source, which, according to the Documentary Hypothesis, is the layer of editing of the biblical text, dated to ca. 850 B.C.E., that reflects a northern or Israelite viewpoint after the division of the kingdom.

egalitarianism. A social system in which persons have equal status.

Elohim. One of the names for the Israelite God in the Bible. Associated with the E-source, it is translated as "God" in English translations of the Bible.

endogamy. A policy of marrying only within a certain identifiable group.

Ephraim. Son of Joseph and the generic political name synonymous with the northern kingdom of Israel.

eschatology. The study of "last things" or events just prior to the end of time.

ethnocentrism. A belief, represented in speech, literature, and attitude, that one's own race or group is superior to all others.

etiology. The study of causes, such as the origin of an event, the background of a place-name, or the basis for a tradition.

execration ritual. An action that curses a person or place.

framework story. A narrative that when analyzed shows an outline structure that can be applied whenever a similar set of events occurs or that can be used as the basis for a drama.

genre. A category of literature (e.g., short story, poetry).

gloss. A scribal addition to a text.

hegemony. A political situation in which a powerful nation or empire exercises extensive influence over the policies and actions of neighboring states.

henotheism. The belief in the existence of many gods but the choice to worship only one.

hesed. "Everlasting love"; a covenantal term used as the basis for Yahweh's willingness to make a covenant with the people.

hieratic. A cursive form of Egyptian writing used for everyday, practical applications. The pictographic hieroglyphic script was reserved chiefly for public and monumental displays.

inclusio. A literary device in which the same thing occurs at the beginning and the end (e.g., ABCDA).

investiture. A ceremony in which a person receives the symbols of office, usually including robes or other garments distinctive to the new position of authority.

J-source. The Yahwist/Jahwist source, which, according to the Documentary Hypothesis, is the first layer of editing of the biblical text, dated to ca. 1000 B.C.E., and that contains a narrative style and reflects the political boundaries of David's kingdom.

Jeroboam's sin. The actions taken by King Jeroboam I to establish a separate identity for the northern kingdom. They were used by the biblical writers as the hallmark of the "evil king."

kosher. A Jewish term for "clean" (i.e., ritually pure) food.

legend. A story that centers on human heroes or founders of nations and that includes superhuman feats or dealings with gods.

liturgy. The outline and stages of a worship service.

Messiah. Hebrew for "anointed"; used for those individuals chosen by Yahweh for particular leadership positions.

midwife. A woman who assists with the birth of children and the instruction of mothers in child care.

motif. A repeated story line in a narrative.

myth. A story that centers on the origins of events or things (see **etiology**) and usually involves the activities of gods.

Nazirite. A Jew (either male or female) who takes an oath to refrain from consuming any product of the grape, from coming in contact with the dead, and from cutting his or her hair.

nepotism. The practice of hiring or appointing one's relatives to jobs or positions of authority.

Nomes. Administrative districts in ancient Egypt, originally independent provinces that were united by the pharaohs of the Old Kingdom.

Ophel. The ridge on the southeastern slope of the Temple Mount in Jerusalem that extends south between the Kidron and Tyropoeon Valleys and has been identified as part of David's city.

oracle. A prophetic speech.

ordination ritual. The set of actions that are used to designate a person as a member of the clergy or as a prophet.

P-source. According to the Documentary Hypothesis, this Priestly Source is the final layer of editing of the biblical text, dated to the eighth century and reincorporated after 500 B.C.E. into the postexilic community's practices. It reflects priestly concern for matters of religious ritual and purity.

pantheon. All of the gods in a religious system.

Pentateuch. The first five books of the Old Testament/Hebrew Bible (Genesis through Deuteronomy).

prophetic immunity. Protection given to a prophet when he or she speaks in a god's name that prevents the people from killing the prophet because of a negative message.

proselytes. Converts to a faith community.

remnant. The portion of the community that will, according to the prophets, survive God's wrath and rebuild the nation.

ritual purification. The steps taken to transform persons or objects into a "clean" or "pure" religious state.

Sabbath. The celebration of Yahweh as the creator God and the commemoration of the creation event by ceasing work one day each week.

Semitic. A term traced to Gen. 10:21–31 relating to Noah's son Shem and referring to a group of languages (Akkadian, Aramaic, Hebrew, Arabic, Ethiopic) and those peoples who spoke them.

Septuagint. The Greek translation of the Hebrew Bible by Alexandrian Jews (fourth–second centuries B.C.E.), which is abbreviated LXX and which contains the Apocrypha/deuterocanon.

seventy elders. The group of men selected to help administer the Israelites and to represent them at major events.

Shema. The statement of faith of the Israelites found in Deut. 6:4.

Sheol. "The pit"; identified with the underworld in Hebrew tradition but not perceived as a place of punishment or reward for the dead.

suzerain. A king or ruler.

symbiotic relationship. In a political sense, the coexistence of two states or groups in cooperation based on trade, mutual defense, or political expediency.

syncretism. The borrowing of cultural ideas and traits from neighboring peoples.

theodicy. An explanation for God's actions. Most often found in the words of the prophets.

theophany. The appearance of God to a human being.

transcendence. A characteristic of a deity who is separate from the creation and is not affected by the forces of nature.

transformation ritual. An event in which a person is changed either physically or culturally by means of a physical or verbal set of actions (i.e., circumcision or religious conversion).

treaty. A formal agreement with a traditional set of sections that defines the relationship between two nations or peoples.

universalism. A theme in the biblical narrative which attempts to demonstrate that Yahweh is a universal god by having a non-Israelite make a statement of faith or remark about Yahweh's power.

Via Maris. The name of an international highway that stretched at least from the Upper Galilee to the Mediterranean coast of Palestine by way of the Jezreel Valley. It may have also extended south along the coast to Egypt and north to Damascus.

xenophobia. The fear of the stranger.

Yahweh. One of the names for the Israelite God in the Bible. It is associated with the J-source. In English translations of the Bible, Yahweh is always translated "LORD."

Bibliography

Abbreviations Used in the Bibliography

AA	*American Anthropologist*
ACEBT	*Amsterdamse Cahiers voor Exegese en Bijbelse Theologie*
AE	*American Ethnologist*
AfO	*Archiv für Orientforshung*
AJA	*American Journal of Archaeology*
AJS	*American Journal of Sociology*
AOAT	*Alter Orient und Altes Testament*
AQ	*Anthropological Quarterly*
ARA	*Annual Review of Anthropology*
Arch	*Archaeology*
ASR	*American Sociological Review*
ATJ	*Ashland Theological Journal*
ATR	*Anglican Theological Review*
AUSS	*Andrews University Seminary Studies*
BA	*Biblical Archaeologist*
BAR	*Biblical Archaeology Review*
BASOR	*Bulletin of the American Schools of Oriental Research*
BBR	*Bulletin for Biblical Research*
Bib	*Biblica*

BibInt	*Biblical Interpretation*
BiOr	*Bibliotheca Orientalis*
BJRL	*Bulletin of the John Rylands University Library*
BK	*Bibel und Kirche*
BN	*Biblische Notizen*
BR	*Biblical Research*
BRev	*Bible Review*
BRT	*Baptist Review of Theology/La Revue Baptiste de Théologie*
BS	*Bibliotheca Sacra*
BTB	*Biblical Theology Bulletin*
BTFT	*Bijdragen: Tijdschrift voor Filosofie en Theologie*
BV	*Biblical Viewpoint*
BZ	*Biblische Zeitschrift*
CA	*Current Anthropology*
CBQ	*Catholic Biblical Quarterly*
CJ	*Concordia Journal*
CR:BS	*Currents in Research: Biblical Studies*
CSR	*Christian Scholars Review*
CTR	*Concordia Theoligical Review*
CurTM	*Currents in Theology and Mission*
ETR	*Etudes Theologiques et Religieuses*
EvQ	*Evangelical Quarterly*
ExpT	*Expository Times*
FCED	*Feminist Companion to Exodus and Deuteronomy*
FCEJS	*Feminist Companion to Esther, Judith and Susanna*
FCG	*Feminist Companion to Genesis*
FCHBNT	*Feminist Companion to the Hebrew Bible in the New Testament*
FCJ	*Feminist Companion to Judges*
FCLP	*Feminist Companion to the Latter Prophets*
FCR	*Feminist Companion to Ruth*
FCRB	*Feminist Companion to Reading the Bible*
FCSK	*Feminist Companion to Samuel and Kings*
FCSS	*Feminist Companion to the Song of Songs*
FCWL	*Feminist Companion to Wisdom Literature*
FH	*Fides et Historia*
GTJ	*Grace Theological Journal*
HAR	*Hebrew Annual Review*
HBT	*Horizons in Biblical Theology*
Hor	*Horizons*
HR	*History of Religions*
HS	*Hebrew Studies*
HTR	*Harvard Theological Review*
HUCA	*Hebrew Union College Annual*
IBS	*Irish Biblical Studies*
IEJ	*Israel Exploration Journal*
Int	*Interpretation*
ISSB	*International Social Science Bulletin*
ITQ	*Irish Theological Quarterly*
JAAR	*Journal of the American Academy of Religion*
JANES	*Journal of the Ancient Near Eastern Society*
JAOS	*Journal of the American Oriental Society*
JATS	*Journal of the Adventist Theological Society*
JBL	*Journal of Biblical Literature*

JBQ	Jewish Bible Quarterly
JCS	Journal of Cuneiform Studies
JEA	Journal of Egyptian Archaeology
JESHO	Journal of Economic and Social History of the Orient
JETS	Journal of the Evangelical Theological Society
JGES	Journal of the Grace Evangelical Society
JHS	Journal of Hellenic Studies
JJS	Journal of Jewish Studies
JNES	Journal of Near Eastern Studies
JNSL	Journal of Northwest Semitic Languages
JQR	Jewish Quarterly Review
JR	Journal of Religion
JSem	Journal for Semitics
JSJ	Journal for the Study of Judaism in the Persian, Hellenistic, and Roman Periods
JSNT	Journal for the Study of the New Testament
JSOT	Journal for the Study of the Old Testament
JSP	Journal for the Study of the Pseudepigrapha
JSQ	Jewish Studies Quarterly
JSS	Journal of Semitic Studies
JTS	Journal of Theological Studies
Jud	Judaism
Levant	
List	Listening
LTQ	Lexington Theological Quarterly
LTS	Lutheran Theological Studies
Ma	Maarav
MQR	Mennonite Quarterly Review
MSJ	The Master's Seminary Journal
NGTT	Nederduits Gereformeerde Teologiese Tydskrif
NT	Novum Testamentum
NTR	New Theology Review
NTS	New Testament Studies
Or	Orientalia
OTE	Old Testament Essays
OTS	Oudtestamentische Studiën
PEGLMBS	Proceedings, Eastern Great Lakes and Midwest Biblical Societies
PEQ	Palestine Exploration Quarterly
PIBA	Proceedings of the Irish Biblical Association
Proof	Prooftexts
PRS	Perspectives in Religious Studies
PSB	Princeton Seminary Bulletin
QR	Quarterly Review
RA	Revue d'assyriologie
RB	Revue Biblique
RQ	Restoration Quarterly
RSO	Revista degli studi orientali
RSR	Religious Studies Review
RTR	The Reformed Theological Review
Scrip	Scriptura
Semeia	
SH	Scripta Hierosolymitana
SJOT	Scandinavian Journal of the Old Testament
SJT	Scottish Journal of Theology

SK	*Skrif en Kerk*
SR	*Studies in Religion*
SVTQ	*St. Vladimir's Theological Quarterly*
TA	*Tel Aviv*
TB	*Tyndale Bulletin*
TBT	*The Bible Today*
TD	*Theology Digest*
TE	*Theological Educator*
Them	*Themelios*
Theo	*Theology*
TJ	*Trinity Journal*
TJT	*Toronto Journal of Theology*
TS	*Theological Studies*
TT	*Theology Today*
TZ	*Theologische Zeithschrift*
UF	*Ugarit Forschungen*
USQR	*Union Seminary Quarterly Review*
VE	*Vox Evangelica*
VT	*Vetus Testamentum*
WA	*World Archaeology*
WO	*Die Welt des Orients*
WTJ	*Wesminster Theological Journal*
ZA	*Zeitschrift fur Assyriologie*
ZAW	*Zeitschrift fur die Alttestamentliche Wissenschaft*
ZNW	*Zeitschrift fur die Neutestamentliche Wissenschaft und die Kunde des Urchristentums*

Ackroyd, P. R. 1968. *Exile and Restoration.* London: SCM Press.

Adams, R. M. 1981. *Heartland of Cities: Surveys of Ancient Settlement and Land Use on the Central Floodplain of the Euphrates.* Chicago: University of Chicago Press.

Aharoni, M., and A. F. Rainey. 1987. "Arad: An Ancient Israelite Fortress with a Temple to Yahweh." *BAR* 13 (2): 16–35.

Aharoni, Y. 1974. "The Building Activities of David and Solomon," *IEJ* 24: 13–16.

Ahlström, G. W. 1991. "The Origin of Israel in Palestine." *SJOT* 2: 19–34.

———. 1993. *The History of Ancient Palestine from the Paleolithic Period to Alexander's Conquest.* JSOTSup 146. Sheffield: Sheffield Academic Press.

Albertz, R. 1994. *A History of Israelite Religion in the Old Testament Period. Vol. 2, From the Exile to the Maccabees.* Louisville, Ky.: Westminster John Knox Press.

Albright, W. F. 1957. *From the Stone Age to Christianity: Monotheism and the Historical Process.* Baltimore: Johns Hopkins University Press.

———. 1968. *Archaeology and the Religion of Israel.* Baltimore: Johns Hopkins University Press.

Andersen, F. I., and D. N. Freedman. 1980. *Hosea: A New Translation with Introduction and Commentary.* New York: Doubleday.

Ash, P. S. 1995. "Solomon's? District? List." *JSOT* 67: 67–86.

———. 1998. "Jeroboam I and the Deuteronomistic Historian's Ideology of the Founder." *CBQ* 60: 16–24.

Avigad, N. 1976. *Bullae and Seals from a Post-Exilic Judan Archive.* Qedem 4. Hebrew University Institute of Archaeology Monograph Series. Jerusalem: Hebrew University Press.

Balentine, S. E. 1996. "The Politics of Religion in the Persian Period." In *After the Exile: Essays in Honour of Rex Mason,* edited by J. Barton and D. J. Reimer. Macon, Ga.: Mercer University Press.

Bar-Adon, P. 1989. "Excavations in the Judean Desert." *Atiqot* 9: 1–88. (Hebrew)

Barstad, H. M. 1997. "History and the Hebrew Bible." In *Can a "History of Israel" Be Written?* edited by L. L. Grabbe. JSOTSup 245. Sheffield: Sheffield Academic Press.

———. 1998. "The Strange Fear of the Bible." In *Leading Captivity Captive: "The Exile" as History and Ideology,* edited by L. L. Grabbe. JSOTSup 278. Sheffield: Sheffield Academic Press.

Bartlett, J. R. 1983. "The 'United' Campaign against Moab in 2 Kings 3:4–27." In *Midian, Moab, and Edom: The History and Archaeology of Late Bronze and Iron Age Jordan and Northwest Arabia,* edited by J. Sawyer and D. Clines. Sheffield: JSOT Press.

———. 1989. *Edom and the Edomites.* JSOTSup 77. Sheffield: Sheffield Academic Press.

Batto, B. F. 1992. *Slaying the Dragon: Mythmaking in the Biblical Tradition.* Louisville, Ky.: Westminster/John Knox Press.

Beaulieu, P. A. 1989. *The Reign of Nabonidus, King of Babylon 556–539 B.C.* New Haven, Conn.: Yale University Press.

Becking, B. 1992. *The Fall of Samaria: An Historical and Archaeological Study.* Leiden: Brill.

———. 1997. "Inscribed Seals as Evidence for Biblical Israel? Jeremiah 40.7–41.15 Par Exemple." In *Can a "History of Israel" Be Written?* edited by L. L.Grabbe. JSOTSup 245. Sheffield: Sheffield Academic Press.

———. 1998. "Ezra's Re-enactment of the Exile." In *Leading Captivity Captive: "The Exile" as History and Ideology,* edited by L. L. Grabbe. JSOTSup 278. Sheffield: Sheffield Academic Press.

———. 1999. "Did Jehu Write the Tel Dan Inscription?" *SJOT* 13: 187–201.

Begg, C. T. 1987. "The Interpretation of the Gedalajah Episode (2 Kgs. 25, 22–26) in Context." *Antonianum* 62: 3–11.

Beit-Arieh, I., and B. Cresson. 1991. "Horvat 'Uza, a Fortified Outpost on the Eastern Negev Border." *BA* 54: 126–35.

Ben Tor, A., and D. Ben-Ami. 1998. "Hazor and the Archaeology of the Tenth Century B.C.E." *IEJ* 48: 1–37.

Ben Zvi, E. 1991. "The Account of the Reign of Manasseh in II Reg 21, 1–18 and the Redactional History of the Book of Kings." *ZAW* 103: 355–74.

Berquist, J. L. 1995. *Judaism in Persia's Shadow: A Social and Historical Approach.* Minneapolis: Fortress Press.

Bickerman, E. J. 1988. *The Jews in the Greek Age.* Cambridge, Mass.: Harvard University Press.

Biran, A., and J. Naveh. 1993. "An Aramaic Stele Fragment from Tel Dan." *IEJ* 43: 81–98.

———. 1995. "The Tel Dan Inscription: A New Fragment." *IEJ* 45: 1–18.

Blenkinsopp, J. 1987. "The Mission of Udjahorresnet and Those of Ezra and Nehemiah." *JBL* 106: 409–21.

———. 1988. *Ezra-Nehemiah: A Commentary.* Philadelphia: Westminster Press.

———. 1991. "Temple and Society in Achaemenid Judah." In P. R. Davies, ed. *Second Temple Studies. Vol. 1, Persian Period.* JSOTSup 117. Sheffield: Sheffield Academic Press.

Bloch-Smith, E., and B. A. Nakhai. 1999. "A Landscape Comes to Life: The Iron Age I." *NEA* 62: 62–92, 101–27.

Borowski, O. 1995. "Hezekiah's Reforms and the Revolt against Assyria." *BA* 58: 148–55.

Briant, P. 1975. "Villages et communautés villageoises d'Asie achéménid et hellénistique." *Journal for Economic and Social History of the Orient* 18: 165–88.

———. 1992. "Persian Empire." *ABD* 5: 236–44.

Brinkman, J. A. 1984. *Prelude to Empire: Babylonian Society and Politics, 747–626 B.C.* Philadelphia: Occasional Publications of the Babylonian Fund, University Museum.

Broshi, M. 1974. "The Expansion of Jerusalem in the Reigns of Hezekiah and Manasseh."
    IEJ 24: 21–26.
———. 1978. "Estimating the Population of Ancient Jerusalem." *BAR* 4 (2): 10–15.
Callaway, J. A. 1983. "A Visit with Ahilud." *BAR* 9 (5): 42–53.
Carneiro, R. 1978. "Political Expansion as an Expression of the Principle of Competitive
    Exclusion." In *Origins of the State: The Anthropology of Political Evolution,* edited by
    R. Cohen and E. R. Service. Philadelphia: Institute for the Study of Human Issues.
———. 1981. "The Chiefdom as Precursor of the State." In *The Transition to Statehood
    in the New World,* edited by G. Jones and R. Krautz. Cambridge: Cambridge Uni-
    versity Press.
Carroll, R. P. 1992. "The Myth of the Empty Land." In *Ideological Criticism of Biblical
    Texts,* edited by D. Jobling and T. Pippin. Semeia 59. Atlanta: Scholars Press.
———. 1998. "Exile! What Exile? Deportation and the Discourses of the Diaspora." In
    Leading Captivity Captive: "The Exile" as History and Ideology, edited by L. L.
    Grabbe. JSOTSup 278. Sheffield: Sheffield Academic Press.
Carter, C. E. 1994. "The Province of Yehud in the Post-Exilic Period: Soundings in Site
    Distribution and Demography." In *Second Temple Studies. Vol. 2, Temple Commu-
    nity in the Persian Period,* edited by T. C. Eskenazi and K. H. Richards. JSOTSup
    175. Sheffield: Sheffield Academic Press.
———. 1999. *The Emergence of Yehud in the Persian Period: A Social and Demographic
    Study.* JSOTSup 294. Sheffield: Sheffield Academic Press.
Cerroni-Long, E. L. 1984. "Marrying Out: Socio-Cultural and Psychological Implica-
    tions of Intermarriage." *Journal of Comparative Family Studies* 15 (1): 25–46.
Chavalas, M. W. 1995. "An Historian's Approach to Understanding the Accounts of Sen-
    nacherib's Invasion of Judah." *Fides et Historia* 27: 5–22.
Clancy, F. 1999. "Shishak/Shoshenq's Travels." *JSOT* 86: 3–23.
Clements, R. E. 1996. "The Deuteronomic Law of Centralisation and the Catastrophe of
    587 B.C.E." In *After the Exile,* edited by J. Barton and D. J. Reimer. Macon, Ga.:
    Mercer University Press.
Cline, E. H. 2000. *The Battles of Armageddon.* Ann Arbor, Mich.: University of Michigan
    Press.
Cogan, M. 1974. *Imperialism and Religion: Assyria, Judah, and Israel in the Eighth and Sev-
    enth Centuries B.C.E.* Missoula, Mont.: Scholars Press.
Cogan, M., and H. Tadmor. 1988. *II Kings.* New York: Doubleday.
Coggins, R. J. 1989. "The Origins of the Jewish Diaspora." In *The World of Ancient Israel,*
    edited by R. E. Clements. Cambridge: Cambridge University Press.
Cohen, C. 1979. "Neo-Assyrian Elements in the First Speech of the Biblical Rab-Šaqê."
    TA 9: 32–48.
Collins, J. J. 1997. *Jewish Wisdom in the Hellenistic Age.* Louisville, Ky.: Westminster John
    Knox Press.
Coogan, M. D. 1974. "Life in the Diaspora: Jews in Nippur in the Fifth Century B.C."
    BA 37: 6–12.
Cook, J. M. 1983. *The Persian Empire.* New York: Schocken Books.
Coote, R. B., and K. W. Whitelam. 1987. *The Emergence of Early Israel in Historical Per-
    spective.* Sheffield: Almond Press.
Cross, F. M. 1973. *Canaanite Myth and Hebrew Epic.* Cambridge, Mass.: Harvard Uni-
    versity Press.
———. 1975. "A Reconstruction of the Judean Restoration." *JBL* 94: 4–18.
Dagan, Y. 1992. "The Shephelah During the Period of the Monarch in Light of Archae-
    ological Excavations and Survey" (in Hebrew). Master's thesis, Tel Aviv University.
Dalley, S. 1985. "Foreign Chariotry and Cavalry in the Armies of Tiglath-Pileser III and
    Sargon II." *Iraq* 47: 31–48.

Dandamaev, M. A. 1969. "Achaemenid Babylonia." In *Ancient Mesopotamia: Socio-Economic History,* edited by I. M. Diakonoff. Moscow: Nauka Publishing House.

———. 1989. *A Political History of the Achaemenid Empire.* Leiden: Brill.

Dandamaev, M. A., and V. G. Lukonin, 1989. *The Culture and Social Institutions of Ancient Iran.* Cambridge: Cambridge University Press.

Davidson, R. 1989. "Covenant Ideology in Ancient Israel." In *The World of Ancient Israel,* edited by R. E. Clements. Cambridge: Cambridge University Press.

Davies, P. R. 1992. *In Search of "Ancient Israel."* JSOTSup 148. Sheffield: Sheffield Academic Press.

———. 1997. "Whose History? Whose Israel? Whose Bible?" In *Can a "History of Israel" Be Written?* edited by L. L. Grabbe. JSOTSup 245. Sheffield: Sheffield Academic Press.

Dearman, J. A. 1989. "Historical Reconstruction and the Mesha Inscription." In *Studies in the Mesha Inscription and Moab,* edited by J. A. Dearman. Atlanta: Scholars Press.

Dever, W. G. 1990. *Recent Archaeological Discoveries and Biblical Research.* Seattle: University of Washington Press.

———. 1992. "Archaeology and the Israelite 'Conquest.'" *ABD* 3: 545–58.

———. 1995a. "Ceramics, Ethnicity, and the Question of Israel's Origins." *BA* 58: 200–213.

———. 1995b. "Will the Real Israel Please Stand Up? Part II: Archaeology and Israelite Historiography." *BASOR* 297: 61–80.

———. 1995c. "Will the Real Israel Please Stand Up? Part II: Archaeology and the Religions of Ancient Israel." *BASOR* 298: 37–58.

———. 1997a. "Archaeology and the 'Age of Solomon': A Case Study in Archaeology and Historiography." In *The "Age of Solomon": Scholarship at the Turn of the Millennium,* edited by L. K. Handy. Leiden: Brill.

———. 1997b. "Archaeology, Urbanism, and the Rise of the Israelite State." In *Urbanism in Antiquity,* edited by W. E. Aufrecht et al. JSOTSup 244. Sheffield: Sheffield Academic Press.

———. 1997c. "Is There Any Archaeological Evidence for the Exodus?" In *Exodus: The Egyptian Evidence,* edited by E. S. Frerichs and L. H. Lesko. Winona Lake, Ind.: Eisenbrauns.

———. 1998. "Archaeology, Ideology, and the Quest for an 'Ancient' or 'Biblical' Israel." *NEA* 61: 39–52.

———. 2001a. "Excavating the Hebrew Bible, or Burying It Again?" *BASOR* 322: 67–77.

———. 2001b. *What Did the Biblical Writers Know and When Did They Know It? What Archaeology Can Tell Us about the Reality of Ancient Israel.* Grand Rapids: Wm. B. Eerdmans.

DeVries, L. F. 1997. *Cities of the Biblical World.* Peabody, Mass.: Hendrickson.

Dion, P. E. 1995. "Syro-Palestinian Resistance to Shalmaneser III in the Light of New Documents." *ZAW* 107: 482–89.

Earle, T. 1987. "Chiefdoms in Archaeological and Ethnological Perspective." *ARA* 16: 279–308.

———. 1989. "The Evolution of Chiefdoms," *CA* 30: 84–88.

———. 1991. "The Evolution of Chiefdoms." In *Chiefdoms: Power, Economy, and Ideology,* edited by T. Earle. Cambridge: Cambridge University Press.

Edelman, D. V. 1984. "Saul's Rescue of Jabesh-Gilead (1 Sam. 11.1–11): Sorting Story from History." *ZAW* 96: 195–209.

———. 1985. "The 'Ashurites' of Eshbaal's State," *PEQ* 117: 85–91.

———. 1988. "Tel Masos, Geshur, and David." *JNES* 47: 253–58.

————. 1991. "Doing History in Biblical Studies." In *The Fabric of History: Text, Artifact, and Israel's Past*, edited by D. V. Edelman. JSOTSup 127. Sheffield: Sheffield Academic Press.

————. 1995. "Solomon's Adversaries Hadad, Rezon, and Jeroboam: A Trio of 'Bad Guy' Characters Illustrating the Theology of Immediate Retribution." In *The Pitcher is Broken: Memorial Essays for Gösta W. Ahlström*, edited by S. W. Holloway and L. K. Handy. JSOTSup 190. Sheffield: Sheffield Academic Press.

————. 1996. "Saul ben Kish in History and Tradition." In *The Origins of the Ancient Israelite States*, edited by V. Fritz and P. R. Davies. JSOTSup 228. Sheffield: Sheffield Academic Press.

Ehrlich, Carl S. 1997. "'How the Mighty Are Fallen': The Philistines in Their Tenth-Century Context." In *The Age of Solomon*, edited by L. K. Handy. Leiden: Brill.

Elat, M. 1975. "The Campaigns of Shalmaneser III against Aram and Israel." *IEJ* 25: 25–35.

Eliade, M. 1959. *The Sacred and the Profane*. San Diego: Harcourt Brace Jovanovich.

Elton, G. R. 1967. *The Practice of History*. New York: Thomas Y. Crowell.

Emerton, J. A. 2001. "Were the Lachish Letters Sent to or from Lachish?" *PEQ* 133: 11–14.

Eph'al, E. 1978. "The Western Minorities in Babylonia in the 6th–5th Centuries B.C.: Maintenance and Cohesion." *Orientalia* 47: 74–90.

Eshel, H. 1987. "The Late Iron Age Cemetery of Gibeon." *IEJ* 37: 1–17.

Eskenazi, T .C. 1988. *In an Age of Prose: A Literary Approach to Ezra-Nehemiah*. Atlanta: Scholars Press.

Eskenazi, T .C., and E. P. Judd. 1994. "Marriage to a Stranger in Ezra 9–10." In *Second Temple Studies. Vol. 2, Temple Community in the Persian Period*, edited by T .C. Eskenazi and K. H. Richards. JSOTSup 175. Sheffield: Sheffield Academic Press.

Eynikel, E. 1997. "The Portrait of Manasseh and the Deuteronomistic History." In *Deuteronomy and Deuteronomic Literature*, edited by M. Vervenne and J. Lust. Leuven: Leuven University Press.

Finkelstein, I. 1985. "Summary and Conclusions: History of Shiloh from Middle Bronze Age II to Iron Age II." *TA* 2: 159–77.

————. 1988. *The Archaeology of the Settlement of Israel*. Jerusalem: Israel Exploration Society.

————. 1989. "The Emergence of the Monarchy in Israel: The Environmental and Socio-Economic Aspects." *JSOT* 44: 43–74.

————. 1994. "The Archaeology of the Days of Manasseh." In *Scripture and Other Artifacts*, edited by M. Coogan et al. Louisville,Ky.: Westminster John Knox Press.

————. 1995. "The Great Transformation: The 'Conquest' of the Highland Frontiers and the Rise of the Territorial States." In *The Archaeology of Society in the Holy Land*, edited by T. E. Levy. Leicester: Leicester University Press.

————. 1996b. "Ethnicity and the Origin of the Iron I Settlers in the Highlands of Canaan: Can the Real Israel Stand Up?" *BA* 59: 198–212.

————. 1996a. "The Archaeology of the United Monarchy: An Alternative View." *Levant* 28: 177–87.

————. 1998. "The Rise of Early Israel: Archaeology and Long-Term History." In *The Origin of Early Israel—Current Debate*, edited by S. Ahituv and E. D. Oren. Beersheva: Ben-Gurion University of the Negev Press.

Freedman, D. N. 1978. "Real Story of the Ebla Tablets: Ebla and the Cities of the Plain." *BA* 41: 143–64.

Freyne, S. 1999. "Behind the Names: Galileans, Samaritans, *Ioudaioi*." In *Galilee through the Centuries: Confluence of Cultures*, edited by E. M. Meyers. Winona Lake, Ind.: Eisenbrauns.

Frick, F. S. 1985. *The Formation of the State in Ancient Israel*. Sheffield: JSOT Press.

———. "Ecology, Agriculture and Patterns of Settlement." In *The World of Ancient Israel*, edited by R. E. Clements. Cambridge: Cambridge University Press.

Galil, G. 1991. "The Babylonian Calendar and the Chronology of the Last Kings of Judah." *Biblica* 72: 367–78.

———. 1995a. "The Last Years of the Kingdom of Israel and the Fall of Samaria." *CBQ* 57: 52–65.

———. 1995b. "A New Look at the `Azekah Inscription,'" *Revue Biblique* 102: 321–29.

———. 1996. *The Chronology of the Kings of Israel and Judah.* Leiden: Brill.

———. 2000. "The Boundaries of Aram-Damascus in the 9th–8th Centuries B.C.E." In *Studies in Historical Geography and Biblical Historiography*, edited by G. Galil and M. Weinfeld. Leiden: Brill.

Gallagher, W .R. 1999. *Sennacherib's Campaign to Judah.* Leiden: Brill.

Galpaz, P. 1991. "The Reign of Jeroboam and the Extent of Egyptian Influence." *BN* 60: 13–19.

Gane, R. 1997. "The Role of Assyria in the Ancient Near East during the Reign of Manasseh." *AUSS* 35: 21–32.

Garbini, G. 1988. *History and Ideology in Ancient Israel.* New York: Crossroad.

Geus, C. H. J. de. 1976. *The Tribes of Israel.* Assen: Van Gorcum.

Gill, D. 1994. "How They Met: Geology Solves Long-standing Mystery of Hezekiah's Tunnel." *BAR* 20 (4): 20–33, 64.

Gitin, S. 1989. "Tel Miqne-Ekron: A Type Site for the Inner Coastal Plain in the Iron Age II Period." In *Recent Excavations in Israel: Studies in Iron Age Archaeology*, edited by S. Gitin and W. Dever. AASOR 49. Winona Lake, Ind.: Eisenbrauns.

———. 1997. "The Neo-Assyrian Empire and Its Western Periphery." In *Assyria 1995*, edited by S. Parpola et al. Helsinki: Neo-Assyrian Text Corpus Project.

———. 1998. "Philistia in Transition: The Tenth Century B.C.E. and Beyond." In *Mediterranean Peoples in Transition: Thirteenth to Early Tenth Centuries B.C.E.*, edited by S. Gitin et al. Jerusalem: Israel Exploration Society.

Glasswasser, O. 1991. "Ancient Egyptian Scribe from Lachish and the Hieratic Tradition of the Hebrew Kingdom." *TA* 18: 248–53.

Glatt-Gilad, D.A. 1996. "The Role of Huldah's Prophecy in the Chronicler's Portrayal of Josiah's Reform." *Biblica* 77: 16–31.

Gnuse, R. 1991. "Israelite Settlement in Canaan: A Peaceful Internal Process." *BTB* 21: 56–66, 109–17.

Goldberg, J. 1999. "Two Assyrian Campaigns against Hezekiah and Later Eighth Century Biblical Chronology." *Biblica* 80: 360–90.

Gottwald, N. K. 1979. *The Tribes of Yahweh: A Sociology of the Religion of Liberated Israel 1250–1050 B.C.E.* Maryknoll, N.Y.: Orbis Books.

———. 1983. "Early Israel and the Canaanite Socio-Economic System." In *Palestine in Transition: The Emergence of Ancient Israel*, edited by D. N. Freedman and D. Graf. Sheffield: Almond Press.

Grabbe, L. L. 1991. "Reconstructing History from the Book of Ezra." *Second Temple Studies. Vol. 1, Persian Period*, edited by P. Davies. JSOTSup 117. Sheffield: JSOT Press.

———. 1992. *Judaism from Cyrus to Hadrian. Vol. 1, The Persian and Greek Periods.* Minneapolis: Fortress Press.

———. 1994. "What Was Ezra's Mission?" In *Second Temple Studies. Vol. 2, Temple Community in the Persian Period*, edited by T. C. Eskenazi and K. H. Richards. JSOTSup 175. Sheffield: Sheffield Academic Press.

———. 1997a. "Are Historians of Ancient Palestine Fellow Creatures—Or Different Animals?" In *Can a "History of Israel" Be Written?* edited by L. L. Grabbe. JSOTSup 245. Sheffield: Sheffield Academic Press.

————. 1997b. "Reflections on the Discussion." In *Can a "History of Israel" Be Written*.

————. 1998. "'The Exile' under the Theodolite: Historiography as Triangulation." In *Leading Captivity Captive: "The Exile" as History and Ideology*, edited by L. L. Grabbe. JSOTSup 278. Sheffield: Sheffield Academic Press.

Graham, J. N. 1984. "'Vinedressers and Plowmen': 2 Kings 25:12 and Jeremiah 52:16." *BA* 47: 55–58.

Gray, J. 1970. *I & II Kings: A Commentary*, 2nd ed. Philadelphia: Westminster Press.

Grayson, A. K. 1975. *Assyrian and Babylonian Chronicles*. Locust Valley, N.Y.: J. J. Augustin.

Guest, P. D. 1998. "Can Judges Survive without Sources? Challenging the Consensus." *JSOT* 78: 43–61.

Haerinck, E. 1997. "Babylonia under Achaemenid Rule." In *Mesopotamia and Iran in the Persian Period: Conquest and Imperialism 539–331 B.C.*, edited by J. Curtis. London: British Museum Press.

Hallo, W. W. 1990. "The Limits of Skepticism," *JAOS* 110: 187–99.

Halpern, B. 1991. "Jerusalem and the Lineages in the Seventh Century B.C.E.: Kingship and the Rise of Individual Moral Liability." In *Law and Ideology in Monarchic Israel*, edited by B. Halpern and D. W. Hobson. JSOTSup 124. Sheffield: JSOT Press.

————. 1996. "The Construction of the Davidic State: An Exercise in Historiography." In *The Origins of the Ancient Israelite States*, edited by V. Fritz and P. R. Davies. JSOTSup 228. Sheffield: Sheffield Academic Press.

————. 1997. "Text and Artifact." In *The Archaeology of Israel*, edited by N. A. Silberman and D. Small. JSOTSup 237. Sheffield: Sheffield Academic Press.

————. 2001. *David's Secret Demons: Messiah, Murderer, Traitor, King*. Grand Rapids: Wm. B. Eerdmans.

Handy, L. K. 1995. "Historical Probability and the Narrative of Josiah's Reform in 2 Kings." In *The Pitcher is Broken: Memorial Essays for Gösta W. Ahlström*, edited by S. W. Holloway and L. K. Handy. JSOTSup 190. Sheffield: Sheffield Academic Press.

————. 1997. "Phoenicians in the Tenth Century B.C.E.: A Sketch of an Outline." In *The Age of Solomon: Scholarship at the Turn of the Millennium*, edited by L. K. Handy. Leiden: E. J. Brill.

Hartley, J. E. 1992. *Leviticus*. Dallas: Word Books.

Hawk, L. D. 1996. "Saul as Sacrifice." *BRev* 12 (6): 20–25, 56.

Hayes, J. H. and J. K. Kuan. 1991. "The Final Years of Samaria (730–720 B.C.)." *Biblica* 72: 153–81.

Heaton, E. W. 1974. *Solomon's New Men: The Emergence of Ancient Israel as a National State*. New York: Pica Press.

Heltzer, M. 2000. "Some Questions Concerning the Economic Policy of Josiah, King of Judah." *IEJ* 50: 105–8.

Hendel, R. S. 1996. "The Date of the Siloam Inscription: A Rejoinder to Rogerson and Davies." *BA* 59: 233–37.

Hengel, M. 1974. *Judaism and Hellenism*. 2 vols. Philadelphia: Fortress Press.

Hillers, D. R. 1969. *Covenant: The History of a Biblical Idea*. Baltimore: Johns Hopkins University Press.

Hobbs, T. R. 1994. "The 'Fortresses of Rehoboam': Another Look." In *Uncovering Ancient Stones*, edited by L. M. Hopfe. Winona Lake, Ind: Eisenbrauns.

Hoffmann, H. D. 1980. *Reform und Reformen*. ATANT 66. Zurich: Theologischer Verlag.

Hoffmeier, J. K. 1997. *Israel in Egypt: The Evidence for the Authenticity of the Exodus Tradition*. New York: Oxford University Press.

Hoglund, K. G. 1991. "The Achaemenid Context." In *Second Temple Studies, Vol. 1, Persian Period*. JSOTSup 117. Sheffield: Sheffield Academic Press.

———. 1992. *Achaemenid Imperial Administration in Syria-Palestine and the Missions of Ezra and Nehemiah.* SBLDS 125. Atlanta: Scholars Press.

———. 1997. "The Chronicler as Historian: A Comparativist Perspective." In *The Chronicler as Historian,* edited by M. P. Graham et al. JSOTSup 238. Sheffield: Sheffield Academic Press.

Holladay, J. S. 1987. "Religion in Israel and Judah under the Monarchy: An Explicitly Archaeological Approach." In *Ancient Israelite Religion,* edited by P. D. Miller et al. Philadelphia: Fortress Press.

Hopkins, David C. 1985. *The Highlands of Canaan.* Sheffield: Almond Press.

Horsley, R. 1991. "Empire, Temple, and Community—But No Bourgeoisie! A Response to Blenkinsopp and Petersen." In *Second Temple Studies, Vol. 1, Persian Period.* JSOTSup 117. Sheffield: Sheffield Academic Press.

Hurowitz, V. 1994. "Inside Solomon's Temple." *Brev* 10 (2): 24–37, 50.

Irvine, S. A. 1995. "The Threat of Jezreel (Hosea 1:4–5)." *CBQ* 57: 494–503.

Ishida, T. 1975. "The House of Ahab." *IEJ* 25: 135–37.

———. 1982. "Solomon's Succession to the Throne of David—A Political Analysis." In *Studies in the Period of David and Solomon,* edited by T. Ishida. Winona Lake, Ind.: Eisenbrauns.

Isserlin, B. S. J. 1983. "The Israelite Conquest of Canaan: A Comparative Review of the Arguments Applicable." *PEQ* 115: 85–94.

Jackson, K. P. 1989. "The Language of the Mesha Inscription." In *Studies in The Mesha Inscription and Moab,* edited by A. Dearman. Atlanta: Scholars Press.

Jacobsen, T. 1976. *The Treasures of Darkness: A History of Mesopotamian Religion.* New Haven, Conn.: Yale University Press.

James, T. G. H. 1984. *Pharaoh's People.* Chicago: University of Chicago Press.

Jamieson-Drake, D. W. 1991.*Scribes and Schools in Monarchic Judah: A Socio-Archaeological Approach.* Sheffield: JSOT Press.

Japhet, S. 1983. "Sheshbazzar and Zerubbabel against the Background of the Historical and Religious Tendencies of Ezra-Nehemiah." *ZAW* 95: 218–29.

———. 1992. "The Israelite Legal and Social Reality as Reflected in Chronicles: A Case Study." In *Sha'arei Talmon,* edited by M. Fishbane et al. Winona Lake, Ind.: Eisenbrauns.

———. 1993. *I and II Chronicles.* Louisville, Ky.: Westminster John Knox Press.

Johnson, A., and T. Earle. 1987. *The Evolution of Human Society: From Forager Group to Agrarian State.* Stanford, Calif.: Stanford University Press.

Joyce, P. M. 1996. "Dislocation and Adaptation in the Exilic Age and After." In *After the Exile,* edited by J. Barton and D. J. Reimer. Macon, Ga.: Mercer University Press.

Katzenstein, H. J. 1997. *The History of Tyre from the Beginning of the Second Millennium B.C.E. until the Fall of the Neo-Babylonian Empire in 539 B.C.E.* 2nd ed. Beer-sheva: Ben-Gurion University of the Negev Press.

Kelso, J. L. 1968. *The Excavation of Bethel 1934–1960.* AASOR 39. Winona Lake, Ind.: Eisenbrauns.

Keown, G. L., P. J. Scalise, and T. G. Smothers. 1995. *Jeremiah 26–52.* Dallas: Word Books.

Kincheloe, J. L., and P. L. McLaren. 1994. "Rethinking Critical Theory and Qualitative Research." In *Handbook of Qualitative Research,* edited by N. K. Denzin and Y. S. Lincoln. Thousand Oaks, Calif.: Sage Publications.

King, P. 1989. "The Great Eighth Century." *Brev* 5 (4): 22–33, 44.

Kitchen, K. A. 1961. *Suppiluliumas and the Amarna Pharaohs.* Liverpool: University of Liverpool Press.

———. 1986. *The Third Intermediate Period in Egypt (1100–650 B.C.).* 2nd ed. Warminster: Aris & Phillips.

————. 1995. "The Patriarchal Age: Myth or History?" *BAR* 21 (2): 48–57, 88, 90–92, 94–95.

————. 1997a. "Egypt and East Africa." In *The Age of Solomon,* edited by L. K. Handy. Leiden: Brill.

————. 1997b. "A Possible Mention of David in the Late Tenth Century B.C.E., and Deity *DOD as Dead as the Dodo?" *JSOT* 76: 29–44.

Kletter, R. 1999. "Pots and Polities: Material Remains of Late Iron Age Judah in Relation to its Political Borders." *BASOR* 314: 19–54.

Knapp, A. B. 1988. *The History and Culture of Ancient Western Asia and Egypt.* Chicago: Dorsey Press.

Knauf, E. A. 1992. "Ishmaelites." *ABD* 3: 513–20.

————. 1995. "Edom: A Socio-Economic History." In *You Shall Not Abhor an Edomite for He Is Your Brother: Seir and Edom in History and Tradition,* edited by D. Edelman. Atlanta: Scholars Press.

————. 1997. "Le roi est mort, vive le roi!: A Biblical Argument for the Historicity of Solomon." In *The Age of Solomon,* edited by L. K. Handy. Leiden: E. J. Brill.

————. 2000. "Jerusalem in the Late Bronze and Early Iron Ages: A Proposal." *TA* 27: 75–90.

Knibb, M. A. 1989. "Life and Death in the Old Testament." In *The World of Ancient Israel,* edited by R. E. Clements. Cambridge: Cambridge University Press.

Knight, D. A. 1995. "Political Rights and Powers in Monarchic Israel." *Semeia* 66: 93–117.

Knohl, I. 1987. "The Priestly Torah versus the Holiness School: Sabbath and the Festivals." *HUCA* 58: 65–117.

Knoppers, G. N. 1990. "Rehoboam in Chronicles: Villain or Victim?" *JBL* 109: 423–40.

————. 1995. "Aaron's Calf and Jeroboam's Calves." In *Fortunate the Eyes That See,* edited by A. B. Beck et al. Grand Rapids: Wm. B. Eerdmans.

————. 1997. "The Vanishing Solomon: The Disappearance of the United Monarchy from Recent Histories of Ancient Israel." *JBL* 116: 19–44.

Kochavi, M., ed. 1972. *Judaea, Samaria, and the Golan: Archaeological Survey 1967–68.* Jerusalem: Survey of Israel. (Hebrew)

Krecher, J. 1993. "The Ebla Tablets and Their Possible Significance for Biblical Studies." In *Biblical Archaeology Today,* edited by A. Biran and A. Paris-Shadur. Jerusalem: Israel Exploration Society.

Kuhrt, A. 1983. "The Cyrus Cylinder and Achaemenid Imperial Policy." *JSOT* 25: 83–97.

Lancaster, S. P., and G. A. Long. 1999. "Where They Met: Separations in the Rock Mass Near the Siloam Tunnel's Meeting Point." *BASOR* 315: 15–26.

Langdon, S. 1912. *Die neubabylonischen Königsinschriften: Vorderasiatische Bibliothek.* Leipzig: J. Hinrichs Buchhandlung.

Lapp, N. L., ed. 1981. *The Third Campaign at Tell el-Full: The Excavations of 1964.* AASOR 45. Cambridge, Mass.: ASOR.

Lasine, S. 1992. "Reading Jeroboam's Intentions: Intertextuality, Rhetoric, and History in 1 Kings 12." In *Reading between Texts: Intertextuality and the Hebrew Bible,* edited by D. N. Fewell. Louisville, Ky.: Westminster/John Knox Press.

————. 1993. "Manesseh as Villain and Scapegoat." In *The New Literary Criticism and the Hebrew Bible,* edited by J. C. Exum and D. J. A. Clines. JSOTSup 143. Sheffield: JSOT Press.

LaSor, W. 1982. "Jerusalem," *ISBE* 2: 998–1032.

Lemaire, A. 1998. "The Tel Dan Stela as a Piece of Royal Historiography." *JSOT* 81: 3–14.

Lemche, N. P. 1988. *Ancient Israel: A New History of Israelite Society.* Sheffield: JSOT Press.

————. 1991. "The Development of the Israelite Religion in the Light of Recent Studies on the Early History of Israel." In *Congress Volume Leuven 1989,* edited by J. A. Emerton. VTSup 43. Leiden: Brill.

———. 1993. "The Old Testament—a Hellenistic Book?" *SJOT* 7: 163–93.

———. 1998. *Prelude to Israel's Past*. Peabody, Mass.: Hendrickson.

Lemche, N. P., and T. L. Thompson. 1994. "Did Biran Kill David? The Bible in the Light of Archaeology." *JSOT* 64: 3–22.

Levine, L. D. 1982. "Sennacherib's Southern Front: 704–689 B.C." *JCS* 34: 28–58.

Levine, L. I. 1999. "The Age of Hellenism: Alexander the Great and the Rise and Fall of the Hasmonean Kingdom." In *Ancient Israel*, edited by H. Shanks. Washington, D.C.: Biblical Archaeology Society.

Lipschits, O. 1997. *The "Yehud" Province under Babylonian Rule (586–539 B.C.E.): Historic Reality and Historiographic Conceptions*. Ph.D. diss., Tel Aviv University. (Hebrew)

———. 1999. "The History of the Benjamin Region under Babylonian Rule." *TA* 26: 155–90.

Luria, B. Z. 1969–70. *Saul and Benjamin: Studies in the History of the Tribe of Benjamin*. Jerusalem: Magnes Press.

Machinist, P. 1983. "Assyria and Its Image in the First Isaiah." *JAOS* 103: 719–37.

———. 1995. "The Transfer of Kingship: A Divine Turning." In *Fortunate the Eyes That See*, edited by A. B. Beck et al. Grand Rapids: Wm B. Eerdmans.

Maidman, M. 1976. *A Socio-Economic Analysis of a Nuzi Family Archive*. Ph.D. diss., University of Pennsylvania.

Maier, G. 1999. "Truth and Reality in the Historical Understanding of the Old Testament." In *Israel's Past in Present Research*, edited by V. P. Long. Winona Lake, Ind.: Eisenbrauns.

Malamat, A. 1950. "The Last Wars of the Kingdom of Judah." *JNES* 9: 218–21.

———. 1965. "Organs of Statecraft in the Israelite Monarchy." *BA* 28: 34–65.

———. 1968. "The Last Kings of Judah and the Fall of Jerusalem." *IEJ* 18: 137–56.

———. 1973. "Josiah's Bid for Armageddon: The Background of the Judaean-Egyptian Encounter in 609 B.C." *JANES* 5: 267–79.

———. 1975. "The Twilight of Judah: In the Egyptian-Babylonian Maelstrom." *VTSup* 28: 123–45.

———. 1988. "The Kingdom of Judah between Egypt and Babylon: A Small State within a Great Power Confrontation." In *Text and Context*, edited by W. Claussen. JSOTSup 78. Sheffield: Sheffield University Press.

———. 1998. "Let My People Go and Go and Go and Go." *BAR* 24 (1): 62–66, 85.

———. 1999. "Caught between the Great Powers: Judah Picks a Side . . . and Loses." *BAR* 25 (4): 34–41, 64.

———. 2001. *History of Biblical Israel: Major Problems and Minor Issues*. Leiden: Brill.

Margalith, O. 1991. "The Political Background of Zerubbabel's Mission and the Samaritan Schism." *VT* 41: 312–23.

Marinkovic, P. 1994. "What Does Zechariah 1–8 Tell Us about the Second Temple?" In *Second Temple Studies. Vol. 2, Temple Community in the Persian Period*, edited by T. C. Eskenazi and K. H. Richards. JSOTSup 175. Sheffield: Sheffield Academic Press.

Master, D. M. 2001. "State Formation Theory and the Kingdom of Ancient Israel." *JNES* 60: 117–31.

Matthews, V. H. 1991. "The King's Call to Justice." *Biblische Zeitschrift* 35: 204–16.

———. 1994. "Female Voices: Upholding the Honor of the Household," *BTB* 24: 8–15.

———. 1995. "The Anthropology of Clothing in the Joseph Narrative." *JSOT* 65: 25–36.

———. 1998. "The Social Context of Law in the Second Temple Period." *BTB* 28: 7–15.

———. 2000. *Old Testament Themes*. St. Louis: Chalice Press.

Matthews, V. H., and D. C. Benjamin. 1993. *Social World of Ancient Israel, 1250–587 B.C.E.* Peabody, Mass.: Hendrickson.

————. 1997. *Old Testament Parallels: Laws and Stories from the Ancient Near East.* 2nd ed. Mahweh, N.J.: Paulist Press.

Mayer, J. 1961. "Jewish-Gentile Intermarriage Patterns: A Hypothesis." *Sociology and Social Research* 45 (2): 188–95.

Mazar, A. 1990. *Archaeology of the Land of the Bible, 10,000–586 B.C.E.* New York: Doubleday.

McCarter, P. K. 1980. "The Apology of David." *JBL* 99: 489–504.

McCarthy, D. J. 1972. *Old Testament Covenant.* Atlanta: John Knox Press.

McEvenue, S. E. 1981. "The Political Structure of Judah from Cyrus to Nehemiah." *CBQ* 43: 353–64.

McNutt, P. M. *The Forging of Israel: Iron Technology, Symbolism, and Tradition in Ancient Society.* Sheffield: Almond Press, 1990.

Mendenhall, G. E. 1973. *The Tenth Generation: The Origins of the Biblical Tradition.* Baltimore: Johns Hopkins University Press.

Merton, R. K. 1941. "Intermarriage and the Social Structure." *Psychiatry* 4: 361–74.

Mettinger, T. N. D. 1971. *Solomonic State Officials: A Study of the Civil Government Officials of the Israelite Monarchy.* Lund: CWK Gleerups Forlag.

Meyers, C. 1997. "The Family in Ancient Israel." In *Families in Ancient Israel,* edited by L. G. Perdue. Louisville, Ky.: Westminster John Knox Press.

————. 1999. "Women and the Domestic Economy of Early Israel." In *Women in the Hebrew Bible: A Reader,* edited by A. Bach. New York: Routledge.

Meyers, C., and E. M. Meyers. 1987. *Haggai, Zechariah 1–8.* New York: Doubleday.

Milgrom, J. 1991. *Leviticus 1–16.* New York: Doubleday.

————. 1992. "Priestly ('P') Source," *ABD* 5: 454–61.

————. 2001. *Leviticus 23–27.* New York: Doubleday.

Millard, A. R. 1985. "Daniel and Belshazzar in History." *BAR* 11 (3): 73–78.

————. 1992. "Ebla and the Bible: What's Left (if Anything)?" *BRev* 8 (2): 18–31, 60, 62.

————. 2001. "Where Was Abraham's Ur? The Case for the Babylonian City." *BAR* 27 (3): 52–53, 57.

Millard, A. R., and Donald J. Wiseman. 1980. *Essays on the Patriarchal Narratives.* Leicester: InterVarsity Press.

Miller, J. M. 1989. "Moab and the Moabites." In *Studies in the Mesha Inscription and Moab,* edited by A. Dearman. Atlanta: Scholars Press.

————. 1991. "Is It Possible to Write a History of Israel without Relying on the Hebrew Bible?" In *The Fabric of History: Text, Artifact, and Israel's Past,* edited by D. V. Edelman. JSOTSup 127. Sheffield: Sheffield Academic Press.

————. 1997. "Separating the Solomon of History from the Solomon of Legend." In *The Age of Solomon,* edited by L. K. Handy. Leiden: Brill.

Miller, J. M., and J. H. Hayes. 1986. *A History of Ancient Israel and Judah.* Philadelphia: Westminster Press.

Miller, P. D., and J. J. M. Roberts. 1977. *The Hand of the Lord: A Reassessment of the "Ark Narrative" of 1 Samuel.* Baltimore: Johns Hopkins University Press.

Miller, R. D. 2001. "Yahweh and His Clio: Critical Theory and the Historical Criticism of the Hebrew Bible." Paper presented to the Social Scientific Criticism of the Hebrew Bible section, Society of Biblical Literature Annual Meeting, Denver, Colorado, November 20.

Moor, J. C. de. 1996. "Egypt, Ugarit, and Exodus." In *Ugarit, Religion, and Culture,* edited by N. Wyatt, W. G. E. Watson, and J. B. Lloyd. Münster: Ugarit-Verlag.

Moran, W. L. 1992. *The Amarna Letters.* Baltimore: Johns Hopkins University Press.

Muhly, J. D. 1982. "How Iron Technology Changed the Ancient World—And Gave the Philistines a Military Edge." *BRev* 8 (6): 40–54.

Muth, R. F. 1997. "Economic Influences on Early Israel." *JSOT* 75: 77–92.

Na'aman, N. 1974. "Sennacherib's 'Letter to God' on His Campaign to Judah." *BASOR* 214: 25–39.

———. 1979. "Sennacherib's Campaign to Judah and the Date of the *lmlk* Stamps." *VT* 29: 61–86.

———. 1986. "Habiru and Hebrews: The Transfer of a Social Term to the Literary Sphere." *JNES* 45: 271–88.

———. 1990. "The Historical Background to the Conquest of Samaria." *Biblica* 71: 206–25.

———. 1991a. "Forced Participation in Alliances in the Course of the Assyrian Campaigns to the West." *Scripta Hierosolymitana* 33: 80–98.

———. 1991b. "The Kingdom of Judah under Josiah." *TA* 18: 3–71.

———. 1993. "Population Changes in Palestine Following Assyrian Deportations." *TA* 20: 104–24.

———. 1995. "The Debated Historicity of Hezekiah's Reform in the Light of Historical and Archaeological Research." *ZAW* 107: 179–95.

———. 1996. "The Contribution of the Amarna Letters to the Debate on Jerusalem's Political Position in the Tenth Century B.C.E." *BASOR* 304: 17–27.

———. 1997a. "King Mesha and the Foundation of the Moabite Monarchy." *IEJ* 47: 83–92.

———. 1997b. "Prophetic Stories as Sources for the Histories of Jehoshaphat and the Omrides." *Biblica* 78: 153–73.

———. 1997c. "Cow Town or Royal Capital? Evidence for Iron Age Jerusalem." *BAR* 23 (4): 43–45, 67.

———. 1999. "The Contribution of Royal Inscriptions for a Re-evaluation of the Book of Kings as a Historical Source." *JSOT* 82: 3–17.

———. 2000. "Three Notes on the Aramaic Inscription from Tel Dan," *IEJ* 50: 92–104.

Nakhai, B. A. 2001. *Archaeology and the Religions of Canaan and Israel.* Boston: American Schools of Oriental Research.

Nicholson, E. W. 1967. *Deuteronomy and Tradition.* Philadelphia: Fortress Press.

Niemann, H. M. 1997. "The Socio-Political Shadow Cast by the Biblical Solomon." In *The Age of Solomon,* edited by L. K. Handy. Leiden: Brill.

———. 2000. "Megiddo and Solomon: A Biblical Investigation in Relation to Archaeology." *TA* 27: 61–74.

Noll, K. L. 2000. "An Alternative Hypothesis for a Historical Exodus Event." *SJOT* 14: 260–74.

Oded, B. 1977. "Judah and the Exile." In *Israelite and Judaean History,* edited by J. H. Hayes and J. M. Miller. Philadelphia: Westminster Press.

———. 1979. *Mass Deportation and Deportees in the Neo-Assyrian Empire.* Wiesbaden: Ludwig Reichert.

———. 1992. *War, Peace, and Empire: Justifications for War in Assyrian Royal Inscriptions.* Wiesbaden: Ludwig Reichert Verlag.

———. 1998. "History vis-à-vis Propaganda in the Assyrian Royal Inscriptions." *VT* 48: 423–25.

———. 2000. "The Settlements of the Israelite and the Judean Exiles in Mesopotamia in the 8th–6th Centuries B.C.E." In *Studies in Historical Geography and Biblical Historiography,* edited by G. Galil and M. Weinfeld. Leiden: Brill.

Ofer, A. 1994. "'All the Hill Country of Judah': From a Settlement Fringe to a Prosperous Monarchy." In *From Nomadism to Monarchy: Archaeological and Historical Aspects of Early Israel,* edited by I. Finkelstein and N. Na'aman. Jerusalem: Israel Exploration Society.

Oredsson, D. 1998. "Jezreel—Its Contribution to Iron Age Chronology." *SJOT* 12: 86–101.

Parker, S. B. 1994. "The Lachish Letters and Official Reactions to Prophecies." In *Uncovering Ancient Stones,* edited by L. M. Hopfe. Winona Lake, Ind.: Eisenbrauns.

————. 1996. "Appeals for Military Intervention: Stories from Zinjirli & the Bible." *BA* 59: 213–14.

Parpola, S. 1987. *The Correspondence of Sargon II, Part I.* SAA 1. Helsinki: Helsinki University Press.

Patrick, D. 1985. *Old Testament Law.* Atlanta: John Knox Press.

Porten, B. 1968. *Archives from Elephantine: The Life of an Ancient Jewish Military Colony.* Berkeley, Calif.: University of California Press.

————. 1979. "Aramaic Papyri and Parchments: A New Look." *BA* 42: 74–104.

————. 1981. "The Identity of King Adon." *BA* 44: 36–52.

————. 1992. "Elephantine Papyri." *ABD* 2: 445–55.

Pritchard, J. 1969. *Ancient Near Eastern Texts Relating to the Old Testament.* 3rd ed. Princeton, N.J.: Princeton University Press.

Rainey, A. F. 1987. "The Saga of Eliashib." *BAR* 13 (2): 36–39.

————. 1994. "Hezekiah's Reform and the Altars at Beer-sheba and Arad." In *Scripture and Other Artifacts: Essays on the Bible and Archaeology in Honor of Philip J. King,* edited by M. D. Coogan et al. Louisville, Ky.: Westminster John Knox Press.

————. 1995. "Unruly Elements in Late Bronze Canaanite Society." In *Pomegranates and Golden Bells,* edited by D. Wright et al. Winona Lake, Ind.: Eisenbrauns.

————. 2000. "Mesha's Attempt to Invade Judah (2 Chron 20)." In *Studies in Historical Geography and Biblical Historiography,* edited by G. Galil and M. Weinfeld. Leiden: Brill.

Redford, D. B. 1992. *Egypt, Canaan, and Israel in Ancient Times.* Princeton, N.J.: Princeton University Press.

Reisch, G. 1995. "Scientism without Tears." *History and Theory* 34: 45–58.

Renfrew, C. 1982. "Socio-Economic Change in Ranked Societies." In *Ranking, Resource, and Exchange: Aspects of Early European Society,* edited by C. Renfrew and S. Shennan. Cambridge: Cambridge University Press.

Rogerson, J., and P. R. Davies. 1996. "Was the Siloam Tunnel Built by Hezekiah?" *BA* 59: 138–49.

Romer, T. C. 1997. "Transformations in Deuteronomistic and Biblical Historiography: On 'Book-Finding' and Other Literary Strategies." *ZAW* 109: 1–11.

Rosenberg, J. 1986. *King and Kin: Political Allegory in the Hebrew Bible.* Bloomington, Ind.: Indiana University Press.

Rosenberg, S. 1998. "The Siloam Tunnel Revisited." *TA* 25: 116–30.

Roth, P. A. 1988. "Narrative Explanations: The Case of History." *History and Theory* 27: 1–13.

Sack, R. H. 1992. "Nabonidu.," *ABD* 4: 973–76.

Saggs, H. W. F. 1984. *The Might That Was Assyria.* London: Sidgwick & Jackson.

Sanders, J. T. 1979. "Ben Sira's Ethics of Caution." *HUCA* 50: 73–106.

————. 1997. "The Exile and Canon Formation." In *Exile: Old Testament, Jewish, and Christian Conceptions,* edited by J. M. Scott. Leiden: Brill.

Sasson, J .M. 1966. "Circumcision in the Ancient Near East." *JBL* 85: 473–76.

————. 1981. "Models for Recreating Israelite History." *JSOT* 21: 3–24.

Schmidt, B. B. 1996. *Israel's Beneficent Dead: Ancestor Cult and Necromancy in Ancient Israelite Religion and Tradition.* Winona Lake, Ind.: Eisenbrauns.

Schneider, T. J. 1996. "Rethinking Jehu." *Biblica* 77: 100–107.

Schniedewind, W. 1996. "Tel Dan Stela: New Light on Aramaic and Jehu's Revolt." *BASOR* 302: 75–90.

Schulte, H. 1995. "The End of the Omride Dynasty: Social-Ethical Observations on the Subject of Power and Violence." *Semeia* 66: 133–48.

Seitz, C. R. 1989. *Theology in Conflict: Reaction to the Exile in the Book of Jeremiah.* Berlin and New York: Walter de Gruyter.

———. 1993. "Account A and the Annals of Sennacherib: A Reassessment." *JSOT* 58: 47–57.

Shaheen, N. 1979. "The Sinuous Shape of Hezekiah's Tunnel." *PEQ* 111: 103–8.

Shanks, H. 1984. "Destruction of Judean Fortress Portrayed in Dramatic 8th Century B.C. Pictures." *BAR* 10 (2): 48–65.

———., ed. 1999. *Ancient Israel.* Rev. ed. Washington, D.C.: Biblical Archaeology Society.

Shavit, A. 1992. *The Ayalon Valley and Its Vicinity during the Bronze and Iron Ages.* Master's thesis, Tel Aviv University. (Hebrew)

Shaw, C. S. 1997. "The Sins of Rehoboam: The Purpose of 3 Kingdoms 12.24A–Z." *JSOT* 73: 55–64.

Shiloh, Y. 1984. *Excavations at the City of David.* Qedem 19. Jerusalem: Institute of Archaeology, Hebrew University.

Singer, I. 1992. "Sea Peoples." *ABD* 5: 1059–61.

Smelik, K. A. D. 1991. *Writings from Ancient Israel.* Louisville, Ky.: Westminster/John Knox Press.

———. 1992. *Converting the Past.* Leiden: Brill.

Smith, D. L. 1989. *The Religion of the Landless: The Social Context of the Babylonian Exile.* Bloomington, Ind.: Meyer-Stone Books.

Smith, M. 1971. *Palestinian Parties and Politics That Shaped the Old Testament.* New York: Columbia University Press.

Smith, M. S. 1990. *The Early History of God: Yahweh and the Other Deities in Ancient Israel.* San Francisco: Harper & Row.

Smith, R. L. 1984. *Micah-Malachi.* Waco: Word Books.

Smith, S. 1924. *Babylonian Historical Texts Relating to the Capture and Downfall of Babylon.* London: Methuen.

Smith-Christopher, D. L. 1994. "The Mixed Marriage Crisis in Ezra 9–10 and Nehemiah 13: A Study of the Sociology of the Post-Exilic Judean Community." In *Second Temple Studies. Vol. 2, Temple Community in the Persian Period,* edited by T. C. Eskenazi and K. H. Richards. JSOTSup 175. Sheffield: Sheffield Academic Press.

———. 1997. "Reassessing the Historical and Sociological Impact of the Babylonian Exile (597/587–539 B.C.E.)." In *Exile: Old Testament, Jewish, and Christian Conceptions,* edited by J. M. Scott. Leiden: Brill.

Soggin, J. A. 1978. "The History of Ancient Israel: A Study in Some Questions of Method." *EI* 14: 44–51.

———. 1984. *A History of Ancient Israel from the Beginnings to the Bar Kochba Revolt, A.D. 135.* Philadelphia: Westminster Press.

Spanier, K. 1998. "The Northern Israelite Queen Mother in the Judaean Court: Athalia and Abi." In *Boundaries of the Ancient Near Eastern World,* edited by M. Lubetski et al. JSOTSup 273. Sheffield: Sheffield Academic Press.

Sparks, K. L. 1998. *Ethnicity and Identity in Ancient Israel.* Winona Lake, Ind.: Eisenbrauns.

Stager, L. E. 1982. "The Archaeology of the East Slope of Jerusalem and the Terraces of Kidron." *JNES* 41: 111–24.

———. 1985. "The Archaeology of the Family in Ancient Israel." *BASOR* 260: 1–35.

———. 1996. "The Fury of Babylon." *BAR* 22 (1): 56–69, 76–77.

Steinberg, N. 1993. *Kinship and Marriage in Genesis: A Household Economics Perspective.* Minneapolis: Augsburg Fortress Press.

Steinmetz, D. 1991. *From Father to Son: Kinship, Conflict, and Continuity in Genesis.* Louisville, Ky.: Westminster/John Knox Press.

Stern, E. 1982. *Material Culture of the Land of the Bible in the Persian Period, 538–332 B.C.* Warminster: Aris & Phillips.

———. 1994. "The Eastern Border of the Kingdom of Judah in Its Last Days." In *Scripture and Other Artifacts*, edited by M. Coogan et al. Louisville, Ky.: Westminster John Knox Press.

———. 2000. "The Babylonian Gap." *BAR* 26 (6): 45–51, 76.

———. 2001a. *Archaeology of the Land of the Bible: The Assyrian, Babylonian, and Persian Periods (732–332 B.C.E.)*. New York: Doubleday.

———. 2001b. "Pagan Yahwism: The Folk Religion of Ancient Israel." *BAR* 27 (3): 20–29.

Stiebing, W. H. 1989. *Out of the Desert?: Archaeology and the Exodus/Conquest Narratives*. Buffalo, N.Y.: Prometheus Books.

Stolper, M. W. 1985. *Entrepreneurs and Empire: The Murašû Archive, the Murašû Firm, and Persian Rule in Babylonia*. Leiden: Uitgaven van het Nederlands Historisch-Archaeologisch Instituut te Istanbul.

Strange, J. 1987. "The Transition from the Bronze Age in the Eastern Mediterranean and the Emergence of the Israelite State." *JSOT* 1: 1–19.

Sun, H. T. C. 1990. *An Investigation into the Compositional Integrity of the So-called Holiness Code (Leviticus 17–26)*. Ph.D. diss., Claremont Graduate University.

Sweeney, M. A. 1991. "A Form-Critical Reassessment of the Book of Zephaniah." *CBQ* 53: 388–408.

———. 1996. "Jeremiah 30–31 and King Josiah's Program of National Restoration and Religious Reform." *ZAW* 108: 569–83.

Tadmor, H. 1958. "The Campaigns of Sargon II of Assur." *JCS* 12: 22–40, 77–100.

———. 1975. "Assyria and the West: The Ninth Century and Its Aftermath." In *Unity and Diversity*, edited by H. Goedicke and J. J. M. Roberts. Baltimore: Johns Hopkins University Press.

———. 1982. "Traditional Institutions and the Monarchy: Social and Political Tensions in the Time of David and Solomon." In *Studies in the Period of David and Solomon and Other Essays*, edited by T. Ishida. Winona Lake, Ind.: Eisenbrauns.

Tadmor, H., B. Landsberger, and S. Parpola. 1989. "The Sin of Sargon and Sennacherib's Last Will." *State Archives of Assyria Bulletin* 3: 3–51.

Talmon, S. 1980. "The Biblical Idea of Statehood." In *The Bible World*, edited by G. Rendsburg et al. New York: KTA Publishing House.

Talshir, Z. 1996. "The Three Deaths of Josiah and the Strata of Biblical Historiography (2 Kings XXIII 29–30; 2 Chronicles XXXV 20–5; 1 Esdras I 23–31)." *VT* 46: 213–36.

Tarler, D., and J. M. Cahill. 1992. "David, City of." *ABD* 2: 52–67.

Tatum, L. 1991. "King Manasseh and the Royal Fortress at Horvat "Uza." *BA* 54: 136–45.

Tcherikover, V. 1972. "Alexander the Great and the Conquest of the Orient." In *The World History of the Jewish People. Vol 6, The Hellenistic Age*, edited by A. Schalit. New Brunswick, N.J.: Rutgers University Press.

Thompson, T. L. 1974. *The Historicity of the Patriarchal Narratives*. BZAW 133. Berlin: Walter de Gruyter.

———. 1992. *Early History of the Israelite People: From the Written and the Archaeological Sources*. Leiden: Brill.

———. 1996. "Historiography of Ancient Palestine and Early Jewish Historiography." In *The Origins of the Ancient Israelite States*, edited by V. Fritz and P. R. Davies. JSOTSup 228. Sheffield: Sheffield Academic Press.

———. 1999. "Historiography in the Pentateuch: 25 Years after Historicity." *SJOT* 13: 258–83.

Toews, W. I. 1993. *Monarchy and Religious Institutions in Israel under Jeroboam I*. SBLMS 47. Atlanta: Scholars Press.

Tomes, R. 1993. "The Reason for the Syro-Ephraimite War." *JSOT* 59: 55–71.

Trigger, B. G. 1998. "Archaeology and Epistemology." *AJA* 102: 1–34.

Tucker, G. M. 1966. "The Legal Background of Genesis 23." *JBL* 85: 77–84.

Ussishkin, D. 1976. "Royal Judean Storage Jars and Private Seal Impressions." *BASOR* 223: 1–13.

———. 1977. "The Destruction of Lachish by Sennacherib and the Dating of the Royal Judean Storage Jars," *TA* 4: 28–60.

———. 1980. "The 'Lachish Reliefs' and the City of Lachish." *IEJ* 30: 174–95.

———. 1983. "Excavations at Tel Lachish, 1978–1983: Second Preliminary Report." *TA* 10: 97–175.

———. 1988. "The Date of the Judaean Shrine at Arad." *IEJ* 38: 142–157.

———. 1990. "Notes on Megiddo, Gezer, Ashdod, and Tel Batash in the Tenth to Ninth Centuries B.C." *BASOR* 277/278: 71–91.

———. 1997. "Lachish." In *The Oxford Encyclopedia of Archaeology in the Near East*, edited by E. M. Meyers. Vol. 3. New York: Oxford University Press.

Van der Toorn, K., and C. Houtman. 1994. "David and the Ark." *JBL* 113: 209–31.

Van Seters, J. 1975. *Abraham in History and Tradition*. New Haven Conn.: Yale University Press.

———. 1992. *Prologue to History: The Yahwist as Historian in Genesis*. Louisville, Ky.: Westminster/John Knox Press.

Vaughn, A. G. 1999. *Theology, History, and Archaeology in the Chronicler's Account of Hezekiah*. Atlanta: Scholars Press.

———. 2001. "Can We Write a History of Israel Today?" Paper presented to the Hebrew Bible, History, and Archaeology section, Society of Biblical Literature Annual Meeting, Denver, Colorado, November 17.

Weidner, E. F. 1939. "Jojachin, König von Juda, in Babylonischen Keilschrifttexten." In *Mélanges Syriens offerts à René Dussaud*. Vol. 2. Paris: P. Geuthner.

Weinberg, J. P. 1992. *The Citizen-Temple Community*. JSOTSup 151. Sheffield: Sheffield Academic Press.

Weinstein, J. M. 1981. "The Egyptian Empire in Palestine: A Reassessment." *BASOR* 241: 1–28.

———. 1998. "Egyptian Relations with the Eastern Mediterranean World at the End of the Second Millennium B.C.E." In *Mediterranean Peoples in Transition: Thirteenth to Early Tenth Centuries B.C.E.,* edited by S. Gitin, A. Mazar, and E. Stern. Jerusalem: Israel Exploration Society.

Weissbach, F. H. 1938. *Das Hauptheiligtum des Marduk in Babylon*. Leipzig: Hinrichs.

Wesselius, J. W. 1999. "The First Royal Inscription from Ancient Israel: The Tel Dan Inscription Reconsidered." *SJOT* 13: 163–86.

Whitelam, K. 1986. "The Symbols of Power: Aspects of Royal Propaganda in the United Monarchy.," *BA* 49: 166–73.

Whybray, R.N. 1990. "The Sage in the Israelite Court." In *The Sage in Israel and the Ancient Near East,* edited by J. G. Gammie and L. G. Perdue. Winona Lake, Ind.: Eisenbrauns.

Williamson, H. G. M. 1982. *1 and 2 Chronicles*. London: SCM Press.

———. 1985. *Ezra, Nehemiah*. Waco: Word Books.

———. 1989. "The Concept of Israel in Transition." In *The World of Ancient Israel*, edited by R. E. Clements. Cambridge: Cambridge University Press.

Willis, T. M. 1991. "The Text of I Kings 11:43–12:3." *CBQ* 53: 37–44.

———. 2001. *The Elders of the City: A Study of the Elders-Laws in Deuteronomy*. Atlanta: Society of Biblical Literature.

Wiseman, D. J. 1956. *Chronicles of Chaldean Kings*. London: Trustees of the British Museum.

———. 1985. *Nebuchadnezzar and Babylon*. Oxford: Oxford University Press.

Wright, D. P. 1992. "Holiness (OT)." *ABD* 6: 237–49.

Wright, G. E. 1962. *Biblical Archaeology*. Philadelphia: Westminster Press.

Yadin, Y. 1968. *The Old Testament against Its Environment*. London: SCM Press.

———. 1972. *Hazor*. London: Oxford University Press.

Yamauchi, E. M. 1980a. "Two Reformers Compared: Solon of Athens and Nehemiah of Jerusalem." In *The Bible World: Essays in Honor of Cyrus H. Gordon*, edited by G. Rendsburg et al. New York: Ktav Publishing House.

———. 1980b. "Was Nehemiah the Cupbearer a Eunuch?" *ZAW* 92: 132–42.

———. 1990. *Persia and the Bible*. Grand Rapids: Baker Book House.

Younger, K. L. 1990. *Ancient Conquest Accounts: A Study in Ancient Near Eastern and Biblical History Writing*. JSOTSup 98. Sheffield: Sheffield Academic Press.

———. 1998. "The Deportations of the Israelites." *JBL* 117: 201–27.

Yurco, Frank J. 1997. "Merenptah's Canaanite Campaign and Israel's Origins." In *Exodus: The Egyptian Evidence*, edited by E. S. Frerichs and L. H. Lesko. Winona Lake, Ind.: Eisenbrauns.

Zadok, R. 1979a. *The Jews in Babylonia during the Chaldean and Achaemenian Periods according to the Babylonian Sources*. Haifa: Haifa University Press.

———. 1979b. "Phoenicians, Philistines, and Moabites in Mesopotamia." *BASOR* 230: 57–66.

———. 1985. "Samarian Notes." *BiOr* 42: 567–72.

———. 1988. *The Pre-Hellenistic Israelite Anthroponymy and Prosopography*. Leiden: Brill.

Zertal, A. 1998. "The Iron Age I Culture in the Hill-Country of Canaan—A Manassite Perspective." In *Mediterranean Peoples in Transition, Thirteenth to Early Tenth Century B.C.E.*, edited by S. Gitin, A. Mazar, and E. Stern. Jerusalem: Israel Exploration Society.

Zevit, Z. 2001. *The Religions of Ancient Israel*. New York: Continuum.

Zimansky, P. 1990. "Urartian Geography and Sargon's Eighth Campaign." *JNES* 49: 1–21.

Zorn, J. R. 1993. *Tell en-Nasbeh: A Re-evaluation of the Architecture and Stratigraphy of the Early Bronze Age, Iron Age, and Later Periods*. Ph.D. diss., University of California, Berkeley.

———. 1997. "Mizpah: Newly Discovered Stratum Reveals Judah's Other Capital." *BAR* 23 (5): 29–38, 66.

Index of Ancient Sources

Non-Biblical Writings

ANNALS OF ADAD
    NARARI III   70
ANNALS OF
    SENNACHERIB   85
ANNALS OF TIGLATH
    PILESER III   72
ARAD LETTERS   56,
        92–93
AZEKAH
    INSCRIPTION   56,
        78–79

BABYLONIAN
    CHRONICLE   72–73,
        91, 93–94, 106
BOOK OF THE
    DEAD   90

CYRUS CYLINDER   59,
        107, 113

DIODORUS
    17.45–51   125

EA 15, 24, 31–32,
    252–54   26
EA 287, 290   47
ELEPHANTINE
    PAPYRI   115, 120–21
    COWLEY 21   115, 121
    COWLEY 30   121–22
    ENUMA ELISH   2

GEZER ALMANAC   38

HERODOTUS
    1.188–91   113, 119

HYMN TO PTAH   2

INSTRUCTION OF
    MERIKARE   24

JOSEPHUS   89, 91, 105
ANTIQUITIES OF THE
    JEWS
    10.74   89, 92
    10.84–86   92
    10.85–88   105

LACHISH
    LETTERS 56, 93, 96–97
LEIDEN
    PAPYRUS 348   27

MERNEPTAH
    STELE   23, 28–29, 32

MESHA STELE	66	12:1	5	41	9
MURASHU		12:1–3	5, 7	48:17–22	9
TEXTS	*107–8*	12:5–7	6	49:8–12	9
		12:6–7	6, 11		
PAPYRUS		12:8	6, 11	**Exodus**	
ANASTASI I	28	12:10–20	9	1:8–14	23
PAPYRUS		13:18	6	1:11	28
ANASTASI VI	9	15	5, 6	2:1–22	23
PAPYRUS HARRIS	22	16:15–16	10	4:24–26	110
		17	5, 6	7–12	33
PAUSANIAS		17:4	51	15:10–18, 21	30
"GUIDE TO		17:5–6	6	17:8–16	33
GREECE" IV, 26	90	17:9–14	110	18:13–26	33
		19:20–38	10	19:4–6	16
PROPHECY OF		19:31–38	10	19:20–25	33
NEFERTI	24	21:8–21	9, 10	24:1–8	33
		21:33	6	24:2	33
SHALMANESER III'S		22:1–20	9	24:4–8	90
BLACK OBELISK	69	23	7	25–31	102
SHALMANESER III'S		23:2–19	11	25:1–22	50
BULL		24:3–4	111, 124	32	62
INSCRIPTION	64	25:1–6	10	32:4	62
SHALMANESER III'S		25:12–16	10	32:27–28	62
MONOLITH		26:34	111	33:12–23	34
INSCRIPTION	65	27:5–17	7	34:12–16	124
SILOAM		27:41–45	10		
INSCRIPTION	56, 83	28	62	**Leviticus**	
		28:1–5	124	11:45	15
TALE OF SINUHE	18, 24	28:11–22	11	17–26	102, 109, 110
TALE OF WENAMON	20	30:1–21	10		
TEL DAN		31:44	8	**Numbers**	
INSCRIPTION	43, 56,	31:44–54	62	6:5–8	102
	68	31:44–55	8	10:35	50
TRIBUTE LIST OF		31:45–46	8	12:1–16	33
ASHURBANIPAL	87	31:46	8	14:1–35	33
		31:47–48	8	16:1–35	33
XENOPHON		31:49–50	8	20:1	30
CYROPAEDIA 7.5.7–32,		31:51–52	8	21:4–9	30
58	113	31:53	8	21:10–22:3	68
		31:54	8	21:21–30	30
Old Testament		33:12–17	10	21:27–30	67
Genesis		34:2–26	11	28–29	102
1–11	2, 13	36:1–5	10		
1:1–2:4a	102	36:1–14	10	**Deuteronomy**	
8:20–21	6	37:2–11	7	5:33	6
10:21–31	134	37:12–36	10	6:4	134
12	62	38	9	7:1–11	124
12–50	3, 13, 15	38:13–26	8	8:14	15
				9–10	8
				12	63

12:2–28	102	18	39	2:11	11
16	63	18:31	11	3:6–30	8
16:2	84			5:1–3	58
18	63	**Ruth**		5:6–12	50
28:36–37	101	4:13–22	124	5:9	47
29	8			6:1–19	50
34:10	34	**1 Samuel**		7:5–16	50
		1:3	11	7:8–11	51
Joshua		3:21	11	7:12–16	51
3 23		4:1–11	39	8	41
3:5–17	50	4:2–11	50	8:16	44
4:14–24	11	4:17	11	9:7	41
6:1–8:29	32	4:19–22	50	10:6	40
6–11	28	7:3–17	36	13:32	44
6:2–21	33	8:11–18	40	14:30	41
6:6–7	50	8:14	41	15:7–10	11
6:6–21	50	9–31	40	15:32–37	8
17:18	38	10:1–8	57	17:25	44
18:1–10	11	10:27	40	18:2	44
19:40–47	39	11:5–14	11	20:1	51, 57
21:13	11	11:12	40	20:1–3	40
24	8	11:17–24	39	20:4–10	8
24:1–28	33, 90	12:13–15	40	20:23	44
24:1–32	11	12:16–25	40		
		13:2	44	**1 Kings**	
Judges		13:2–4	40	1:5–53	7
1:19	36, 37, 38	13:8–14	40	1:15–21	8
1:20	11	13:10–15	40	2:3a, 12	58
1:21	50	13:20–21	37	2:11	11
2:11–14	66	14:24–46	40	2:13–35	44
3:1–2	36	14:50	44	2:26	41
4–5	37	15:2	39	3:1	46
4:4–5	36	15:12–23	11	4:1–19	44, 50
4:12–15	39	15:28	40	4:2–19	44
4:17–22	8	16:1	40	4:7–19	45, 58
5:13–18	36	16:1–13	7	4:20–21	45
5:15b–17	37	17:26	110	5–6	50
6:2–6	39	18:7	40	5:16–6:38	46
6:11	39	22:1–2	44	6:1	29
7:2–23	33	22:7–8	41	8:1–9	51
8:22–23	36	23:1–5	44	9:1–9	50
9:5	69	25:14–35	8	9:11–14	45
11:1–3	27	30:1–20	39	9:15	46
11:4–33	39	30:21–25	44	9:15–19	49
11:12–33	36	30:26–31	44	9:16	46
12:1–6	36	31:4	110	11–12:19	59
13–16	23	**2 Samuel**		11:14–25	55
14:3	110	2:3–4	7	11:17–22	56
17–18	62	2:9	44		

1 Kings (*cont.*)
11:26–40	55
11:29–39	57, 59
11:37–38	60
11:40	57
11:43	58
12:1	58
12:1–17	11
12:3–4	40
12:15	59
12:16	57
12:20	54
12:26–32	61
12:28	62
12:29	11
13	129
13:1–10	62
14:6	54
14:7–14	64
14:19	54
14:25–26	56, 60
15:23	54
15:25–31	64
15:31	54
16:8–13	64
16:14	64
16:14, 20	54
16:16–17	54
16:21–28	64
16:31	67
18:18	34
18:20–40	33
19:2–9	33
19:17	68
20:32–34	65
21	49
21:1–40	66
22	69
22:1–38	69
22:29–40	66
22:39	54
22:45	54

2 Kings
1:2–16	33
3	56, 69
3:4–27	67
3:14	69

6:24–7	66
8:7–15	66, 68
8:18	69
8:20–22	67
8:26	65
9	56, 64
9:1–13	51
9:7, 32–37	85
9:14–28	68
9:30–37	70
10:1–25	68
11:1–3	69, 70
11:17	54
12:1–16	70
12:17–18	70
14:7	70
14:11–14	71
14:19	51
14:19–21	71
14:21	54
14:25, 28	71
15:8–14	71
15:19–20	71
15:29–30	71
16:5–9	72
16:6	72
16:10	92
17:3–6	72, 73, 80
17:4	73
17:6	74
17:24	73
18	84
18:1–10	80
18:4	30, 81, 82
18:8	82
18:9	73
18:9–12	72
18:10	73
18:13	73, 80
18:13–37	56
18:21	84
18:22	84
18:27–35	84
19:29–34	84
20:1–11	80
20:12–15	79
20:20	56, 82
21:1–7	86

21:23	51
21:23–24	88
22:3	97
22:3–7	89
22:8	90
22:8–20	89
22:15–20	90
23:1–3	33, 89
23:2–3	54
23:4–7	89
23:8–9	89
23:10–14	89
23:15–20	89
23:21–23	89
23:25	90
23:28–30	91
23:29–30	91
23:31–34	92
23:34–35	92
24:1	94
24:1–6	94
24:10, 13–17	56, 93
24:12	94
25:1–25	97
25:6–7	97
25:22	97
25:22–26	97
25:26	98
25:27–30	94, 106

1 Chronicles
2:16	44

2 Chronicles
4	46
10:2	58
10:15	59
11:5–10	60
13:4–12	59
20	67
20:31–37	69
21:5–6	69
22:2	65
29–32	82, 89
29:25	81
30:1–2	81
30:13–14	81
31:1	81
31:5–7	81

31:15	81	5:4–10	122	6:13–15	34
31:19	81	6:6–7	122	7:12–14	11
32:20–23	85	7:1–4	122	21:9	104
32:28	81	8:1–12	33, 90, 120	24:2–10	102
32:30	82	8:13–18	120	26:20–23	94
33:1–20	86	10:30	122	27–28	95
33:11	87	13	124	27:3	95
33:12–14	87	13:4–31	122	28	33
34:3b–4	89	13:23–24	123	29	95, 102
34:6–7	89	13:23–30	111	29:10–14	33
34:8–13	89	13:23–31	118	30–31	91
34:14–28	89			32:1–15	7

Psalms

35:1–19	89	37	118	32:6–25	102
35:20–24	91	47:9	92	34:6–7	56, 93
36:20–21	99, 104	49	118	34:7	97
		52	118	36:20–26	94

Ezra

1:8–11	114	73	118	37:11	96
4:1–5	105	78:42–43	16	38:22	96
4:1–16	114	78:60	11	37:12–16	96
4:2	114	137	107	39:1–10	97
4:3	111	137:7	95	39:3	106
5:1–6:15	115	137:7–9	56, 93	40:5	97
6:1–12	115			40:7–41:15	97
6:2–5	115	**Isaiah**		40:11–12	98
6:4–5	118	7:1–9	72	41:5	105
7:12	120	10:5	77, 84	42:7–12	98
7:12–24	120	11	91	51:34–35	107
7:14	120	11:1	101	51:59	95
7:14–15, 20	118	14:20	73	52:1–30	97
7:19	120	14:28–29a	80	52:30	104
7:21	116	20	56, 79		
7:25	120	28:1–16	34	**Ezekiel**	
7:26	118	30:1–7	79	8:1	105
8:15–34	120	40:1–5	33	11:15	107
8:25	118	40:1–11	99	11:16	107
9	124	40:3–5	114	30:22	92
9–10	120	40:12–31	33	30:22–26	92
9:1–10:44	120	42–53	16	33:30–33	105
9:1–4	111	45:1–6	114	37:24–28	91
10:6–12	118	45:1–8	33		
		45:6	114	**Daniel**	
Nehemiah		49:1–6	103, 111	1–6	33, 111
1:11	123	56:1–8	111	2	9
2:1–10	117	58:13–14	110	4	9
2:5–8	122				
2:19	122	**Jeremiah**		**Hosea**	
3–5	122	2:18, 36	89	1:4	68
5:1–4	118, 121	3:16–17	51	4:12–19	64
				5:10	71

Hosea (*cont.*)

7:11–16	71
8:4	34
9:15	11
11:1	16

Amos

1:3–5	69
2:6–12	64
4:4	11
7:10–13	11
7:10–17	33

Obadiah

1:10	95

Micah

4:11–13	82
6:4–8	34

Haggai

1:2–11	119
1:4	114
2:14	111

Zechariah

1–8	103, 119
1:16	119

Deuterocanon

1 Maccabees

1:27–29	33

1 Esdras

25–32	89

New Testament

Luke

15:11–32	7

Author Index

Ackroyd, P. R., 108
Adams, R. M., 106
Aharoni, M., 90
Aharoni, Y., 46
Ahlström, G. W., 28, 31, 124, 126
Albertz, R., 118
Albright, W. F., 3
Andersen, F. I., 71
Ash, P. S., 41, 45, 58, 60, 63
Avigad, N., 116

Balentine, S. E., 108, 116, 118
Bar-Adon, P., 86
Barstad, H., xiii, 3–4
Bartlett, J. R., 67, 95
Batto, B. F., 2
Beaulieu, P.-A., 106, 112–13

Becking, B., 68, 73–74, 97–98, 120
Begg, C. T., 98
Beit-Arieh, I., 86
Ben-Ami, D., 45
Benjamin, D. C., 1, 36
Ben Tor, A., 45
Ben Zvi, E., 86
Berquist, J. L., 108, 116–18, 120
Bickerman, E. J., 126
Biran, A., 43, 68
Blenkinsopp, J., 107, 118, 123
Bloch-Smith, E., 31, 38
Borowski, O., 80–81
Briant, P., 118, 120
Brinkman, J. A., 78–79, 88

Broshi, M., 77, 86, 104
Cahill, J. M., 47
Callaway, J. A., 37
Carneiro, R., 38, 40
Carroll, R. P., 114
Carter, C. E., 104, 114, 116–19
Cerroni-Long, E. L., 111
Chavalas, M. W., 83, 85
Clancy, F., 57, 60
Clements, R. E., 102
Cline, E. H., 17, 91
Cogan, M., 70, 88, 90, 92, 97
Coggins, R. J., 103
Cohen, C., 84
Collins, J. J., 118, 126
Coogan, M. D., 107

Cook, J. M., 120, 125
Coote, R. B., 23, 38–39
Cresson, B., 86
Cross, F. M., 62, 116

Dagan, Y., 86
Dalley, S., 74
Dandamaev, M. A., 116, 117, 125
Davidson, R., 6, 8
Davies, P. R., xii–xiii, 3, 47, 83
Dearman, J. A., 67–68
Dever, W. G., xiii, 3, 30–32, 46, 90, 105
DeVries, L. F., 6
Dion, P. E., 65–66

Earle, T., 38–41, 43
Edelman, D. V., xiii, 39–41, 44, 55–57
Ehrlich, C. S., 41
Elat, M., 66
Eliade, M., 6
Elton, G. R., xiii
Emerton, J. A., 96
Eph'al, E., 108
Eshel, H., 98
Eskenazi, T. C., 122–23
Eynikel, E., 86

Finkelstein, I., 30–31, 37, 39, 46, 86, 87
Freedman, D. N., 4, 71
Freyne, S., 105
Frick, F. S., 31, 43–44

Galil, G., 69, 73, 76, 79, 94
Gallagher, W. R., 78–79
Galpaz, P., 57
Gane, R., 87
Garbini, G., 45
Geus, C. H. J. de, 31
Gill, D., 82
Gitin, S., 48, 60, 86
Glasswasser, O., 43
Glatt-Gilad, D. A., 91

Gnuse, R., 38
Goldberg, J., 73, 80
Gottwald, N. K., 31, 39
Grabbe, L. L., xiii, 2, 105, 120–21
Graham, J. N., 99
Gray, J., 70
Grayson, A. K., 73, 79, 94
Guest, P. D., 29

Haerinck, E., 113
Hallo, W. W., xiii
Halpern, B., xiii, 7, 68, 82
Handy, L. K., 45, 90
Hartley, J. E., 109
Hawk, L. D., 41
Hayes, J. H., xii, 73, 88–89
Heaton, E. W., 44
Heltzer, M., 88
Hendel, R. S., 83
Hengel, M., 126
Hillers, D. R., 8
Hobbs, T. R., 60
Hoffmann, H.-D., 63
Hoffmeier, J. K., 24
Hoglund, K. G., 104, 111, 114, 116–18, 121–23
Holladay, J. S., 90
Hopkins, D. C., 38
Horsley, R., 119
Houtman, C., 50
Hurowitz, V., 46

Irvine, S. A., 68
Ishida, T., 44, 64
Isserlin, B. S. J., 31

Jackson, K. P., 66–67
Jacobsen, T., 6
James, T. G. H., 44
Jamieson-Drake, D. W., 43, 47
Japhet, S., 86, 104, 116, 124
Johnson, A., 39
Joyce, P. M., 107
Judd, E. P., 123

Katzenstein, H. J., 73, 88, 95
Kelso, J. L., 98
Keown, G. L., 95, 105
Kinchloe, J. L., xiii
King, P. J., 70
Kitchen, K. A., 4, 21, 41, 43, 46, 60, 68
Kletter, R., 87–88, 90
Knapp, A. B., 17
Knauf, E. A., 10, 46, 48
Knibb, M. A., 6
Knight, D. A., 63
Knohl, I., 109
Knoppers, G. N., 46, 59, 62–63
Kochavi, M., 117
Krecher, J., 4
Kuan, J. K., 73
Kuhrt, A., 106, 112–13

Lancaster, S. P., 82
Landsberger, B., 79
Langdon, S., 107
Lapp, N. L., 98
Lasine, S., 63, 86
LaSor, W., 104
Lemaire, A., 68
Lemche, N. P., xii, 3, 6, 39, 47, 68
Levine, Lee I., 127
Levine, Louis D., 80
Lipschits, O., 95–98, 104
Long, G. A., 82
Lukonin, V. G., 117
Luria, B. Z., 41

Machinist, P., 59, 77
Maidman, M., 7
Maier, G., xiii
Malamat, A., xiii, 27, 43, 92, 94–97
Margalith, O., 105, 115, 120
Marinkovic, P., 119
Master, D. M., 46, 49, 57
Matthews, V. H., 1, 8–9, 36, 49, 52, 111
Mayer, J., 123

Mazar, A., 90
McCarter, P .K., 41
McCarthy, D. J., 6
McEvenue, S. E., 102
McLaren, P. L., xiii
McNutt, Paula M., 37
Mendenhall, G. E., 31
Merton, R. K., 123
Mettinger, T. N. D., 41
Meyers, C., 8, 116
Meyers, E. M., 116
Milgrom, J., 102, 109
Millard, A. R., 4–5, 112
Miller, J. M., xii, 43, 45, 67,
    88–89
Miller, P. D., 50
Miller, R. D., xiii
Moor, J. C. de, xiii, 22, 28
Moran, W. L., 26, 47
Muhly, J. D.. 37
Muth, R. F., 37, 39

Na'aman, N., 27, 45–49, 54,
    66–68, 73, 78, 81–82, 84,
    86–89, 92–93
Nakhai, B. A., 6, 31, 38
Naveh, J., 43, 68
Nicholson, E. W., 90
Niemann, H. M., 45–46
Noll, K. L., 29–30

Oded, B., 73–74, 85, 97,
    105
Ofer, A., 48
Oredsson, D., 46, 49

Parker, S. B., 72, 96
Parpola, S., 79
Patrick, D., 90
Porten, B., 94–95, 121–23

Rainey, A. F., 27, 67, 81, 90,
    96
Redford, D. B., 19, 21, 29, 32,
    46, 78, 84, 87, 92, 95–96
Renfrew, C., 39
Roberts, J. J. M., 50

Rogerson, J., 83
Romer, T. C., 90–91
Rosenberg, J., 44
Rosenberg, S., 82
Roth, P. A., xii

Sack, R. H., 112
Saggs, H. W. F., 93
Sanders, J. T., 108–9, 126
Sasson, J. M., xiii, 110
Scalise, P. J., 95, 105
Schmidt, B. B., 7
Schneider, T. J., 64, 69
Schniedewind, W., 68
Schulte, H., 64–65
Seitz, C. R., 98
Shaheen, N., 82
Shanks, H., xii, 83
Shavit, A., 86
Shaw, C. S., 59
Shiloh, Y., 47
Singer, I., 22
Smelik, K. A. D., xiii, 96
Smith-Christopher, Daniel L.,
    104, 106–7, 123
Smith, Daniel L., 107
Smith, Mark S., 31
Smith, Morton, 121, 124
Smith, R. L., 82
Smith, S., 112
Smothers, T. G., 95, 105
Soggin, J. A., xii, 72
Spanier, K., 70
Sparks, K. L., 108
Stager, L. E., 32, 37, 47, 94
Steinberg, N., 9
Steinmetz, D., 9
Stern, E., 62, 77, 90, 99, 104,
    115–16, 117
Stiebing, W. H., 29
Stolper, M. W., 107
Strange, J., 31
Sun, H. T. C., 109
Sweeney, M. A., 91

Tadmor, H., 58, 65, 67, 70,
    73, 78–79, 90, 92, 97

Talmon, S., 44
Talshir, Z., 92
Tarler, D., 47
Tatum, L., 87
Tcherikover, V., 125–26
Thompson, T. L., xii, 3, 47, 68
Toews, W. I., 62
Tomes, R., 71–72
Trigger, B. G., xiii
Tucker, G. M., 7

Ussisskin, D., 46, 60, 82–83,
    86, 90, 96

van der Toorn, K., 50
Van Seters, J., 3
Vaughn, A. G., 4, 80, 82

Weidner, E. F., 95
Weinberg, J. P., 104
Weinstein, J. M., 28, 57
Weissbach, F. H., 106
Wesselius, J.-W., 43
Whitelam, K., 23, 38–39, 45,
    51
Whybray, R. N., 43
Williamson, H. G. M., 87,
    103, 120
Willis, T. M., 36, 58
Wiseman, D. J., 4, 92–94,
    104, 106
Wright, D. P., 109
Wright, G. E., 3

Yadin, Y., 46
Yamauchi, E. M., 108, 121,
    123
Younger, K. L., xiii, 72, 74,
    105
Yurco, Frank J., 28

Zadok, R., 74, 87, 107–8
Zertal, A., 37, 39
Zevit, Z., 5, 101, 105, 110
Zimansky, P., 70
Zorn, J. R., 98

Subject Index

Aaron, 11, 33, 62, 102
Abdi-Heba, 47
Abiathar, 44
Abigail, 8
Abimelech, 69
Abner, 44
Abraham, 2–11, 13, 51, 62, 109
Absalom, 11
Achish, 41
Adad-guppi, 106, 112
Adonijah, 44, 58
adoption, 6–7
agriculture, 37–38
Ahab, 43, 55–56, 64–68
Ahaz, 72, 79–80, 89, 92, 101
Ahaziah, 43, 56, 68–69
Ahijah, 57, 59, 64

Ahmose I, 23
Ai, 32
Akhenaton, 16, 21, 26, 112
Akhetaten, 24, 26
Alexander of Macedon, 19, 103, 118, 125–27
altar, 6, 11, 81, 89, 110
Amalekites, 33
Amaziah, 70–71
Amel-Marduk, 106
Amenophis III, 26
Ammon, 10, 95, 115
Ammonites, 22, 36, 39, 67, 87, 122
Amorite, 19, 30, 67
Amos, 11, 33, 64
anachronism, 5, 63, 67, 131

Anatolia, 17, 19–22, 68, 70, 112, 117
annals, 55, 63–65, 68, 71–73, 81, 83–84, 88, 90, 110
'Apiru, 27–28
Apries, 95–96
Arabia, 10, 20, 48, 87–88, 112
Arad, 55, 81, 90, 92, 95
Aram, 55–56, 65–70
Aramaic, 84, 94, 109, 120
archaeology, 3, 23, 29–32, 37–39, 46–49, 77, 81–83, 86–88, 90, 96–99, 104, 116–18
architecture, 32, 46–47, 77
ark of the covenant, 11, 50–51, 61–62, 102, 131

army, 44–45, 50, 61, 64, 68,
    117–19, 121
Arnon River, 66–69
Artaxerxes I, 103, 115–16,
    118, 120
Ashdod, 29, 38, 41, 46,
    55–56, 71, 77–79, 85
Ashkelon, 28–29, 38, 55
Ashurbanipal, 19, 78, 86–88
Ashurnasirpal II, 65
assassination, 51–52, 63, 71,
    88, 98, 104, 115, 125
assimilation, 107, 123, 131
Assyria, 17, 19, 22, 43,
    47–48, 54–56, 60–61,
    64–74, 77–80, 82–91, 93,
    96, 105–6, 118
Athaliah, 65, 69–70
Athens, 115–16, 118–20
Avaris, 24
Azekah, 78–79, 93, 97

Baasha, 64
Babylon, 2, 17, 19, 33, 59,
    73, 80, 82, 88, 94–96,
    102, 103, 106–7, 112–15,
    119, 125
Babylonians, 55, 56, 61,
    78–79, 86–88, 92–99, 102,
    104–7, 110, 113, 115, 118
Bashan, 54, 69
Bathsheba, 8
Beersheba, 6, 55, 81, 86,
    89–90
Belshazzar, 106, 112
Benaiah, 44
Ben-Hadad, 65–66
Ben Sira/Sirach, 109, 117,
    126
Bethel, 6, 11, 54, 61–62, 89,
    98
Beth-shean, 27, 54
Beth-shemesh, 70, 104
bureaucracy, 40, 43–44,
    49–50, 61, 63–64,
    114–17, 119–21, 123, 132
burial, 7, 11, 77
Byblos, 26

Caleb, 11
calendar, 6, 38, 61, 63, 110
Cambyses II, 114–15, 122
canon, 108–9, 132
Carchemish, 91–94, 106
cedar forest, 19–20
Chaldean, 5, 19, 78, 87
chiefdom, 39–40, 44–45,
    48–49, 56, 132
Chronicler, 59, 67, 80, 85,
    91, 104, 114, 132
circumcision, 108, 110
circumscription, 38, 40–41,
    132
city-state, 17, 19, 23, 27, 38,
    40, 95, 115, 119–20,
    132
climate, 23, 54
coins, 118–19, 126
copper, 48
covenant, 2, 5–10, 13, 15–16,
    34, 50–51, 77, 89–90,
    102, 108–9, 120, 124–25,
    132
Cyprus, 22, 48
Cyrus, 19, 33, 59, 103, 106,
    112–15, 119

Damascus, 65–67, 69–70, 72,
    92, 126
Dan, 11, 54, 61–62, 68–69
Daniel, 9, 33, 107
Darius, I, 19, 114–16, 119
Darius II, 115–16, 121
Darius III, 125
David, 7–8, 11, 40–41,
    43–44, 47–51, 54, 56–60,
    62–63, 67–68, 81, 90–91,
    95, 98, 101, 104, 118, 124
Deborah, 36–37
decalogue, 51, 132
Delian League, 121
deportation, 72, 74, 78, 83,
    86–87, 98, 104–6
deuteronomist, 41, 45–46,
    49–50, 53–54, 57, 59–64,
    67, 71, 86, 90, 101, 104,
    109, 132

Diadochi, 126, 132
diaspora, 99, 103, 108,
    110–11, 113, 124,
    132
Dibon, 67
diplomacy, 20, 22, 26, 38, 69,
    72, 79, 84, 96
divine warrior, 8, 33, 50–51,
    133

Ebla, 4
Edom, 9–10, 22, 55–56,
    67–68, 70, 72, 78, 87, 93,
    95, 123
education, 63, 110–11
Egypt, 17–24, 26–32, 41,
    43–46, 54, 56–57, 60,
    71–73, 78–79, 83–85, 87,
    89, 91–96, 98, 103, 110,
    112–23, 125–26
Ein-gedi, 90, 99
Ekron, 29, 38, 41, 48, 55, 79,
    84–86, 94
Elam, 78, 86, 88, 115
El Amarna, 19, 21, 24,
    26–27, 47
elders, 7, 11, 36–37, 39–40,
    44, 58–59
Eli, 11
Elijah, 33–34, 69
Eliphantine, 120, 122–23
Elisha, 34, 69
endogamy, 108, 111, 123–24,
    133
Esarhaddon, 86
Esau, 7, 10
espionage , 20–21
ethnocentrism, 24, 53, 133
etiology, 2, 6, 16
everlasting covenant, 50–51,
    59, 101
exile, 7, 13, 16, 33, 61, 74,
    86, 90, 93, 95, 97–99,
    102–11, 113, 115,
    117–19, 122–23
Ezekiel, 107–8
Ezra, 103, 111, 115, 117–20,
    123–24

figurines, 81, 87, 90

gate, 46, 77, 96
Gath, 29, 41, 44, 55
Gaugamela, 125
Gaza, 29, 38, 41, 54, 71, 83, 85
Geba, 89–90
Gedaliah, 97–98, 104
Gezer, 28, 38, 46, 86
Gibeon, 39
Gideon, 33, 36, 39, 69, 98
Gilead, 36, 54
Gilgal, 11
Gôlâh, 107, 113
Greece, 115–16, 119, 125
Greeks, 110, 115–21, 125–26
Gudea, 20
Gulf of Aqaba, 48, 67, 72

habiru, 21, 27
Hagar, 10
Haggai, 103, 114
Hamath, 65–66, 93–94
Hammurabi, 17, 19
Hananiah, 33, 95
Harran, 5, 91, 106, 112
Hattusas, 22
Hattusilis III, 8, 21, 58
Hazael, 56, 66, 68–70
Hazor, 46
Hebron, 6–7, 11, 55, 58
hegemony, 17, 19, 21, 28, 32, 47–48, 65–67, 69–70, 85, 92, 94, 113, 116, 119, 133
Herod, 48, 110
Hezekiah, 30, 41, 56, 63, 73, 75, 78–86, 90, 102
high place, 61, 63, 89, 110
Hilkiah, 89–90
Hiram, 45
Hittite, 5, 8, 19–23, 26–27, 30, 32, 37, 110–11
Holiness Code, 102, 108–10
Horus, 2, 24
Hosea, 11, 64, 71
Hoshea, 71–73, 80
Huldah, 89–90, 92

Hurrian, 20, 26–27
Hyksos, 18–19, 23–24

idolatry, 62–63
Inarus, 116, 121
Irhuleni, 65–66
iron, 37
Isaac, 3–4, 7, 10
Isaiah, 16, 79, 84–85, 103, 110, 113–14
Ishmael, 10

Jabesh-Gilead, 11
Jacob, 3–4, 7–8, 10–11, 62
Jael, 8
Jehoash, 70
Jehoiachin, 94–95, 103, 106
Jehoiakim, 92, 94, 106
Jehoram, 43, 56, 65–70
Jehoshaphat, 65, 67, 69
Jehu, 54, 56, 64, 66, 68–69
Jephthah, 27, 36
Jeremiah, 7, 11, 33, 89, 94–96, 1–2, 108
Jericho, 32–33, 90, 104
Jeroboam, 11, 54–55, 57–64, 89
Jeroboam II, 71
Jeroboam's Sin, 60–63, 71, 133
Jerusalem, 7, 13, 21, 27, 29–30, 33, 41, 45–51, 54–56, 58–63, 69–71, 78, 80–90, 92–94, 96–99, 102–7, 109–11, 114–17, 119–24, 127–27
Jesse, 51, 57
Jewish Identity Movement, 102, 104, 108–11, 122–24
Jezebel, 64, 67, 70
Jezreel, 46, 49, 77
Jezreel Valley, 46, 70, 91
Joab, 8, 44
Jonathan, 44
Joseph, 3–4, 7, 9–10, 23
Joshua, 11, 17, 28, 32–33, 36, 50, 68

Josiah, 33, 78, 86, 88–93, 96, 102

Kadesh, 22
Kadesh-Barnea, 30
Karnak, 22, 28–29
Kassite, 19
King's Highway, 67
Kish, 17

Laban, 8
Lâbâši-Marduk, 106, 112
Lab'ayu, 26–27
labor service, 58–59, 64, 66, 106–7
Lachish, 46, 55–56, 71, 82–83, 86, 95–97, 104
Lagash, 17
Leah, 10
Levites, 24, 62–63, 81, 89, 122, 124
lmlk jars, 82
Lot, 10
Lydia, 112, 115

Machpelah, 7
Manasseh, 85–89, 101
Marathon, 115–16, 119
Marduk, 2, 106–7, 112–14
Mari, 3, 5, 17, 26
marriage, 45–46, 64–65, 67, 69, 103, 108, 111, 118, 122–24
Medes, 92, 107, 112, 114–15
Megabyzus, 116
Megiddo, 29, 46, 49, 54, 60, 77–78, 91–94
Memphis, 2
Menahem, 71–72
Mephibosheth, 58
Merodach-baladan, 78–80
Mesha, 43, 66–68
Midianites, 10, 33, 39
Mitanni, 3, 19, 21, 27
Mizpah, 97–98, 104
Moab, 10, 43, 56, 66–68, 78, 87, 95
Moabites, 22, 39, 108

monarchy, 39–41, 43–45, 47–53, 57–58, 78, 91, 93, 101
Moses, 16, 23, 30, 33–34, 36, 50, 62
Mt. Carmel, 33
Mt. Gerizim, 103, 126
Mt. Horeb, 33
Mt. Sinai, 33, 62
Mursilis, 21

Nabonidus, 59, 106, 112–13
Nabopolassar, 92–93
Naram-Sin, 19
Nathan, 81
Nebuchadnezzar, 9, 17, 19, 46, 56, 78, 93–98, 103, 106–7, 112, 116, 121
Necho II, 78, 91–92, 94
Negev, 86–87, 90
Nehemiah, 103–4, 107, 111, 115–18, 121–24
nepotism, 44, 50, 134
Neriglissar, 106, 112
Nineveh, 83, 105
Nippur, 17, 107
Niqmaddu II, 21
Noah, 6
Nuzi, 3, 7

Omri, 43, 54–55, 64–70, 73
Osorkon IV, 78

Passover, 81, 89, 91, 115, 121
Peace of Callias, 120
Pekah, 71–72
Peloponnesian War, 116
Persepolis, 125
Persia, 17, 19, 98, 103–4, 106–7, 109, 111–26
Philistines, 11, 22–23, 29–30, 32, 36–41, 44–46, 48–49, 54–55, 57, 70–71, 78–79, 82–84, 86, 94–95, 108, 110, 115, 118
Phoenicians, 19, 22, 45–46, 48–49, 60, 64, 67, 70, 87–88, 108, 118

Pi-Rameses, 27
Plataea, 120
priestly source, 102, 109–10, 134
prophet, 50, 52, 56–57, 59, 62, 64, 69, 77, 89–90, 92, 96, 114, 119
Psammeticus I, 87
Psammeticus II, 94–95
Ptolemy, 19, 126

Qarqar, 56, 65, 67

Rabshakeh, 83–85
Rachel, 10
Ramesses II, 8, 22, 27–29, 58
Ramesses III, 22–23
Ramesses VI, 32
Rebekah, 7–8, 10
Rehoboam, 11, 57–60
Rib-Hadda, 26
ritual purity, 108–10, 134

Sabbath, 108, 109, 122, 124, 134
sacred space, 6, 103, 110
sacrifice, 6, 62, 102, 105, 110, 122
Salamis, 115 120
Samaria, 54, 61, 64, 71–73, 77–78, 80–81, 86–87, 89, 98, 104–5, 114–16, 121, 126
Samaritan, 103–5
Samuel, 11, 36
Sanballat, 122
Sarah, 7, 10
Sargon II, 19, 56, 72–74, 78–80, 105
Sargon of Akkad, 19, 23
satrap, 104, 116, 120
Saul, 7, 11, 39–41, 44, 47–50, 57–58
scribe, 43, 49, 120
Scythians, 88
Sea Peoples, 22–23, 29–32, 37, 45, 48
Seleucus, 19, 126

Semitic, 17, 19, 24, 134
Sennacherib, 19, 41, 56, 78–87, 96
Senwosret I, 24
Septuagint, 57, 59, 134
Servant Songs, 16
Shabaka, 78, 84
Shalmaneser III, 19, 56, 64–66, 68–69, 72
Shalmaneser V, 72–73
Shasu, 9, 28–29
Sheba, 51, 57
Shechem, 6, 11, 21, 27–28, 33, 58–59, 62, 103, 105, 126
Shephelah, 29, 32, 38, 55, 57, 60, 82, 86–87
Sheshbazzar, 114, 116
Shiloh, 11, 49, 105
Shishak, 45, 56–57, 60
Siamun, 41, 46
Sidon, 22, 45, 69, 95, 125
Sin (moon god), 106, 112
Sippar, 94
Solomon, 7, 29, 41, 44–49, 51, 54–59, 62, 80, 89, 97
Sparta, 116
Sumer, 17, 19
Suppululiumas, 21
Susa, 116
synagogue, 110
Syria, 19–22, 27, 65, 72, 92, 125
Syro-Ephraimite War, 72

taxation, 64, 88, 92, 99, 116–19
temple, 45–46, 48, 50–51, 54, 60, 81, 89–90, 97, 99, 102–5, 107, 109–11, 113–15, 117–20, 122, 126
Thebes, 19
Themistocles, 119
theodicy, 8, 84, 99, 108, 113, 134
theophany, 11, 134
Thutmosis III, 20–21, 29

Tiglath-Pileser I, 20
Tiglath-Pileser III, 19, 43,
   71–73, 80, 92
Tirzah, 38, 61
Tobit, 105
trade, 17, 20, 22, 28, 38,
   48–49, 67, 70, 72, 82,
   86–87, 99, 112, 118
treaty, 5, 8, 21–22, 26, 58,
   65, 135
Tyre, 22, 45, 69, 73, 87, 95,
   125

Ugarit, 19, 21–22, 30, 45, 48
Ur, 5, 17

Urartu, 70, 78
Ur-Nammu, 19
Uruk, 17
Uzziah, 71

vassalage, 20–21, 26–27,
   67–68, 73, 78–79,
   83–84, 87, 89, 92, 94,
   113, 120
Via Maris, 54, 67, 135

Wadi Tumilat, 9, 24
warfare, 73, 79, 81–85, 89,
   91, 93–97, 113, 125
water tunnel, 56, 82

wilderness, 16, 30, 33–34

Xerxes, 19, 115–16, 119

Yehud, 103, 110, 114,
   116–18, 120–24

Zechariah, 103
Zedekiah, 56, 93–97
Zerubbabel, 115–16
Ziklag, 41
Zimri, 64
Zion, 51